The Composer's Workshop

II

The Composer's Workshop

Serie's editor: Gianmario Borio

Editorial board:
Denis Herlin
Ulrich Mosch
Friedemann Sallis

Marco Cosci

Egisto Macchi:
The Assassination of Trotsky

Sources of the Creative Process

BREPOLS

Translation by Sally Davies and Samantha Stout

© 2022, Brepols Publishers n.v., Turnhout, Belgium.

All rights reserved. No part of this publication may be reproduced stored in a retrieval system, or transmitted, in any form or by any means, electronic, mechanical, photocopying, recording, or otherwise, without the prior permission of the publisher.

ISBN 978-2-503-59351-7

D/2022/0095/332

Printed in the EU on acid-free paper.

Table of Contents

9	INTRODUCTORY ESSAY
	«What goes on behind those eyes?»: Egisto Macchi through the silver screen
11	Bad tales
12	New sounds on the screen
17	Interpreting reality through music
21	Losey, Trotsky, Macchi
25	Inside the composer's workshop
30	Appendix 1 – Filmography
32	Appendix 2 – Egisto Macchi, [Writing the score for a film]
35	Appendix 3 – *The Assassination of Trotsky* (1972): Film credits
37	CHAPTER I
	In search of the right sound
39	Document 1: List of Music & Records
45	Document 2: Sequenza B.
51	Document 3: Letter to Egisto Macchi from Joseph Losey, 30 March 1972
54	Document 4: Music
56	Document 5: *Bandera roja*, fair copy, notes, typescript
62	Document 6: II Banda, draft and fair copy
69	CHAPTER II
	From the opening credits to the bullfight
71	Document 7: Titoli, draft
77	Document 8: Titoli, fair copy
83	Document 9: M. 5/2 I versione, sketch
86	Document 10: M. 5/2 I versione, fair copy
88	Document 11: M. 5/2 II versione, draft
91	Document 12: M. 5/2 II versione, fair copy
94	Document 13: M. 5/2 versione definitiva, fair copy
96	Document 14: M. 6/1, draft
99	Document 15: M. 6/1, fair copy
103	CHAPTER III
	Alternative routes
105	Document 16: M. 3/2, sketch
109	Document 17: M. 3/2 I versione, II versione, III versione, fair copies

114	Document 18: M. 3/3 I versione, draft
117	Document 19: M. 3/3 I versione, fair copy
122	Document 20: M. 3/3 II versione, draft
128	Document 21: M. 3/3 II versione, fair copy
133	Document 22: M. 8/1 I versione, draft
136	Document 23: M. 8/1 I versione, fair copy
141	Document 24: M. 8/1 II versione, draft
145	Document 25: M. 8/1 II versione, fair copy
151	BIBLIOGRAPHY

Acknowledgements

The research project that led to this volume began when I was a Ph.D. candidate at the Department of Musicology and Cultural Heritage at the University of Pavia. At that time, Egisto Macchi's archival materials were preserved by his son, Lamberto, and by his widow, Sylvaine Couquet Macchi, in two different private locations in Rome. Without their generosity, I would not have been able to start my research project on Macchi. Kindly supported by Giovanni Alliata di Montereale, I continued during my Research Fellowship at the University of Pavia, in collaboration with the Institute of Music at the Giorgio Cini Foundation (to which Macchi's documents were donated in 2013).

During all these years, I benefitted from the academic guidance of Gianmario Borio, who conceived this series of volumes, and followed all the stages of this book: without his supervision, advice, and continuous encouragement, it would never have seen the light. I also wish to thank Johan Van der Beke from Brepols Publishers for his precious suggestions and his attention to this project. My genuine thanks go to the staff at the Institute of Music at the Giorgio Cini Foundation, for the professional and personal help they never failed to offer while I was researching and writing the book: Agnese Bonini, Angela Carone, Giulia Clera, Tommaso Maggiolo, and Francisco Rocca. Sally Davies, Samantha Stout, and Matteo Broccoli oversaw the translation and the graphic layout offering a precious contribution with their professionalism and commitment. I am also very grateful for the kind assistance offered by personnel at the British Film Institute, and I particularly wish to thank Johnny Davies, former curator of the Joseph Losey Collection, and Storm Patterson, Special Collections Coordinator. Special thanks are due to Candida Mantica for reading the translation, suggesting many improvements, and Antonio Calvia for his insights on several editorial issues. Finally, I would like to thank all the scholars, colleagues, and friends who helped me in various ways during the work that led to this book. In particular: Alessandro Bratus, Roberto Calabretto, Alessandro Cecchi, Maurizio Corbella, Giulia Cosci, Elena Mosconi, Emilio Sala, Alice Tavilla, Silvia Timitilli, and Giada Viviani.

INTRODUCTORY ESSAY

«What goes on behind those eyes?»: Egisto Macchi through the silver screen

Bad tales

At the seventieth edition of the Berlin International Film Festival *Favolacce* (*Bad Tales*, 2020), the film by the D'Innocenzo brothers not only won the award for best screeplay, but it also attracted the critics' attention for its soundtrack. Described by the cinema scholar Gianni Canova as «one of the most beautiful and bold and stunning soundtracks of recent years», it is based on a little-known album of library music from the 1970s: Egisto Macchi's *Città Notte* (1972), «a music full of clangs, screeches, arrhythmias and obsessive repetitions of notes [which creates] an adequate sound kit for the uneasiness, the disquiet, the frustration of hopeless lives and of an adolescence without any future».[1] Thirty years after his death, with this return to the silver screen, Macchi is still proven to be one of the most singular voices in Italian cinema.

And yet, compared to the great names of Italian film music, in particular Nino Rota and Ennio Morricone, Macchi has yet to receive due attention from the scientific community. Of course, his career was not lacking in illustrious moments. Just think of his collaborations with directors such as Joseph Losey for *The Assassination of Trotsky* (1972) and *Mr. Klein* (1976), but also with Paolo and Vittorio Taviani for *Padre padrone* (*Father and Master*, 1977), Bernardo Bertolucci for the industrial film *La via del petrolio* (1967) and Gregory Markopoulos, who edited the television version of the experimental work *A(lter)A(ction)*, broadcast on the third channel of Bayerishen Rundfunk in 1968.[2] Nonetheless, his compositional activity has never been the subject of a systematic study to identify its impact on post-World War II film production. Therefore, I think it is useful to focus on some of the reasons that have contributed to Macchi's position as a background figure in the panorama of Italian film music. Although the main goal of this study is not to restore him to his "rightful" place in history, it will help to reposition his collaboration with Joseph Losey on *The Assassination of Trotsky*.

It is worth starting with a statement by the Italian director Cecilia Mangini, which seems to be partially at odds with what has been said so far. According to Mangini: «if you read our opening credits carefully, you will find that there are often many recurring names. The one that appears with the greatest frequency is that of Egisto Macchi, a musician who knew how to musically interpret images».[3] The director is referring to a particular genre, namely the documentary, an aptly selected field for Macchi's compositional activity. There is no doubt that in terms of quantity and quality for documentaries produced in Italy, Macchi is one of the most prolific composers of music. It is hard to calculate the exact number of films to which he contributed with his music: the list drawn up by Macchi himself indicates at least a thousand titles. Although this high number can be partially reduced if we consider serial productions,

---

[1] Gianni Canova, *Favolacce*, https://welovecinema.it/2020/05/12/favolacce-la-regia-di-damiano-e-fabio-dinnocenzo/.

[2] For more on the soundtrack of *Padre padrone* see Mark Graham, *Padre Padrone and the Dialectics of Sound*, «Film Criticism», 1, 1981, pp. 21-30: 26; Marco Cosci, *La voce del padrone e i suoni del popolo. Identità musicali e processi d'ibridazione tra universi etnici, colti e popular in* Padre Padrone, «Cinema e Storia», III/1, 2014, pp. 55-68; Roberto Calabretto, Giovanni De Mezzo, *Il paesaggio sonoro nel cinema sardo. Banditi a Orgosolo di Vittorio De Seta e Padre padrone dei fratelli Taviani*, «L'avventura. International Journal of Italian Film and Media Landscapes», 4/1, 2018, pp. 19-40. As regards his collaboration with Markopoulos see Elena Salza, *Egisto Macchi and Antonin Artaud: from* A(lter)A(ction) *to* München-Requiem *and Beyond*, «Archival Notes», 3, 2018, pp. 97-118; Marco Cosci, *La scena media(tizza)ta: teatro, cinema e televisione in* A(lter)A(ction), in Gianmario Borio, Giordano Ferrari, Daniela Tortora (eds), *Teatro di avanguardia e composizione sperimentale per la scena in Italia: 1950-1975*, Venice: Fondazione Giorgio Cini, 2017, pp. 235-257.

[3] Gianluca Sciannameo, *Nelle Indie di quaggiù: Ernesto De Martino e il cinema etnografico*, Bari: Palomar, 2006, p. 152.

which saw the widespread and continuous reuse of the same materials in different audiovisual contexts. It is still worth trying to understand what the documentary genre meant for Macchi and the reasons behind his dedicated approach. In fact, at the same time Macchi was beginning his activity as a composer of film music, he was also starting to take his first steps in the musical avant-garde environment in Rome. During the 1950s and the 1960s, he contributed to many activities that show the centrality of experimentation in his compositional work and, more generally, in his cultural initiatives. In 1959, he joined the editorial board of the journal *Ordini*, dedicated to new music – along with Franco Evangelisti, Domenico Guaccero and Antonino Titone. Precisely this initiative was the launchpad for one of the main Italian associations for contemporary music – Nuova Consonanza – together with the aforementioned Evangelisti and Guaccero, joined by Mario Bertoncini, Mauro Bortolotti and Daniele Paris.[4] The Nuova Consonanza association soon became one of the most important centres for the diffusion of new music in Italy, devising a series of musical events that also benefitted from exchanges with Palermo's Settimane Internazionali di Nuova Musica [International Weeks of New Music] (1960-68). Macchi's personal commitment and organisational capacity was reflected in his organization of other institutions such as Rome's Compagnia del Teatro Musicale,[5] which he founded together with Guaccero and Sylvano Bussotti and was active in until 1970. In 1967, Macchi joined the improvisation group Nuova Consonanza (created in Rome by Evangelisti in 1964), with whom he collaborated until 1985;[6] in 1968 he was among the founders of Studio R7, an electronic music laboratory (1968-73), together with Walter Branchi, Evangelisti, Guaccero, Guido Guiducci, Gino Marinuzzi Jr and Paolo Ketoff. Macchi's engagement on all these fronts, just when he took his first steps in the field of cinema, is not so significant in the milieu of film production. As James Wierzbicki recently pointed out, «being a film composer and at the same time a composer for the concert hall 'is much more about doing many different things in parallel than about trying to fuse them into new musical forms, genres, or practices'».[7] Morricone, to whom I will return shortly, seems to confirm this hypothesis. And yet, as soon as I contemplate his enormous documentary production, Macchi's case invites us to set aside the idea, applicable to many of his colleagues, of a double compositional life, and to hypothesise a possible common horizon between the film sector and concert music. In the next paragraphs, I will examine the production context and the aesthetic assumptions underlying Macchi's compositional work in the 1960s, and then proceed to consider how fundamental these experiences were to his collaboration with Losey in the early 1970s.

New sounds on the screen

The existence of a close relationship between compositional activity for the cinema and the concert hall is an interpretative path that Macchi himself followed. During a Nuova Consonanza season in the 1980s, Macchi presented a series of his compositions to the public in a monographic concert. He introduced one of his key compositions from the 1960s, *Morte all'orecchio di Van Gogh* (1964)[8] with the following explanation:

> In '59 [...] the cinema got me, grabbed me and never left me. But to demonstrate

---

[4] See Daniela Tortora, *Nuova Consonanza. Trent'anni di musica contemporanea in Italia*, Lucca: Lim, 1990.

[5] The activities of Rome's Compagnia del Teatro musicale have recently been reconstructed by Alessandro Mastropietro in *A Survey of New Music Theatre in Rome, 1961–1973: 'Anni favolosi'?*, in Robert Adlington (ed.), *New Music Theatre in Europe: Transformations between 1955-1975*, New York: Routledge 2019, pp. 177-202.

[6] Note that Ennio Morricone will also be part of the group from 1964 onwards.

[7] James Wierzbicki, *Introduction*, in Id. (ed.), *Double Lives: Film Composer in the Concert Hall*, New York: Routledge, 2020, pp. 1-6: 6.

[8] This is also the title of the homonymous short film directed by Sergio Tau in 1964 and the composition for narrator, harpsichord, magnetic tape and chamber orchestra, which premiered in Milan, Pomeriggi Musicali, Teatro dell'Opera, 1964, under the conduction of Daniele Paris.

perhaps to myself, not to you, that something interesting can be done even within that activity, I want you to hear a recorded piece that comes from a cinematographic opportunity, that is a documentary by Sergio Tau, with a text by Allen Ginsberg. [...] I made a score of concrete music for him, that is, I used a series of pre-established sound objects, already existing: I chose them with care and assembled them carrying out painstaking work that took many days of editing and which eventually gave rise to a surprising, albeit very interesting, result. I took the opportunity to create a piece for voice, tape, harpsichord and chamber orchestra on this score.[9]

These remarks lead us to the following two observations. First of all, the cinematographic field, whose very nature imposes far more limits than free composition, constituted a creative stimulus for Macchi that was useful for developing extra-cinematographic compositions.[10] He did not just re-elaborate a film score into a concert suite for a particular performance or recording project, but rather he exploited the compositional project for cinema as a hypotext for a fully-fledged art music composition.[11] Macchi reworked *Morte all'orecchio di Van Gogh* into an independent composition for the concert hall. Secondly, the attitude he cultivated forsook a relatively widespread sentiment among composers operating within the tradition of art music that viewed cinema as a place naturally resistant to musical research.

As regards Italian composers, there were quite a few leading names who approached cinema with scepticism or cynicism. Goffredo Petrassi gives cinematic experience a relatively short shrift (a couple of pages) in his autobiography:

> However, preparing the music for pictures bored me to death, I felt as if I were in prison. Later cinematographic musical language evolved, because serious musicians like Egisto Macchi elaborated it in a new way, achieving more than acceptable results, but back then, around 1950, making the background music for a film seemed an unbearable obligation.[12]

Petrassi was not alone in his aversion to rigorously fixed lengths for reasons of synchronisation, and his reluctance to use coded solutions to facilitate an alleged correspondence between music and images. The history of cinema is full of similar examples, showing the dissatisfaction of more or less established composers with the technological-production limitations imposed by the prevailing cinema aesthetics. Petrassi's voice is not the only one heard on the Italian scene during those years. For example, let us turn to what the composer Gino Marinuzzi Jr had to say in one of the first Italian books dedicated entirely to film music following the VII International Music Conference in Florence in 1950.[13] Marinuzzi Jr ends his article with a list of programmatic points that would have guaranteed the advent of "a golden age" for film composers. He calls for total freedom of action, eliminating any production constraints, essentially granting free rein to the composer in interpreting a film and

---

[9] Egisto Macchi, *Presentazione del concerto dell'8 ottobre 1984,* Stagione Nuova Consonanza, Concerto monografico dedicato a Egisto Macchi, Rome, Auditorium RAI del Foro Italico, quoted in Daniela Tortora (ed.), *Egisto Macchi*, «Archivio Musiche del XX secolo», Palermo: CIMS-Centro di iniziative musicali in Sicilia, 1996, p. 33. Unless otherwise indicated translations of quotations are those of the book's translator.

[10] One could even reverse the question and point out that, faced with the lack of linguistic-musical grids following the dissolution of tonality, the external conditioning imposed by the cinematographic system can actually be a valid help for the film composer in overcoming the compositional "anxiety" typical of the twentieth century.

[11] In fact, very few studies have investigated this compositional possibility. For example, see the activity of a composer like Erich Wolfgang Korngold, who, despite the great difference in terms of style, offers an interesting perspective on the subject: Robert Van der Lek, *Concert Music as Reused Film Music: E. W. Korngold's Self-arrangements*, «Acta Musicologica», LXVI/2, 1994, pp. 78-112.

[12] Goffredo Petrassi, *Autoritratto. Intervista elaborata da Carlo Vasio*, Rome-Bari: Laterza, 1991, pp. 51-52.

[13] Gino Marinuzzi Jr, *Aspetti della musica per film*, in Enzo Masetti (ed.), *La musica nel film*, Rome: Bianco e Nero Editore, 1950, pp. 35-39. For an in-depth study on Marinuzzi Jr see Maurizio Corbella, *Gino Marinuzzi Jr: Electronics and Early Multimedia Mentality in Italy*, «Musica/Tecnologia», 8-9, 2014-2015, pp. 95-133.

the consequent musical choices. Here too, in addition to continually underscoring the problems related to the constraints of synchronisation, he also pays attention to the issues raised by Petrassi regarding the evolution of musical language. Rather more eloquently, and using the musical innovations of opera as a privileged term of comparison, Marinuzzi Jr observes:

> It must be borne in mind that the artist has always made use of *the means of their time* [emphasis in the original] even when he/she wanted to revive images and situations from even very distant times. Opera is conceived and built on the basis of this principle: it is therefore unclear why such a principle cannot survive also and above all in the cinema, an extremely young form or art and therefore in full evolution. Basically, we are witnessing a curious fact: opera, from its origins to the today, has always been evolving many "leading" musicians (Hindemith, Strawinsky, Berg etc.) have dedicated part of their artistic life to it. Cinema on the other hand [...] has for years been dragging its outmoded and depressing burden of dejected and demeaning music, rich in formulas and poor in ideas [...].[14]

What could be read between the lines in Petrassi's words assumes a more defined form in Marinuzzi Jr's reasoning. In fact, it is not simply a question of regaining an autonomous space, but of rethinking the musical contribution in a different technical-compositional perspective under the lens of history. As Edgard Varèse stressed a decade earlier, «a new dramatic situation in a motion picture will call for a corresponding new use of organised sound, its direct purpose being to achieve an adequate response».[15] Cinema is therefore viewed with curiosity as the youngest art which, thanks to the potential of modern techniques of sound reproduction and transformation, is capable of constantly renewing its creative means. Simultaneously, narrative cinema, aside from the break with tradition promoted by the avant-garde, is represented as an art that was born old from a musical point of view. It is detached from the historical developments of the Arts because it followed certain late nineteenth-century formulas and stylistic codes. What is to be done is to definitively write *contemporary* film music, in the emphatic sense, meaning music capable of keeping up with the changes in sound introduced in the historical present. Marinuzzi Jr's wishes largely fell on deaf ears in the decades to come; they had a far less revolutionary impact than their utopian aspirations hoped for.

There are many reasons for this difficulty. On the one hand, composers often complain about producers' and directors' scarce musical knowledge. On the other, musicians and composers themselves are in part responsible for not breaking down the perceived boundaries between art and film music. With regard to the latter, Morricone's position was emblematic. He always claimed that there was a clear boundary between music intended for concert performance and cinema. In a conversation with Sergio Miceli on Hans Werner Henze's compositional activity for the cinema, Morricone stated: «In cinema, I adopt double aesthetics and I still don't know whether it's my choice or the only way forward. [...] If he keeps on "only doing Henze" they're right to rarely call him because they won't make money, just like those films for which I unambiguously wrote the music of my ideals did not make any money».[16] This time, the creator of the characteristic sound of the "spaghetti western" used the case of Nino Rota as an example of an effective possibility of continuity of writing between concert, cinema, and opera, describing that, unlike Henze, Rota «had a simpler, much more naive and therefore immediate writing».[17]

Within the terms set by Morricone, we can therefore place Macchi on the side of the composers represented by Henze and Rota. But are they such isolated cases? It is worth investigating the historical-production context of the 1960s to appreciate

---

[14] Marinuzzi Jr, *Aspetti della musica per film*, p. 38.
[15] Olivia Mattis, *Varèse's Multimedia Conception of "Déserts"*, «The Musical Quarterly», LXXVI/4, 1992, pp. 557-582: 556-557.
[16] Sergio Miceli, *Colloquio con Ennio Morricone*, in *Musica e cinema nella cultura del Novecento*, Rome: Bulzoni, 2010, pp. 479-502: 501.
[17] Ibidem.

how Macchi is not an atypical figure on the Italian music scene, quite the contrary, he shares common pathways with other leading figures who appeared on the scene in those same years. His entry into the world of cinema took place in 1958. That was a key moment for Italian cinema and its rethinking in sound, which peaked during the 1960s. On the one hand, composers called for greater freedom of action, updating compositional techniques under historical reasons – as we learned from Marinuzzi Jr. On the other hand, the 1960s witnessed the arrival of a new entity on the scene under whose aegis the thrust of Italian musical renewal seems to coagulate, namely, the avant-garde.

During the 1960s, there was an increasingly massive presence of composers committed to carrying out, on different fronts, experiences of musical renewal which found their driving force in Rome. The particular topographical situation of this city favoured the capitalisation of the cultural fervour that characterised this period within the film industry. Indeed, it is clear that cinema holds great attraction, perhaps more so as a source of income than for purely artistic interests. In some cases, it turned out to be a very particular activity because it was flexible and ready to absorb the transformations in musical life. Therefore, the filmographies of influential directors of the time feature, alongside Macchi, compositions by Daniele Paris, Vittorio Gelmetti, Ivan Vandor, Franco Potenza, and the rising star Ennio Morricone.[18]

A sort of alliance between the Roman musical avant-garde and cinema is not, however, a fact that comes to light just by sifting through the biographical background of those composers who crossed the threshold of Cinecittà. Indeed, the figure of a possible new coalition – or perhaps, it would be more correct to define it as a revival of issues that had already animated the very foundation of the seventh art – finds a clearer and more manoeuvrable proposal in the contemporary debate. The numerous articles found, for example, on the pages of the journal *Filmcritica*, which repeatedly returns to the topic, are symptomatic of this trend. With the glaring exception of the hybrid figure Vittorio Gelmetti, who was to some extent not such an institutional figure, it is within film criticism rather than within the ranks of the musical avant-garde itself that there is an attempt to establish a dialogue between the two worlds based on a number of assumptions. As Giovanni De Mezzo highlights, the directional lines around which the various contributions on the subject develop are traced by the director Armando Plebe.[19] Articles, such as *La musica per film e l'avanguardia musicale* [*Film music and musical avant-garde*][20] begin once again to air a series of grievances, that have already been mentioned in part, about the banality and obsolescence of musical composition when confronted with the visual research in films such as *8 ½* (Federico Fellini, 1963) or *Il Gattopardo* (*The Leopard*, Luchino Visconti, 1963). Moreover, electronic music – which Plebe considered to be increasingly unsuitable for enjoyment in the form of pure listening – was identified as the privileged field for a transfusion of avant-garde sounds into cinema: only through the union with other expressive forms is it possible to create a context of fruition capable of producing meaning. In both cases, however, the avant-garde is the "institutional" referent capable of ensuring a process of rejuvenation for Italian film music.

Macchi himself clearly expressed his thoughts on the close relationship between the avant-garde and music for the cinema. During a television programme by national broadcaster RAI about the avant-garde of the 1960s, he answered some questions that went beyond the subject matter of the third episode, namely the Nuova Consonanza Association experience. In this programme curated by Alfredo Di Laura, Macchi more widely explored the relationship between the avant-garde and society, in a country like Italy, which boasted one of the lowest rates of musical knowledge in Europe. The transcript of the passage from the interview, which specifically focused on Macchi's

---

[18] See Maria Francesca Agresta, *Il suono dell'interiorità. Daniele Paris per il cinema di Liliana Cavani, Luigi Di Gianni, Lorenza Mazzetti*, Lucca: Lim, 2010.

[19] See his article on Vittorio Gelmetti's writings and the debate around sound cinema on *Filmcritica*: Giovanni De Mezzo, *Teoria e prassi negli scritti cinematografici di Vittorio Gelmetti*, «Musica e Storia», XVII/3, 2009, pp. 637-677.

[20] Armando Plebe, *La musica per film e l'avanguardia musicale*, «Filmcritica», XIV/135-136, July-August 1963, pp. 447-451.

relationship with the cinema in his creative experience, follows.

> Q: For example. For example, yesterday or for example today, or rather your activity and your language …
> A: Since then, my activity has basically developed along two lines. One, that of pure music, let's say of music not for everyone and the other instead music for everyone, that is film music and television music.
> Q: Don't you feel a bit like an industrial music designer?
> A: In what sense?
> Q: In the sense that you make an object that serves the consumer industries …
> A: Yes yes, I feel a bit like that.
> Q: And it didn't give you anything, precisely this being a designer at the service of the industry?
> A: No, it bothered me. A lot. A great deal of annoyance. It didn't give me anything else. I tried to give something to the medium.
> Q: What?
> A: That is, having lived for quite a long period in the name of the avant-gardes, which you are dealing with, led me naturally to try to transfer, to bring into cinematographic language that is a language let's say for the masses, for large classes of public, to convey in this language a language that is more high-flown, more difficult, more complicated in musical terms, more experimental than avant-garde music. I was amazed the first time I did this, to see how the public, when the image becomes a vehicle for sound, welcomes sound solutions that at the Festival were not accepted, approved, understood and which become immediately clear if they are there to support the image. That is, the image somehow explains the sound. That is, the image somehow guarantees that that sound is authentic, that sound is right, that sound is good, because it joins forces with the film, do you get it? And this is an operation that interested me very much and which I've done whenever possible. It is obvious that in order to do this, the other part, that is your partner, must be a person of quality.
> Q: That is?
> A: Whether his name is for example Losey, Taviani, Bertolucci, then when the interlocutor is of this quality, the project I was telling you about before of transporting that language into an environment in which that language does not automatically have the right to citizenship is all too possible. Indeed, wonderful I'd say.[21]

The avant-garde is indeed useful for the cinema, but, as Macchi reminds us in this interview, cinema is also useful for the avant-garde. Within the audiovisual context, a certain "musical message" is more effective in reaching the same audience, which typically would not be willing to listen to the same music during a traditional kind of concert. However, as Macchi pointed out once more, such an operation can only happen with directors willing to welcome or imagine new sounds within their films. Individual authorial sensibility apart, I think it is appropriate to underline how this phenomenon falls within a broader cinematic perspective typical of that specific historical period in which Macchi took his first steps.[22] The articulated debate that developed around the concept of cinematic modernity during the 1960s stressed the soundtrack's expressive modalities. The questioning of new possible ways of organising sound is somehow a reflection on the awareness of the potentialities of the gaze that characterised the 1960s.

Cinema has represented modern art *par excellence* ever since its inception, mirroring social phenomena concerning the transformations that the twentieth century brought in terms of the acceleration of technology, innovation, and the epochal changes that overwhelmed society.[23] At the centre of the debate amongst the avant-garde theorists of the 1920s, this perspective had the merit of linking the concept of "modern" to

---

[21] *Avanguardie 60, Per es. Nuova Consonanza* (Episode n. 3), 17 September 1979, Rai Uno.

[22] For an overview of the phenomenon see Arved Ashby, *Modernism Goes to the Movies*, in Id. (ed.), *The Pleasure of Modernist Music: Listening, Meaning, Intention, Ideology*, Rochester: Rochester University Press, 2004, pp. 345-386.

[23] See Jacques Aumont, *Moderne: comment le cinéma est devenu le plus singulier des arts*, Paris: Cahiers du cinéma, 2007, p. 8.

that of "crisis" and "revolution". However, it has somehow yoked the discourse to a direct link between art and society. From this assumption, it follows that cinema is in itself modern.[24] It is only from the 1960s onwards that, thanks to a combination of theoretical reflection on the one hand and artistic practice on the other, that a series of connections began to congeal affecting the formal status of cinema and placing the question of modernity at the centre of the debate within the self-same revolution in language.

Giorgio De Vincenti has identified two fundamental traits in the large quantity of films that, just before the 1960s, were commonly classified with the label of "New International Cinema". Apart from their aesthetics, which are of course extremely different from each other, according to De Vincenti, these common traits are to be connected to two instances at the basis of André Bazin's critical and theoretical activity from the 1940s to the 1960s: the redemption of the reproductive aspect of the cinematographic device, and the development of a self-reflective awareness, which introduces a strong metalinguistic component into the filmic text.[25] The cinema of modernity thus takes shape as a cinema that openly investigates the mechanisms of the reproduction of reality, and consequently, the formal and linguistic mechanisms that permit the construction of that reproduction. The debate about sound and its profound renewal can be considered as one of the crucial elements within film criticism and theory, following the practice of the directors of the 1960s who questioned the reproductive and constructive instruments of cinema.

> Recovering the reproductive aspect of cinema implies the assumption, at the level of the individual activity of directing, of the problematic nature of the relationship between the camera and reality, with the resulting implicit or explicit (mostly explicit) problematisation of the gaze, how the eye of the camera formalises the world.[26]

And, I would add, of the way in which even the *ears* of that camera, through the composer's contribution, are able to shape the world on the screen.

Interpreting reality through music

Macchi's compositional activity for cinema fits well into this new aesthetic horizon. He took his first steps within the film genre that, more than others, deals with reality: documentary film.[27] Before we consider the relationship between the representation of reality and the strategies for adding the soundtrack to a film, I should note that non-fiction cinema was already perceived as a field that offered a wealth of extremely interesting musical possibilities. This attitude was typical of someone like Petrassi. He never appreciated his work for cinema, but he was quite ready to defend his documentary experience – «whose music I do not disdain at all»[28] – which includes Edmondo Cancellieri's *Musica nel tempo* (1941), Corrado Pavolini's *La creazione del mondo* (1948), as well as Virgilio Sabel's *Una lezione di geometria* (1948) up to Glauco Pellegrini's *La porta di S. Pietro di Manzù* (1964).[29] Within the debate on sound in film, which developed in Italy from the 1950s onwards, the documentary represents a particularly fertile field to critically rethink the role and contribution of the composer. A glimpse of this trend can be detected within the pages of the aforementioned volume

---

[24] Giorgio De Vincenti, *Il concetto di modernità nel cinema*, Parma: Pratiche Editrice, 2000, p. 13.
[25] See André Bazin, *What is Cinema?*, vol. 1, Berkeley-Los Angeles: University of California Press, 2005.
[26] De Vincenti, *Il concetto di modernità nel cinema*, p. 19.
[27] See Marco Cosci, *Listening to Another Italy: Egisto Macchi's New Music for Italian Documentaries of the 1960s*, «Journal of Film Music», VIII/1-2, 2015 [2019], pp. 109-125.
[28] Petrassi in Luca Lombardi, *Conversazioni con Petrassi*, Milan: Suvini Zerboni, 1980, p. 74.
[29] On the presence of avant-garde composers in industrial film see Alessandro Cecchi, *Creative Titles. Audiovisual Experimentation and Self-Reflexivity in Italian Industrial Films of the Economic Miracle and After*, «Music, Sound, and the Moving Image», VIII/2, 2014, pp. 179-194; on Luigi Nono's film experience, almost completely unknown until a few years ago, see Roberto Calabretto, *Luigi Nono e il cinema. «Un'arte di lotta e fedele alla verità»*, Lucca: Lim, 2017.

on film music, edited by Enzo Masetti. Indeed, Roberto Gervasio and Roman Vlad specifically focus on the documentary.[30] Both composers adopt a strictly pragmatic approach, starting from concrete examples drawn from their active experience. Their writings show how documentary music involves a series of differences of a productive and aesthetic nature that allow the musician in charge to find new compositional strategies, that would be unthinkable in fictional feature films. As Vlad observes:

> More than in normal length films, where the multiplicity and complexity of the spectacular elements at play increase the coefficients of distraction and limit the field of action, it is precisely in *shorts* that music finds the greatest opportunities to do its utmost, often surpassing [...] the limits of its possibilities.[31]

However, the optimism that is apparent in the excerpt from Vlad's article should not lead us to think that the documentary is a field with complete artistic liberty. The standard Italian documentary film is the result of a series of conventions which are in turn intertwined with legislative initiatives. First of all, a number of particularly favourable conditions are created for non-fiction, suffice to cite the October 1945 law which combined the documentary with the screening of a fictional feature film, reserving 3% of box office takings for the production company. This policy remained unaltered in the subsequent legislative acts of 1947 and 1949, only to be slowly dismantled during the time before the 1965 law establishing quality bonuses, abolishing the percentage on revenue, and proceeding to cause the slow death of the genre.[32] While this led producers to attempt to and cut corners – documentaries almost never exceeded a 300 metre-long roll of film, corresponding to eleven minutes in running time[33] – it also gave more creative control to directors and musicians. From the sound point of view, there were two other unavoidable technological issues. First of all, the most widely used camera, the Arriflex 35 mm, did not allow live sound recording. The inability to record the original soundscape live was therefore a real and significant obstacle even though, as Vittorio De Seta's early work[34] with external equipment shows, it was not always inevitable. Faced with the silence imposed by the technical apparatus, the composer's main task above all was to recreate an alternative sound dimension from scratch. The second was to include the so-called speaker, a voice-over who had the task of explaining the contents of the image, whose continued presence was mostly imposed by the production and often opposed by both director and the composer.

These were not the only contextual factors that made documentary film a particularly interesting sector for composers. It was also primarily the topic being investigated that caused a different creative approach for documentaries from the one used in the traditional music of feature films. For example, I agree with Mario Nascimbene who observed that «unlike the feature film, where the obligatory theme is the story, the drama, that is man, this type of documentary, even if it still decides in favour of man, generally excludes him from a declared dramatic function, providing documentary evidence of his hard work and a certain way of life».[35] Documentary films are not

---

[30] Roberto Gervasio, Roman Vlad, *La musica nel documentario*, in Masetti (ed.), *La musica nel film*, pp. 69-77. On these topics, see also the chapters always by Vlad dedicated to music for film and documentary in Roman Vlad, *Modernità e tradizione nella musica contemporanea*, Turin: Einaudi, 1955; for a preliminary overview of Vlad's applied compositional activity, see Francesco Maria Ricci, *La musica di Roman Vlad per il cinema, la televisione e il teatro*, «Nuova Rivista Musicale Italiana», IV, 2008, pp. 499-522.

[31] Vlad, *La musica nel documentario*, p. 77.

[32] See Adriano Aprà, *Itinerario personale nel documentario italiano*, in Lino Miccichè (ed.), *Studi su dodici sguardi d'autore in cortometraggio*, Turin: Associazione Philip Morris Progetto Cinema-Lindau, 1995, pp. 281-295.

[33] See Roberto Nepoti, *L'età d'oro del documentario*, in Sandro Bernardi (ed.), *Storia del cinema italiano: 1954-1959*, Venice: Marsilio, 2004, pp. 185-194: 185.

[34] See for example Marco Bertozzi, *Storia del documentario italiano. Immagini e culture dell'altro cinema*, Venice: Marsilio, 2008, pp. 156-158; Ivelise Perniola, "Vittorio De Seta tra antropologia visiva e poesia," in Sandro Bernardi (ed.), *Storia del cinema italiano: 1954-1959*, pp. 275-281.

[35] Mario Nascimbene, *Malgrè moi, musicista*, Spinea: Edizioni del Leone, 1992, p. 109.

products that merely provide information. At the same time, the privileged and ambiguous relationship that the documentary also maintains with the documentation of reality tends to overshadow its constructive component. The documentary is never, and cannot really be, a neutral reproduction of the world captured but it is always the fruit of its representation.[36] Thus, although the distinction between fiction and non-fiction is a discriminating element that characterises the documentary domain, these two paradigms, in practice, tap into the same pool of filmic techniques and structures. Not by chance, one of the most important documentary scholars, Bill Nichols, has repeatedly resorted to the paradoxical formula «a fiction (un)like any other».[37]

Not only have both camera and video camera never been limited to recording what they observe without any authorial filter, but the sound component has also never been simply the reproduction of the soundscape that the image inhabits. For purely technical reasons or clear authorial choices, this has always been a cornerstone of representative strategies from the very beginning. As theorists have long shown, a documentary film goes beyond the boundaries imposed by the restitution of a reality that is as objective as possible, with an exclusive purpose to convey information. In this regard, Michael Renov has identified four reference categories that can be of help in understanding the variety of intersecting and overlapping trends that account for the multiformity of documentary practice: 1) record, reveal or preserve; 2) persuade or promote; 3) analyse or question; 4) express.[38] While the first three categories, albeit with different nuances, may somehow fall into an informative macro-category, the fourth expressive category is probably one of the most underestimated aesthetic functions in documentary studies.

Documentary production is often traced back to the scientific field, overlooking the aesthetic aspects that are instead in the forefront of narrative feature films. Fiction and non-fiction, understood as two adjacent categories, interpenetrate each other according to the style, the subject and the decisions for their representation. As we will see in the next paragraphs, the representation of reality in *The Assassination of Trotsky* finds a fundamental role in music. The ability to generate an emotional response or aesthetic pleasure through formal solutions, at each of the expressive levels inherent in the medium, is not a distraction from the main event, but is itself a part of its message.[39] It is therefore clear that music can be understood within an expressive need which the various makers of documentary films, with different results and purposes, have taken upon themselves in collaboration with the composers. In its broadest sense of organised sound, music «is part of the heart and soul of film form that strives to represent what it feels like to experience the world from a particular angle, with specific people, in specific places and at specific times»[40]. And the role undertaken by many of Macchi's compositions finds itself situated in precisely in this particular angle.

In fact, it is not by chance that Macchi collaborated with a new generation of directors who were deeply interested in using the camera to filter reality in a novel way, in contrast with the audiovisual strategies explored by fictional cinema. This is mainly the group of the "Demartinian" directors, so called because they were strongly influenced by the studies on Southern Italy carried out by the anthropologist and historian Ernesto De Martino.[41] These directors covered an extremely wide range of topics from ethnographic films to historical documentaries. All their works share the idea of offering an alternative account of reality, and raising public awareness of issues that are not dealt with by contemporary narrative cinema. Take, for example,

---

[36] See the extensive discussion offered by Bill Nichols, *Representing Reality: Issues and Concepts in Documentary*, Bloomington: Indiana University Press, 1991; for a more synthetic version, see instead Id., *Introduction to Documentary*, Bloomington: Indiana University Press, 2010.

[37] See Nichols, *Representing Reality*, pp. 107-109.

[38] See Michael Renov, *Towards a Poetics of Documentary*, in Id. (ed.), *Theorizing Documentary*, New York-London: Routledge, 1993, pp. 12-36: 21.

[39] Renov, *Towards a Poetics of Documentary*, p. 35.

[40] Bill Nichols, *Preface*, in Holly Rogers (ed.), *Music and Sound in Documentary Film*, New York-London: Routledge, 2015, pp. ix-xi: xi.

[41] See Bertozzi, *Storia del documentario italiano*, pp. 146-150.

Lino Del Fra's 1962, *La fata morgana*,[42] winner of the *Leone di San Marco* Award for Best Documentary at the Venice Film Festival. The documentary investigates the very timely phenomenon of farmers who decided to emigrate to the North during the years of the Italian economic miracle.

> Rifts in human relationships, in traditions, in models of behaviour, brutal impact with an "other" universe, new questions and new conflicts would remain, at least for the cinema, almost unnoticed. In fiction, only two or three titles could be recalled: [such as] Visconti's *Rocco* (1960).[43]

Faced with these contradictions, an awareness originating from the paradigm shift typical of cinematic modernity grew in these directors who also started to think up alternative audiovisual solutions. Furthermore, precisely through their awareness of the ability to easily manipulate the visible through music, these directors decided to focus on experimental music above all. Luigi Di Gianni who, together with other documentarians such as the aforementioned Mangini and Del Fra, or Gianfranco Mingozzi, established a close dialogue with the musical avant-garde of the Rome area, makes emblematic remarks in this regard:

> I decided to choose contemporary music because it had to give a particular kind of sound colour... Someone spoke of music from a horror film. This definition is a bit too simple and shows little knowledge of contemporary music in general... The music chosen for my documentaries participates in the visual text without making use of easy melodic and sentimental effects. It is a music that aims at underlining the hidden aspects of a reality that is itself dissonant and "disrupted".[44]

It is easy to understand from Di Gianni both the central role attributed to music in articulating the meaning of documentaries, and the need to get as far away as possible from the musical means adopted within fictional films. Not accidentally, there is substantial similarity between the directors' topics and the positions developed by Theodor W. Adorno and Hanns Eisler on film music's new possibilities. The influential book *Composing for the films* contains a concise, yet methodical discussion of the contribution that "the new musical material" could give to cinema. Adorno and Eisler start from an assumption that is certainly not new, namely the discrepancy between contemporary cinema and the usual underscoring. Then, in the compositional techniques developed in the last thirty years – let us recall that the first edition of the text dates back to 1947 – they see a possible way out of the opportunism and unoriginality of tonal language use in films, now already fossilised around clichés and formulas. Adorno and Eisler's goal is not to introduce a type of post-tonal writing at all costs, which would recover lost ground with respect to certain compositional trends of the twentieth century, but rather to uncouple the current rules of audiovisual construction. In the cinematic remediation of what was expressed by composers such as Arnold Schoenberg, Igor Stravinsky and Béla Bartók, Adorno and Eisler saw the chance to break the vicious cycles currently occurring within the mechanisms of audio-spectator consumption. Only through new musical means can one avoid triggering audiovisual associations dependent on established automatisms. But above all «breaking through the soberly objective surface of the picture and releasing latent suspense» can only happen if the tonal system is abandoned.[45] In the pages dedicated to the new musical material, the idea that going beyond the tonal system determines a sort of drying up of rhetoric and emotion turns up again and again. Everything that

---

[42] The documentary in DVD format is attached to Mirko Grasso (ed.), *Scoprire l'Italia: inchieste e documentari degli anni Cinquanta*, Calimera (LE): Kurumuny, 2007.

[43] Quoted in Mirko Grasso, *Operai del nord e immigrati: la storia orale. Fata Morgana di Lino Del Fra*, in Id. (ed.), *Scoprire l'Italia*, pp. 103-121: 115.

[44] Domenico Ferraro (ed.), *Tra magia e realtà: il meridione nell'opera cinematografica di Luigi Di Gianni*, Rome: Squilibri, 2001, p. 17.

[45] See in particular the third chapter, *The new musical resources*; Theodor W. Adorno, Hanns Eisler, *Composing for the Films*, New York-London: Continuum, 2005, p. 33.

falls within the order of the superfluous, of the optional, is eliminated. The history of tonal music naturally tends towards the development of large forms, but with the lack of long-term architectural functions it is the fragmentation, the indispensable, which finds its *raison d'être* in the irregular cinema framework. The fragmentary logic is a direct consequence of the prosaic nature of cinema, which rejects the principle of symmetrical repetition, characteristic of traditional classical forms. Within this anti-formalistic dimension lies music's ability to interact with images in each single occurrence's autonomy, which naturally prevents the establishment of direct and continuous links with the rest of the musical material. Following this new constructive logic, the focus of the argument is still the communicative purpose. In fact, the abandonment of consolidated formulas does not involve into an emotional dampening of the narrative, but rather it avoids any emotional restraint by means of predetermined stylisations. From the two authors' perspective, the processes of signification are freed from the previous codifications, consequently producing an enhancement of the means that are already available. The abandonment of formulaic baggage gives rise to two results: on the one hand, the musical material tends towards an immeasurable expression of certain emotions – for example, sadness can become despair, anguish, panic – on the other hand, one can find unprecedented modes of expression in the range of inexpressiveness itself, such as peacefulness and indifference.

This is the path that Macchi and the Italian documentary makers explored when they set up successful audiovisual partnerships in the name of musical experimentation. They were inspired by the need to show the transformations of Italy after World War II. In order to do this, they reviewed the visual and sound representation methods adopted until then. Furthermore, as has been already observed, due to a series of production circumstances, as well as for particular authorial sensibilities, the documentary film lent itself to be the film genre's point of reference for experimenting with new means.

Losey, Trotsky, Macchi

During the 1960s, Macchi's name became a reference in the endless production of documentary films, in which he found a way to maintain an extremely high rate of production also thanks to the reuse of already composed pieces. A comparative examination of his documentary production shows how he very often created new musical soundtracks through "compilations" of previously written music, adapted from time to time for new visual and narrative contexts. This practice explains the evident discrepancy between the scores actually kept by the composer and the number of documentaries bearing his signature. Beyond the creative strategies he employed, the great number of projects he was involved in consolidated Macchi's image as a composer of music for experimental films, or at least as an alternative to the compositional standards typical of film production. This obviously did not prevent Macchi from collaborating on more conventional projects, such as the adventure film *Le prigioniere dell'Isola del diavolo* (1962) or the "spaghetti western" *Bandidos* (1968). However, the name "Macchi", even if only in terms of quantitative data, remained linked to documentary production, and more generally to the possibility that the new sounds typical of the second half of the twentieth century could also be conveyed via the silver screen.

Understanding Macchi's position within the Italian film industry helps us to better understand his involvement in Joseph Losey's film project about Leon Trotsky. His involvement was also made possible by the type of productions that governed the last phase of Losey's career. Of the director's last nine feature films, six are international co-productions, including *The Assassination of Trotsky* in 1972 and *Mr. Klein* in 1976. The film about Trotsky was in fact an Italian-French-English co-production – with the contribution of Dino De Laurentiis Cinematografica and Alessandra Cinematografica (Rome), Cinétel (Paris) and Joseph Shaftel Productions (London) – with the Italian capital as the reference centre for the entire post-production phase, which goes to explains why Losey was looking for an Italian composer for the score.

As my comments on the sources preserved in the Joseph Losey Collection at the

British Film Institute (London) will show, after some hesitation, Losey chose Macchi to compose the music for his film, mainly because he was one of the few composers on the Italian scene that could have offered him something different than standard film music. It is no coincidence that all the other composers mentioned in Losey's notes – perhaps with the sole exception of Morricone (cf. Document 1) – were not keen on using a post-tonal musical language. In short, we are dealing with the same issues mentioned before in Adorno and Eisler's seminal book. Interestingly, Losey had the first chance to familiarise himself with a series of film music issues thanks to a project related to *Composing for the films*.

Losey is well-known for his distinct, albeit controversial, musical sensitivity, most clearly supported by his famous film of Mozart's *Don Giovanni* (1979), which is one of the most famous opera-films in the history of cinema.[46] When we step away from Mozart's masterpiece, Losey's name enjoys less notoriety, and one is struck by an almost total absence of a reflection on the sound dimension of his films. Yet his arrival in the cinema is marked by a very prestigious collaboration with Hanns Eisler within the Film Music Project supported by the Rockefeller Foundation: the project within which Eisler was able to start carrying out his research on film music, which was then incorporated in the book *Composing for the Films*.[47] In fact, the young Losey directed the documentaries *Pete Roleum and His Cousins* (1939) and *A Child Went Forth* (1940), for which «the musical problem was to save [them] from the usual saccharine sentimental and humorous romanticism of magazine stories about children».[48]

The attention paid to the different aspects involved in the construction of these films, from the carefully balanced running time ratios of every scene to the musical reworkings of the American children's songs at the base of the score, undoubtedly represented a crucial learning moment for Losey. Exchanging ideas with Eisler gave him the opportunity to question the audiovisual processing procedures mediated by sound and music. During his extensive career, he collaborated with prominent American composers, such as John Barry, and alongside established European musicians, including Michel Legrand and the aforementioned Eisler. No less interesting is his attention to the dramaturgical organisation of sounds, verbal and otherwise. As James Leahy has shown,[49] films like *The Servant* (1963), *Accident* (1967) or *The Go-Between* (1970) highlight significant points of interest in the construction of the ambient soundscape; in the relationships between silences, jump-cuts and the actors' lines; in the importance that certain sounds – the ringing phone or a leaking sink, for example – play in the narrative evolution of the films.

Within this awareness of sound that he had matured over the years, Losey opted to involve Macchi, as a composer who could offer him something new and not trivial. A few years later, during a television programme about the different jobs in the film industry (in an episode entirely dedicated to music which also features Rota and Gelmetti), Macchi himself provided more detail on the tacit agreement he stipulated with Losey:

> Making *Trotsky*, Losey called me saying «I've made a film – he told me – that stands on its own and I think it doesn't need sticks or crutches of any kind. But I believe that if there is a musician who can invent a particular sound, this sound could probably

---

[46] See Marcia Citron, *Opera on Screen*, New Haven: Yale University Press, 2000, pp. 161-204. The director's interest in the sound-musical sphere can also be detected through his brief comments about his films collected in Joseph Losey, *L'œil du Maître*, Textes réunis et présentés par Michel Ciment, Paris-Arles: Institut Lumière/Actes Sud, 1994. In particular see le *Notes sur le but e les utilisations des chansons de Billie Holiday dans Eva*, pp. 124-126; *Notes sur le son*, pp. 147-148.

[47] See Sally Bick, *Unsettled Scores: Politics, Hollywood, and the Film Music of Aaron Copland and Hanns Eisler*, Urbana: University of Illinois Press, 2019, pp. 81-126. For a detailed analysis of the Film Music Project see Breixo Viejo, *Música moderna, para un nuevo cine. Eisler, Adorno y el Film Music Project*, Madrid: Akal, 2008.

[48] Adorno, Eisler, *Composing for the Films*, pp. 141. A digital copy of the film is attached to the German edition of the book (Theodor W. Adorno, Hanns Eisler, *Komposition für den Film*, Frankfurt am Main: Suhrkamp, 2006).

[49] See a first proposal to study sound in Losey's work in the sixth paragraph *Ricominciare dal suono* by James Leahy, *L'arte di Joseph Losey: un viaggio personale*, in Luciano De Giusti (ed.), *Joseph Losey. Senza re, senza patria*, Milan: Il castoro, 2010, pp. 74-92: 87-91.

help my film a lot in some weak spots. You're a musician and I'm a director, if you bring me interesting things I will be happy to accept you, otherwise it means that the film will remain, as after all I had conceived it with the noises and its effects and some street music». Losey's position here was very interesting, quite clear which gave the musician a great responsibility. So this was one of the few times I felt really free to make my score, knowing that only a particular score could convince someone like Joseph Losey [...] and that instead a score of a cautious nature, conservative, ordinary would have certainly driven him away. I understood that he wanted music and not background music. [...] It's perfect when the musician can use his own language for the film presented to him.[50]

The freedom Macchi talks about did not mean he could indiscriminately choose the sequences to set to music or that there were no running time restrictions. The dramaturgy of the film, for example, required him to compose pieces for bands or choirs for diegetic events – the "street music" mentioned in the quotation – which called for a musical style that was "dictated" by the particular cinematic situation. Nevertheless, for all the so-called nondiegetic musical cues, Macchi could instead adopt more personal musical solutions, thus creating sounds with «extraordinary tension, richness and beauty» so appreciated so much by Losey that he called Macchi again for the music of *Mr. Klein*.

Both films are inspired by real events that took place in the 1940s: the assassination of Stalin's famous opponent and the *Grande Rafle* of 1942.[51] Given the importance of the documentary genre in Macchi's film career, it would be plausible to try and look for the expressive potential of Macchi's unconventional scores in the analysis of the non-fictional reality underlying those feature films. In line with the statement by Di Gianni mentioned above, from this point of view, Macchi's music could help shed light on the problematic, hidden aspects of specific historical facts and, in doing so, could help to bring out their non-fictionality according to a model that has also been explored on other creative fronts, for example, by Kurt Weill or by Eisler. A leading expert on Losey like Colin Gardener[52] seems to go in this direction when, in analysing *Mr. Klein*, he emphasises the affinity between the two films and «Macchi's visceral soundtrack» observing how «Macchi chose the same pseudo-electronic rhythm and dissonant chords in the style of Ligeti that he had used in Losey's film *The Assassination of Trotsky*, thus linking the dark and immanent forces of bureaucratic indifference to the monstrous Stalinist gulag of the previous film».[53] Moreover, especially for *The Assassination of Trotsky*, it must be noted that the political dimension plays quite an influential role in the poetics of an openly leftist director, forced to move to Europe during the McCarthy era. More specifically, as Losey himself admitted, the Trotsky project forced him to rethink his positions on Stalinism and the policies of the Soviet Union.[54] In fact, critics welcomed the film with a certain scepticism, accusing Losey of not being able to give the right artistic aura to the narrative precisely because it was excessively biased towards the historical-political representation of events.[55]

However, beyond the account of the statesman's last days in exile in Mexico, the film finds its poetic centre in the figure of the hitman Franck Jackson (Alain Delon) sent to kill Trotsky (Richard Burton), and in the relationship the former has with a girl (Romy Schneider) from the communist circle, who is often found at the statesman's house. Although Jackson is increasingly consumed with guilt over the task

---

[50] *Come si fa il cinema*, La musica, RAI, 1988.

[51] The sweeping raid carried out between 16 and 17 July 1942, during which the French police arrested and rounded up 13,000 Jews in the Vélodrome d'Hiver, and then deported them to Nazi concentration camps.

[52] See Colin Gardner, *Joseph Losey*, Manchester: Manchester University Press, 2004.

[53] Colin Gardner, *La storia senza pietà: Mr. Klein e i cristalli del tempo*, in De Giusti (ed.), *Joseph Losey. Senza re, senza patria*, pp. 160-178: 163.

[54] Gardner, *Joseph Losey*, pp. 265-266.

[55] One of the few discordant voices is undoubtedly that of the critic Maurizio Porro who, on the contrary, appreciates Losey's ability to give life to a political cinema that is also poetic and not enclosed in an ideological schema; see Maurizio Porro, *Joseph Losey*, Milan: Contemporanea cinema, 1978, pp. 81-82.

he must perform, he carries out his mission. And it is precisely around this conflictual relationship – that is, the relationship between victim and executioner, a popular theme in Losey's filmography – that Macchi's music seems to find an operational space.

The film presents an extremely varied musical soundscape: in addition to the nondiegetic pieces composed by Macchi, there are several examples of diegetic music – especially in the form of revolutionary songs for the opening sequences of the street demonstrations. The original pieces by Macchi make it hard to clearly define what is (nondiegetic) musical sound and what are instead (diegetic) noise-based sounds, employed mainly through the extensive use of the Synket, a synthesiser capable of reproducing the timbres of noise-like sounds widely used in Italian cinema of the 1960s and 1970s. In fact, it is used on the soundtrack of *The Assassination of Trotsky* to produce the timbre of the chirping crickets that recalls the natural sound landscape in which Trotsky's fortified villa stands. Despite these ambiguities, the music Macchi made for Losey ends up being different not only from the music *in* films but also from the music *for* films in the traditional sense of the term, especially considering the canons of the Italian scene of that period.

Therefore, what is the role entrusted to this sound component of an interstitial nature? On the one hand, it is clearly different from the music normally heard in a film, and, on the other, it seems to ambiguously emerge from the soundscape itself within the portrayed situation. To answer this question, let us recall some of Gilles Deleuze's illuminating reflections outlined in the first part of his famous study devoted to cinema, *The Movement-Image* (*L'image-mouvement*, 1983). Deleuze dedicates a paragraph to Losey, indicating him as one of the great naturalist authors capable of achieving the impulse-image's purity. According to the French philosopher, the characteristic feature of Losey's films is his ability to create a particular kind of violence: an enacted violence, even before it engages action. The forces that pass through the protagonists of his films are static since the act of violence is always self-reflective. Although Deleuze has not openly discussed *The Assassination of Trotsky*, the trajectory of a character like Trotsky's assassin clearly shows the extent to which he is dominated by and becomes the victim of the violence of his impulses. From a visual perspective, the film presents recurring elements that thematise the question of the gaze and invite the viewer to investigate the underlying dynamics from an openly self-reflective perspective: the numerous mirrors in Jackson's room, the camera-looks, and, above all, Delon's eyes filtered by dark glasses, symbol of a present but hidden gaze. The central role of this last element in the portrayal of the character is suggested by a policeman asking the hitman a question in the lead-up to the attack: «What goes on behind those eyes?» a question that remains unanswered verbally, but which could find a possible resolution in the close synchronisation with Macchi's music.

The theme of seeing, and what lies behind the very act of seeing, is therefore directly connected to the act of listening to Macchi's music, which is not only complex in its stratification and ambiguity of sound levels, but also offers a sound experience based on static sound masses, without any clear temporal vectorisation.

The itinerary that marks this reflective spiral towards the complete annihilation of the protagonist follows audiovisual paths. The tensions of the impulse-image act at a subcutaneous level, establishing a link between the eye and a musical mental dimension that captures what cannot be put into words. As the film progresses, this process becomes more and more evident, eventually colliding with the frame's impenetrable emptiness determined by Delon's silent and increasingly petrified gaze, animated only by the soundtrack. Shortly before Trotsky is killed, a dense network of verbal-musical dialogues emerges between Romy Schneider's voice and the music conceived by Macchi. Beneath a continuous series of long, held notes a constant exchange characterised by the woman's questions and the man's (missing) answers occurs. In managing the overall audiovisual balance, Macchi thus creates a polyphony that interconnects the instrumental lines that lack any directionality in the score, the fragments of the woman's dialogue and the emptiness of the man's petrified gaze.

Evidence of these processes comes from the audiovisual strategy chosen to express the elimination of Franck's identity, once the assassination has been carried out. When the police officer asks him «Who are you?», the now devastated man answers: «I killed Trotsky». This creates an overlap between the impulse and the identity of the character himself, underlined by the dialogues and "incorporated" by the soundtrack of the last shot of the film, made up of a still image that captures Delon's camera look. An electroacoustic track suspended in a liminal zone of music-effects-dialogues stresses this last shot. Macchi obtains it by electroacoustically reworking the babble of a boys' choir – another sound element suspended between the diegetic and the nondiegetic domains – that was already heard at the beginning of the film, during the opening credits, and the bullfighting sequence (cf. Documents 7-13), a crucial moment in which Jackson's strife is audiovisually mirrored through a spectacle in the arena. It is no coincidence that Peter Handford, the sound recordist for Losey's previous film, *The Go-Between* (1971) defined that track as «one of the most impressive uses of sound, as soon as I think about it, certainly one of the most amazingly effective things I've ever heard on a film soundtrack».[56]

Inside the composer's workshop

As we have seen in the previous paragraph, the uniqueness of the music composed by Macchi must not only be traced in its experimental nature *per se*, but also in the stratification of sound events that tended to question the traditional boundaries of dialogues, music, and effects within the balance of the soundtrack. Behind the collaboration between Macchi and Losey lays the will to pursue new creative strategies through music, extending the field of compositional techniques to post-tonality and questioning all levels of audiovisual communication in a fully integrated perspective. But how did this collaboration start? What was its outcome? And what aspects can be reconstructed through the sources that remain? To answer these questions, this book is organised in three chapters which aim to retrace some of the crucial stages of the creative process of music through the reproduction of facsimiles and commentary on a selection of sources relating to *The Assassination of Trotsky*. Almost all of Egisto Macchi's musical sources are housed in the Egisto Macchi Collection at the Institute of Music, Giorgio Cini Foundation in Venice (EMC),[57] which served as the starting point for this research. The materials preserved in the Joseph Losey Collection held by the British Film Institute in London (JLC) are also of great importance, serving to shed light on the genesis of the collaboration. These are not specifically musical sources, but rather letters, notes and production materials that help to understand Losey's intentions on the musical side. The first chapter – *In search of the right sound* – is dedicated to the preliminary stages of the soundtrack genesis. A number of documents in the Losey Collection allow us to understand how, at the start of the project, Macchi was not contemplated as the composer. They show the director's great difficulty in choosing a music collaborator. As an international production, Losey was, in fact, forced to find the composer he needed from the Italian scene and his messages to the rest of the production staff indicate his dissatisfaction. This does not mean that Losey was dealing with second-rate composers – quite the contrary. From the lists initially drawn up to scrutinise the names of possible composers to be involved, we can see that those considered were the leading names in the sector, such as Morricone, Rota and Lavagnino. By contrast, it emerges how Macchi, precisely because he was an eccentric figure on the Italian cinema scene, was functional to Losey's particular audiovisual project. Nevertheless, Macchi still had to oversee the arrangement of more conventional choral pieces for the street sequences. But he was mainly asked to compose a series of modernist pieces that had to go beyond the musical conventions of the cinematic field, but which inevitably had to be adapted to fit the extra-musical soundscape already endorsed by the director. As Losey told

---

[56] Patricia Losey, *Mes années avec Joseph Losey*, Paris: Éditions L'Âge d'Homme, 2015, pp. 236-237.
[57] For an overview of the collection see the site: https://archivi.cini.it/istitutomusica/archive/IT-MUS-GUI001-000008/egisto-macchi.html.

the producers, the collaboration between the two ran smoothly, not only in the preparatory phase of the music, but also in the mixing stages. Not surprisingly, in March 1972 the director officially assigned Macchi:

> any full contractual authority to approve or disapprove the final dubbing and mix of the Italian version of my film THE ASSASSINATION OF TROTSKY. I am most grateful to you for understanding this task and I am sure that your decision will be the same as mine would have been had I been available since you are now certainly as familiar with the picture and the mixing problems as I am myself.[58]

A crucial step because the director's choice allowed Macchi to achieve one of his greatest goals, namely:

> Entrusting the responsibility for the soundtrack to the composer would be an act of wisdom for the benefits it would bring to the cinematographic work and at the same time an act of faith in the musician who still today is frequently sacrificed on altars erected from time to time to the god of cinema to appease him for the serious mistakes made by others than the musician.[59]

This is in fact what Macchi had to say in one of his rare writings – reported in full in the appendix – regarding the usefulness of entrusting the composer to oversee the balance between all the sound components. Like many of the other leading figures of the period,[60] Macchi was aware that the harmonisation of the various sound components in the mixing room is a crucial moment that often risks becoming a battleground between the different departments. With this awareness, Macchi theorised and adopted a pragmatic attitude aimed at establishing the right balance between noises and dialogues already in the composition, in order to avoid discussion and unwelcome changes during mixing. The search for the right sound for *The Assassination of Trotsky* should therefore be understood not only in strictly musical terms, but also in relation to the other sounds present on the soundtrack and, obviously, in relation to the visual details of the sequences set to music.

In the second and third chapters, Macchi's "integrated" compositional approach is discussed through an analysis of the available musical sources, from two different perspectives. In the chapter *From the opening credits to the bullfight*, there are two reasons why I make an in-depth analysis of the piece that accompanies the opening credits. First of all, it allows us to observe what was actually Macchi's typical *modus operandi*, at least for this film. As a rule, it sees him setting down a sketch, and then proceeding with the orchestration and the final drafting of the cues for the recording sessions. Secondly, the theme music for the opening credits occupies a particular position in the structure of the film, because it is reused in a key sequence (the aforementioned bullfight sequence), followed by two other pieces, which, although they are short, reveal insights on the synchronisation strategies Macchi adopted in the capillary structuring of the audiovisual scene. In this regard, unlike the collections of other composers from the same period, the Macchi Collection contains no notebooks with written notes for the editing stage.[61] The scholar therefore has to deal with this lacuna and exploit other textual and paratextual elements embedded in the sources – such as dynamic or chronometric indications – to better understand the creative process adopted in relation to a precise sequence, consequently inferring structural elements.

In the third chapter, *Alternative routes*, I examine the compositional strategies behind some paradigmatic cues by analysing the different versions of the same piece

---

[58] Letter sent from Joseph Losey to Egisto Macchi on 30 March 1972 (Joseph Losey Collection, JWL/1/19/12); cf. Document 3.

[59] See Appendix 2.

[60] Alessandro Cecchi, *Tecniche di sincronizzazione nella musica per film di Angelo Francesco Lavagnino: una prospettiva musicologica*, «Musica/Tecnologia», 8-9, 2014-2015, pp. 57-93: 63.

[61] One of the few exceptions is the notepad relating to the film *Bronte: cronaca di un massacro che i libri di storia non hanno raccontato* (Florestano Vancini, 1972); see Marco Cosci, *Vancini, Macchi and the Voices for the (Hi)story of Bronte*, «Archival Notes», 2017, pp. 65-81.

from a comparative perspective. Among the materials pertaining to *The Assassination of Trotsky* we also find the drafts and the fair copies of the pieces not included in the film. This is certainly not a feature that is exclusive to his compositional process, but it should be noted that Macchi's particular type of writing, as compared to other authors, prevents the director from imagining the overall result by simply listening to it on the piano, for example. The only way to test the musical material in the film and make deliberate choices with the director is through a full-blown performance. Even in the absence of the original tapes, it is still possible to recreate the peculiarity of the listening experience for the discarded versions thanks to an album that includes various materials not used in the film.[62] Through these recordings and the manuscript sources of the alternative versions, not only can we better understand the forces at play when Macchi and Losey were selecting the final version, but we also obtain a better understanding of the essential aspects of the audiovisual construction, which were the result of discussions between composer and director. Moreover, we can also see how Macchi finds different compositional solutions within these restraints depending on which visual and sound elements he decides to favour through the musical lens.

Such avenues of investigation are made possible precisely by the provisional nature and craftsmanship of creative processes, which are defined in the moment when they are put down on paper. This allows us to make several conclusive remarks on the textual status of film music materials and the potential offered by facsimile copies.

«It has often been remarked that a major barrier to effective film-music scholarship lies in the absence of published editions of the scores»[63], observed Ben Winters, introducing one of the main problems faced by anyone who is preparing to study original film music scores. The lack of an official editorial channel that transmits a textual form noted down on paper is actually one of film music's congenital problems and, with the uniqueness of the case, part of the profound change affecting musical textualities especially in the late twentieth century.

Although Winters sought to identify problems and possible solutions to elaborate a critical edition, the lack of a printed transmission can be a peculiarity that offers great potential to critical investigation. In other words, what can be inferred about compositional thought and the production process from manuscript materials and what are the new links that exist between text and performance? And how do they condition and redefine each other?

These questions reveal the great relevance of the theory put forward by McLuhan more than half a century ago, according to which the medium is the message.[64] The message is determined precisely by the very nature of the medium, by its form. Of course, there is no intent to neglect its content, but to focus on the ways in which the content is produced, stored, and enjoyed, according to the forms of knowledge that the musical medium determines. As McLuhan teaches us, media are never neutral entities, but they condition and modify our lifestyles and perceptions; therefore, precisely in light of the detailed debate on textuality, one needs to be clear about the musical transformations put into practice. Since Macchi was an established composer in the field of art music, this awareness is helpful to stress the particularity of his work in the film world.

Obviously, the first observation has to do with time schedules. Macchi's music composed for film cannot be understood within the usual paradigms of creative freedom. This is something that perhaps goes without saying, but which might be taken for granted, especially within a tangential field to the musical expression of art. Composing film music has understandable repercussions in composing faster and, consequently, in the type of materials available. The phases of the compositional process are marked by the maximum exploitation of the forces at hand. It is therefore

---

[62] The album released in 1990 by Beat Records features seven tracks. It groups together some of the pieces composed by Macchi, often also including the alternative versions; Egisto Macchi, *L'assassinio di Trotsky – Il delitto Matteotti*, Beats Records Company, CDCR 15.

[63] Ben Winters, *Catching Dreams: Editing Film Scores for Publication*, «Journal of the Royal Musical Association», CXXXII/1, 2007, pp. 115-140: 115.

[64] Marshall Mcluhan, *Understanding Media: The Extensions of Man*, Cambridge: MIT Press, 1964.

not surprising to observe a reduction in the number of pre-compositional materials, in contrast with the proliferation of sketches and drafts typical of the twentieth century: the speed of cinema consumption reflects a fast-paced genesis, based on the efficient use of materials at all levels. Although there are very few pieces of evidence that can bear witness to the compositional stages preceding the drafting of the "actual" score, it is the fair copy manuscript that often becomes the privileged *witness* through which we can observe the variety of creative processes that have been put into practice. Writing for the cinema is never an activity aimed at formalising a text to be kept in printed form, in view of possible future performances that substantiate its sound material. The score for a film is a compositional project conceived exclusively to record a soundtrack that will be synchronised with the images. And it is thanks to the provisional nature of its notational form, written on paper, that we can reconstruct the layering of compositional processes in and out of the recording studio.

This is the sense of Nicholas Cook's attempt to relate the score to the performance. The hypothesis that considers the score as more of a script, as a starting point for a new chain of performative acts of a creative nature becomes highly relevant. Although the field of film music is unfortunately not covered by the scope of his investigation, which mainly focuses on the paradigm of art music, it highlights how the actual act of the performance, and its fixation on a support, is not a simple reproduction of the text, but an act of production that helps to rethink the music and the creative processes involved.[65] In the light of this awareness, Ilario Meandri's sagacious words offer intriguing insights into the topic:

> The score is therefore in this case a heterotopic text (even if the improper projection of criticism often transforms it into a utopian text). It contributes to realise the compositional project but does not coincide with it. The variation that happens between the initial conception, of which the written document is undoubtedly the proof, and *the music*, is the norm. Film music only exists within this complex relationship. The other extreme – considering recording as being the only relevant document – is an equally worrying philological aberration [...]: «if the recording can sometimes be the extemporaneous fixation of a process, we have to ask ourselves, which recording? Passed from hand to hand, from transcription to transcription, the interventions of various instruments and operators have been stratified, in a cycle of re-mediation that does not allow arbitrary simplification.[66]

Studying Macchi's compositional workshop does not mean attributing the plurality of creative contributions exclusively to the composer. He was operating in the diversified production field of film music, which involved consistent and commendable contributions by several other figures. Likewise, it does not mean that the creative process of the music for *The Assassination of Trotsky* exhausts itself in the textual level handed down on paper. Through the analysis and interpretation of several documents, this study aims to shed light on the sound component of the film that follows in the wake of that "integrated approach" theorised by William Kinderman in the context of so-called genetic criticism.[67] The surviving traces of the composer's experience deposited in the archives help to situate and understand the work in the context of its creation. They enlighten the methodologies of analysis that are capable of interconnecting the different artistic spheres. Philological investigation can make a decisive contribution not only to understanding the genesis of the film in question, but also to revealing and defining the contours of aesthetic assumptions at the basis of the composer's collaboration with Losey. Macchi's compositional filter and his

---

[65] For a preliminary theoretical framework of the topic, see Nicholas Cook, *Between Process and Product: Music and/as Perfomance*, «Music Theory Online», VII/2, 2001, accessible at http://www.mtosmt.org/issues/mto.01.7.2/mto.01.7.2.cook.html. These premises were then elaborated in Nicholas Cook, *Beyond the Score. Music as Performance*, Oxford-New York: Oxford University Press, 2013.

[66] Ilario Meandri, *Internatinal Recording (1959-1969). Indagine sulle memorie orali*, Turin: Kaplan, 2013, p. 87.

[67] See William Kinderman, Joseph E. Jones (eds), *Genetic Criticism and the Creative Process. Essays Music, Literature and Theater*, Rochester: University of Rochester Press, 2009, pp. 1-16; Friedemann Sallis, *Music Sketches*, Cambridge: Cambridge University Press, 2015, pp. 9-11.

working materials for *The Assassination of Trotsky* highlight the crucial relationship that intertwines analysis, theory, and history, and shed light on what it meant, in a particular historical moment, for the world of cinema to open up to experimental sound practices.

Appendix 1
Filmography

Feature films

A proposito di quella strana ragazza, Marco Leto, 1989.
Antonio Gramsci. I giorni dal carcere, Lino Del Fra, 1977.
Bandidos, Max Dillman, 1968.
Bronte, cronaca di un massacro che i libri di storia non hanno raccontato, Florestano Vancini, 1972.
Charlotte, Frans Weisz, 1980.
Circuito chiuso, Giuliano Montaldo, 1978.
Cronaca di un gruppo, Ennio Lorenzini, 1972.
Diary of a Mad Old Man, Lili Rademakers, 1987.
E cominciò il viaggio nella vertigine, Tony De Gregorio, 1974.
E se per caso una mattina, Vittorio Sindoni, 1973 (in collaboration with the improvisation group Nuova Consonanza).
Educatore autorizzato, Luciano Odorisio, 1979.
Gangster '70, Mino Guerrini, 1968.
Giallo alla regola, Stefano Roncoroni, 1988.
Gli amici degli amici hanno saputo, Fulvio Marcolin, 1973.
Havinck, Frans Weisz, 1988.
I vecchi e i giovani, Marco Leto, 1978.
Il delitto Matteotti, Florestano Vancini, 1973.
Il fratello, Massimo Mida Puccini, 1975.
Il giustiziere dei mari, Domenico Paolella, 1962.
Il tempo dell'inizio, Luigi Di Gianni, 1974.
Layla, ma raison, Taïeb Louhichi, 1989.
L.S.D. Un'atomica nel cervello, Mike Middleton, 1967.
L'inchiesta, Gianni Amico, 1971.
L'ombre de la terre, Taïeb Louhichi, 1982.
L'ultima carica, Leopoldo Savona, 1964.
La coda del diavolo, Giorgio Treves, 1986.
La prova generale, Romano Scavolini, 1968.
La torta in cielo, Lino Del Fra, 1973.
La villeggiatura, Marco Leto, 1973.
Le cercle des passions, Claude D'Anna, 1982.
Le due croci, Silvio Maestranzi, 1988.
Le prigioniere dell'Isola del Diavolo, Domenico Paolella, 1962.
Mascara, Patrick Conrad, 1987.
Menuet, Lili Rademakess, 1982.
Mort à…, Leon Desclouzeu, 1983.
Mr. Klein, Joseph Losey, 1976.
Nell'occhio della volpe, Antonio Drove, 1979.
November Mond, Alexandra von Grote, 1984.
Padre padrone, Paolo e Vittorio Taviani, 1977.
Partenaires, Claude D'Anna, 1984.
Salome, Claude D'Anna, 1986.
Ten to survive, 1979 (in collaboration with Nino Rota, Ennio Morricone, Franco Evangelisti, Luis Bacalov; music for two episodes).
The Assassination of Trotsky, Joseph Losey, 1972.
Tre nel Mille, Franco Indovina, 1971 (in collaboration with Ennio Morricone and Giorgio Nataletti).

Une pierre dans la bouche, Jean Louis Leconte, 1983.
Volontari per una destinazione ignota, Alberto Negrin, 1977.

Television dramas

All'ombra dei Savoia, Giorgio Treves, 1982.
Bambole: scene di un delitto perfetto, Alberto Negrin, 1980.
Cambiamento d'aria, Gian Pietro Calasso, 1991.
Educatore autorizzato, Luciano Odorisio, 1980.
ESP, Daniele D'Anza, 1973.
I vecchi e i giovani, Marco Leto, 1979.
I monti di vetro, Sergio Tau, 1972.
Il cancelliere Krehler, Luigi Di Gianni, 1972.
Il caso Lafarge, Marco Leto, 1973.
Il delitto Notarbartolo, Alberto Negrin, 1979.
Il giudice istruttore, Florestano Vancini, 1990.
Il nocciolo della questione, Marco Leto, 1983.
Il picciotto, Alberto Negrin, 1973.
Il processo, Luigi di Gianni, 1978.
Il ritorno, Giorgio Treves, 1980.
Il viaggio difficile, Giorgio Pelloni, 1986.
Io e il duce, Alberto Negrin, 1985.
Indagine su una rapina, Gian Pietro Galasso, 1972.
Ipotesi su un omicidio, Gian Pietro Calasso, 1971.
L'attentato al papa, Giuseppe Fina, 1986.
L'avvoltoio sa attendere, Gian Pietro Calasso, 1991.
L'enigma Borden, Gian Pietro Calasso, 1982.
La gentile morte di Giovanni, Marco Leto, 1983.
La promessa, Alberto Negrin, 1980.
La quinta donna, Alberto Negrin, 1982.
Le due croci, Silvio Maestranzi, 1988.
Le lunghe ombre, Gianfranco Mingozzi, 1987.
Nucleo centrale investigativo, Vittorio Armentano, 1974.
Patto con la morte, Gian Pietro Calasso, 1982.
Quaderno proibito, Marco Leto, 1980.
Spia – Il caso Philby, Gian Pietro Calasso, 1977.
Storie dell'anno mille, Franco Indovina, 1973.
Una pistola nel cassetto, Gianni Bongiovanni, 1974.

Appendix 2
Egisto Macchi, [Writing the score for a film][68]

Writing the score for a film (be it full-length or short) means solving a series of problems that affect not only the musical structure of the score and its relationship with the images for which it is composed, but also the relationships and interplay with the other components of the film's soundtrack, namely the effects and the spoken part. In other words, this is a restriction on the composer's autonomy that can only be accepted insofar as it occurs or should occur within a collaborative relationship between the composer himself and the technicians in charge of the other production departments and, first of all, the director.

The biggest gap, in this regard, is in the relationship between music-effects-dialogues. It apparently seems quite feasible to have a constant exchange of ideas between the technicians of the three departments in order to create the perfect soundtrack, in which each of these three elements has the necessary importance, the right balance that alone can guarantee the effectiveness of the soundtrack itself. In actual fact, the exchange of ideas either does not occur at all, or, if it does, it is limited to noticing what could be noticed even by just viewing the images, where an explosion necessarily brings with it its sound equivalent and the movement of the actors' lips the equivalent dialogue. What is absolutely missing is the fusion of the results of the three departments. The director, who as such should have the most precise vision of his film, often does not have the technical possibility of intervening to reunite these three important elements; when he does so, in the mixing room, it's already too late. Then it is only a question of sacrificing the other two elements to the element deemed most important, eliminating or reducing the effects or the music or eliminating (as sometimes happens) the dialogue, in order to obtain the best compromise that is going to save the soundtrack at this or that point. More than important, the problem is essential, fundamental. I believe that the best way to solve it is to entrust the musician with overall responsibility for the soundtrack. The musician should approach his score bearing in mind the dialogue and effects. The score should be composed based on:

1. on the timing of the film sequence (general tempo and partial timings)

2. on the timing of the dialogue (beginning and end of the dialogue, tones of voice (male, female, high-pitched, low, gentle, shrill, etc., intensity of emission)

3. on the timing of the effects (beginning and end of the effects, timbric quality, rhythm, intensity)

Such a score would have a layout like this:

---

[68] Unpublished and undated manuscript, original text in Italian [Scrivere la partitura per un film]; Venice, Giorgio Cini Foundation, Egisto Macchi Collection.

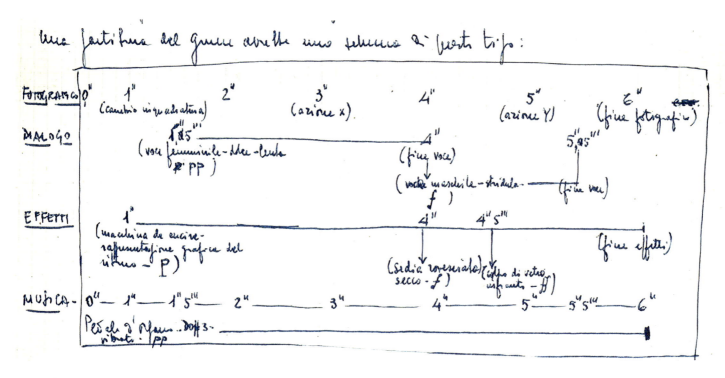

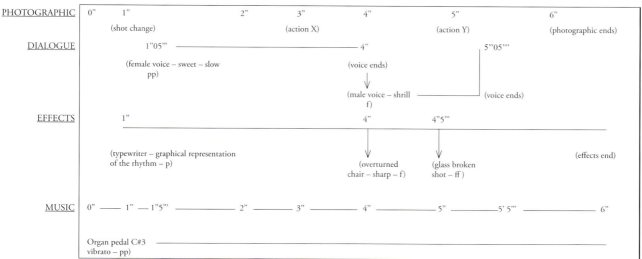

PHOTOGRAPHIC	0"	1"		2"	3"	4"		5"		6"	
		(shot change)			(action X)			(action Y)		(photographic ends)	
DIALOGUE		1"05'"				4"		5"05'"			
		(female voice – sweet – slow pp)				(voice ends)					
						↓					
						(male voice – shrill f)		(voice ends)			
EFFECTS		1"				4"	4"5'"				
		(typewriter – graphical representation of the rhythm – p)				↓	↓			(effects end)	
						(overturned chair – sharp – f)	(glass broken shot – ff)				
MUSIC	0"	1"	1"5'"	2"	3"	4"		5"	5'5'"		6"
	Organ pedal C#3 vibrato – pp)										

    The graph clearly shows how, if the soundtrack were entrusted to the musician, attention could be paid to every detail. In the example reported (absolutely imaginary) there is mainly, for example, a combination of dialogue and effects. In this case the composer can choose between eliminating all the background music and the insertion of a musical element that emphasises the general character of the piece or instead follows the two actors in their acting or again serves as a support for the sound effects. In the first case (absence of music) it is particularly important to search for the sound effects, knowing in advance that they will function as a basic soundtrack, which means they will have to accompany the dialogue. In the other case (presence of music) the composer will take care to compose a piece that joins in with the other elements without disturbing them, which increases their effectiveness and is not spoiled by them. In the specific case (a sewing machine in action, a woman's gentle voice in *pianissimo*, running time 4") an organ pedal vibrato *piano* could blend well with the whole scene: the fast chugging sound of the needle would effectively stand out on the low held note, the slowness of the female voice would integrate well with the fast rhythm of the needle, for its high-pitched tone with the low tone of the organ and its intensity (*pianissimo*) would not be disturbed by the other elements (*piano* the machine, *pianissimo* the organ).

    I've said and repeated *usque ad nauseam* that a film is a collaborative work, the result of the work of a team, whose members are independent in their actions, but all intent on one purpose under the director's coordinating leadership. That they are all totally responsible for the result (and therefore all the collaborators have the right to intervene) is a universally accepted principle, with no exception. We are certainly not going to distance ourselves from this position which we generally acknowledge as being right, even though, in this regard, it would be interesting to launch a debate that would better specify the *rights and duties* of the director and collaborators, with a reorganisation of responsibilities, merits, demerits, contributions, etc. Instead, what we wish to discuss are the difficult conditions in which the musician is forced to work within that team, in the workings of a collaboration that is so highly sought-after, but so little put into practice. My personal experience, things my colleagues have told me, the results of environmental surveys that each of us gets the chance to carry out for work reasons, tell us that this difficult condition is not typical of the musician alone but that it extends to all the other members of the film crew. The time factor, along with the economic one, is at the origin of the precarious situation within which the specialists of the various departments are forced to move, each of them tormented by the duo of «low cost» and «faster» than «low cost». And this is not just a question of causing damage to the work of each single person, but, and let me emphasise this, it particularly damages the collaboration which, by definition, is essential to the success of the film. It doesn't seem to me that this point is sufficiently taken into account during the making of the film: individualism tends to take over and I don't think that this is solely due to the difficulties mentioned above. In each of the collaborators there is an instinctive propensity to dominate, to perfect their own product, without bearing in mind that this selfsame supposed perfection benefits the perfection of others and the extent to which two perfect products are able to amalgamate, fortifying each other, instead of clashing with each other, damaging each other and removing the effectiveness of the end result. The principle of collaboration has yet to be fully understood and it is by no means as 'peaceful' as one might think and as it should be. Collaboration is conquest, it is a work of humbleness and intelligence, not a contest of virtuosity or a struggle for dominance. All too often, however, you have to work without knowing the work of others, without others knowing your work, forced to give your best as if the film were made up only of effects, or music or dialogue. The meeting (far too often, the confrontation) takes place during mixing and is almost always an unpleasant eye-opener for everyone. The result of the 'collaboration' far from having been assessed a priori in all its details, is almost completely left to chance, to uncertainty whose control possibilities are frequently reduced to a minimum. The claim that, despite everything, films continue to come out and that among these one can come across works of considerable artistic value, quite simply doesn't hold water: in most of these cases (the usual *exceptions* have to do with the *exceptional* skills of the directors) a slightly less superficial analysis would reveal the lack of preparation conducted simultaneously and homogeneously on several lines. One can never obtain a decent soundtrack until its component elements are entrusted to a single person in charge who takes care of the levels 'a priori'. Once the dialogues have been recorded and edited, the technician in charge of recording and editing the effects should proceed, bearing in mind the dialogue track. The musician, the last to intervene, should be able to work taking into account the images, dialogue and sound effects tracks, deciding, in perfect harmony with the director, the type of soundtrack deemed most suitable for the individual pieces of the film. It seems to me that it is really important that the concepts of dialogue, effects and music are once and for all merged into a single concept of soundtrack. All too often the musician happens to write extremely difficult pieces, extremely elaborate from a formal point of view, conceived as if they were detached from any other non-musical element and therefore structured in such a way as not to tolerate interference of any kind, and then in the mixing stage, he is forced to witness the completely unexpected intervention of a speaker and which would have required totally different background music, seriously compromising not so much and not only the piece of music in question but the structure of the film itself. Entrusting the responsibility for the soundtrack to the composer would be an act of wisdom for the benefits it would bring to the cinematographic work and at the same time an act of faith in the musician who still today is frequently sacrificed on altars erected from time to time to the god of cinema to appease him for the serious mistakes made by others than the musician.

Appendix 3
The Assassination of Trotsky (1972): Film credits

Director: Joseph Losey
Assistant Director (English version): Carlo Lastricati
Assistant Director (Italian version): Carlo Cotti
Continuity (English version): Pamela Davies
Continuity (Italian version): Carla Ferroni
Production: Josef Shaftel Productions Limited (London), Company C.I.A.C. - Compagnia Internazionale Alessandra, Dino De Laurentiis Cinematografica (Rome), Cinétel (Paris)
Executive Producer: Josef Shaftel
Producers: Norman Priggen, Joseph Losey
Executive in Charge of Production: Alessandro Tasca
Production Manager: Riccardo Coccia
Production Secretary (Italian version): Carlo Castelli
Production Secretary (Italian version): Giuseppe Bruno Bossio
Made at: De Laurentiis Studios (Rome), Estudios Churubusco
Casting Director: Guidarino Guidi
Screenplay by (English version): Nicholas Mosley
Screenplay by (Italian version): Masolino D'amico
Original Screenplay: Ian Hunter
Director of Photography: Pasqualino De Santis
Camera Operators: Henri Tiquet, Mario Cimini
Camera Assistant (Italian version): Marcello Mastrogirolamo
Editor (English and French versions): Reginald Beck
Editor (Italian version): Roberto Silvi
Production Designer: Richard Macdonald
Art Director: Arrigo Equini
Set Dresser: Pierluigi Basile
Costume Designer: Annalisa Nasalli Rocca
Make-up: Ron Berkeley, Franco Freda
Hairdresser: Maria Miccinilli
Music Composed and Conducted by: Egisto Macchi
Sound Recordist (English and French versions): Peter Davies
Sound Recordist (Italian version): Gaetano Testa
Sound Mixing: Federico Savina
Sound Re-recording: International Recording Studios (Rome)
Sound System: Westrex Recording System
Dubbing Editor (English version): Garth Craven
Dubbing Director (Italian version): Mario Maldesi
Mexican Murals by: Orozco, Jose Clemente Mexican, Diego Rivera
Characters and cast: Jacques Jacson/Frank Jackson (Alain Delon), Lev Davidovic "Leon" Trotsky (Richard Burton), Gita Samuels (Romy Schneider), Natasha Fedeva Trotsky (Valentina Cortese), Ruiz (Luigi Vannucchi), Alfred Rosmer (Jean Desailly), Marguerite Rosmer (Simone Valère), Felipe (Duilio Del Prete), Otto (Peter Chatel), Ed/Lou (Powers Hunt), Jim (Mike Forrest), Sheldon Harte (Carlos Miranda), Sam (Gianni Loffredo), Pedro (Pierangelo Civera), Seva (Marco Lucantoni), Salazar (Giorgio Albertazzi)
Duration: 103'
Distribution: Cic (Italy), Valrio Films (France), Mgm-Emi (United Kingdom)
Colour: colour

Editorial note

All the documents from the Joseph Losey Collection (JLC) and from the Egisto Macchi Collection (EMC) reproduced in this book are identified by a document number followed by a progressive letter, and the indication of recto (r) and verso (v). In staff paper folios, I have indicated the ruled side of the sheet as recto.

CHAPTER I

In search of the right sound

Document 1: List of Music & Records
JLC, 4 ff. (all versos blank). Blue ballpoint pen on squared paper, 225 x 160 mm

Joseph Losey had yet to decide on a composer for *The Assassination of Trotsky* even as the film was ready for editing: the director had reached a standstill. Leadership for the Anglo-Italo-French production resided in Italy, where Dino De Laurentiis kept a close eye on development, and their contract called specifically for an Italian composer. In a note to Pamela Davies, his trusted continuity supervisor,[1] Losey expressed his frustration: «Trotsky has gone for negative cutting, and I think it's pretty good. Big problems about the music – both because I don't really like any of the Italian composers, and also because I don't really know what do about it».[2] Losey's writings from January 1972 underline that the director had yet to define the film's soundscape, and that he doubted what the Italian market had to offer. But to what market was he referring? A list compiled by the production team shows us exactly which names they were screening at the end of 1971. There are two versions of this document: a manuscript – reproduced here – and a subsequent typewritten copy which omits the films' directors. Though the original titles are almost always cited (in the original Italian or in English for the international productions), the list refers specifically to soundtrack titles, such as *La ballata di Sacco e Vanzetti* and the *Concerto Grosso per i New Trolls*; in two other cases – *La Gioconda* and *Apollo II* – the list refers instead to Luis Bacalov's compilation *Pitturamusica*.

The list reads like a Who's Who of the most prominent figures on the Italian music scene, from Riz Ortolani to Angelo Francesco Lavagnino; and the names of Nino Rota and Ennio Morricone certainly stand out. Titles from the composers' films are selected by genre as a means of identifying stylistic parallels with *The Assassination of Trotsky*. The list ranges from historical films (*Waterloo*, dir. Sergej Bondarčuk, 1970) to biographical ones (*The Naked Maja*, dir. Henri Koster, 1958), and from crime (*We Still Kill the Old Way*, dir. Elio Petri, 1967) to romantic-drama (*The Garden of the Finzi-Continis*, dir. Vittorio De Sica, 1970). Understandably, there are few comedies or light-hearted works, and yet there is no shortage of genre films such as Spaghetti Westerns (*A Fistful of Dollars*, dir. Sergio Leone, 1964) – added in the typewritten version – or mondo films (*Africa: Blood and Guts*, dir. Gualtiero Jacopetti, Franco Prosperi, 1966). As another production note suggests, this list was likely narrowed down to three composers: De Sica, Ortolani, and Lavagnino, and the director received a copy of their recordings. The production team's documents suggest that the most likely candidate was Manuel De Sica, son of the famous director Vittorio De Sica. In a letter dated 1 December 1971, Jacques Goyard – De Sica's agent, on behalf of the William Morris Organization S.P.A. – acted as middleman for the composer, delivering a custom-made recording to the director and setting up a meeting between the two men:

> Dear Mr. Losey,
>
> here is a record that Manuel De Sica has made especially for "Trotsky". He hopes very much that you will like it and he would like, if possible, to meet with you to know what you think of it.
>
> Sincerely yours.
> Jacques Goyard[3]

Unfortunately, it is impossible to determine the nature of the recorded music, but the piece was likely consistent with the material De Sica produced for his other films. The despondent tone of Losey's note to Pamela Davies makes it clear that the director sought something different. His audiovisual conception for a film on Lev Trotsky does not seem compatible with the composers who, both then and now, could be considered the main exponents of the 1960s and 70s cinematographic "sound" in Italy.

It was not surprising then that in the following two months a composer who had not previously been considered entered into the equation. Although he was initially overlooked, Egisto Macchi had a musical vision that transcended the Italian standard of the time and thus could put forward a unique proposal for a composition. The first official account of this development is Losey's letter to De Sica where the director informs him of the change and final decision. On 3 February 1972, he wrote:

> Dear Signor De Sica,
>
> I have been terribly inconsiderate in not writing to you before to thank you for the music which you composed and recorded as a thought for my TROTSKY film. Unfortunately, but not surprisingly under the circumstances, your music was very far removed from any concepts which I had for this film.
>
> It is only now that I have had enough time to get around thanking you for your work, and to informing you that Maestro Egisto Macchi is doing the score for the film.
>
> I trust that we can meet and talk about work on another occasion.

---

[1] Davies was the assistant director who kept track of what was filmed based on the script and made sure that continuity between the filming of the different scenes was maintained.

[2] London, British Film Institute, Joseph Losey Collection, JWL/1/19/12.

[3] Typewritten letter dated 1 December 1971, London, British Film Institute, Joseph Losey Collection, JWL/1/19/12.

Yours sincerely,
Joseph Losey[4]

Transcription of the list, supplemented – wherever necessary – with the English title of the film, the director, and the production year:

List of Music & Records

Nino Rota
Waterloo – Direct. Sergej Bondarčuk [*Waterloo*, 1970]
I Clowns – [Federico] Fellini [*The Clowns*, 1970]

Manuel De Sica
Per Trotsky
Io e Dio [*Io e Dio*, Pasquale Squiltieri, 1970]
Il Giardino dei Finzi Contini – Vittorio De Sica [*The Garden of the Finzi-Continis*, 1970]
A Place for Lovers [*A Place for Lovers*, Vittorio De Sica, 1968]
Cose di Cosa Nostra – Roberto Amoroso [*Cose di cosa nostra*, Steno, 1971]
Le Coppie – Vittorio De Sica [*Le coppie*, Episode: *Il leone*, 1970]

Ennio Morricone
La Ballata di Sacco e Vanzetti [*Sacco & Vanzetti*, Giuliano Montaldo, 1971]
La Tenda Rossa – Mikhail Kalatozov [*The Red Tent*, 1969]

Stelvio Cipriani
L'Anonimo Veneziano – Enrico Maria Salerno [*The Anonymous Venetian*, 1970]

Carlo Rustichelli
Satyricon – Gian Luigi Polidoro [*Satyricon*, 1969]

[Angelo Francesco] Lavagnino
I Tabu – [Romolo] Marcellini [*Taboos of the World*, 1963]
Venere Imperiale – Jean Delannoy [*Imperial Venus*, 1962]
Falstaff – Orson Welles [1966]
La Maja Desnuda – Henri Koster [*The Naked Maja*, 1958]
Che Gioia Vivere – René Clément [*Che gioia vivere*, 1961]
Il Relitto – Giovanni Paolucci [*The Wastre*, and Michael Cacoyannis, 1961]

Riz Ortolani
Confessione di un Commissario di Polizia Al Procuratore della Repubblica – Damiano Damiani [*Confessions of a Police Captain*, 1971]
Woman Times Seven – Vittorio De Sica [*Woman Times Seven*, 1967]
Africa Addio – [Gualtiero] Jacopetti [*Africa: Blood and Guts*, and Franco Prosperi, 1966]
Addio Zio Tom – " [*Addio Zio Tom*, Gualtiero Jacopetti, Franco Prosperi, 1971]
The 7th Dawn – Lewis Gilbert [*The Seventh Dawn*, 1964]
Yellow Rolls Royce – Anthony Asquith [*Yellow Rolls Royce*, 1964]
Madron – Jerry Hopper [*Madron*, 1970]

[Luis] Bakalov
Quien Sabe [*A Bullet for the General*, Damiano Damiani, 1967]
Concerto Grosso per I New Trolls (La Vittima Designata) [*The Designated Victim*, Maurizio Lucidi, 1971]
L'Amica [*L'amica*, Alberto Lattuada, 1963]
Non-Commercial:
La Gioconda [*La Gioconda*, from *Pitturamusica*, 1971]
Apollo II [*Apollo II*, from *Pitturamusica*, 1971]
Non-Commercial:
La Noia [*The Empty Canvas*, Damiano Damiani, 1963]
Vangelo [*The Gospel According to St. Matthew*, Pier Paolo Pasolini, 1964]
A Ciascuno il Suo [*We Still Kill the Old Way*, Elio Petri, 1967]

---

[4] Typewritten letter dated 3 February 1972, London, British Film Institute, Joseph Losey Collection, JWL/1/19/12.

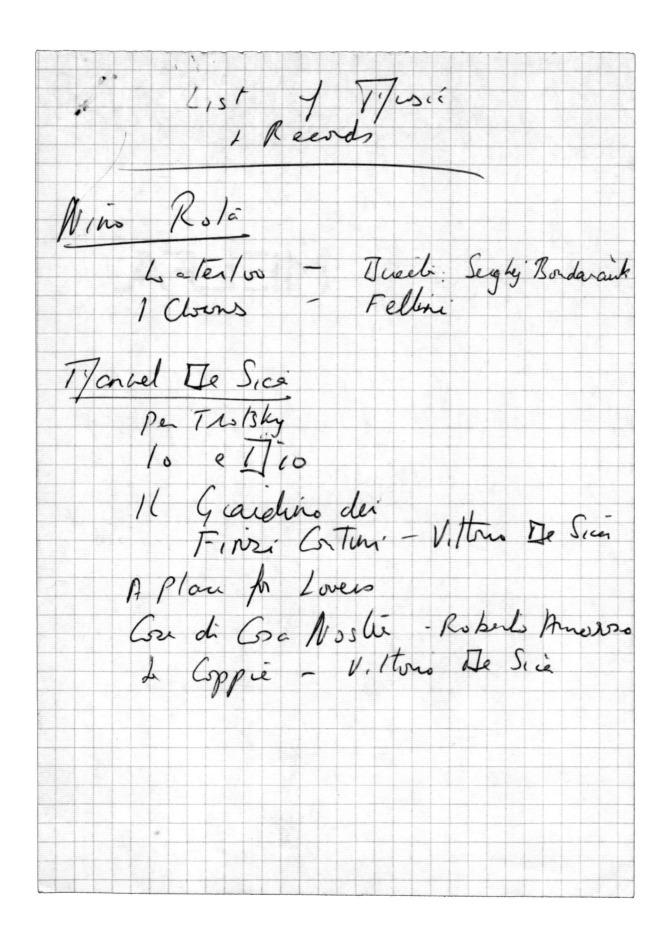

Document 1, Ar

Ennio Morricone
La Ballata di Sacco e Vanzetti –
La Tenda Rossa – Michail Kalatozov

Stelvio Cipriani
L'Anonimo Veneziano – Enrico Maria Salerno

Carlo Rustichelli
Satyricon – Gian Luigi Polidoro

Lavagnino

I Tabu	–	Marcellini
Venere Imperiale	–	Jean Delannoy
Falstaff	–	Orson Welles
Le Maja Desnuda	–	Henry Koster
Che Gioia Vivere	–	Rinè Clement
Il Relitto	–	Giovanni Paolucci

Riz Ortolani

Confessioni di un Commissario di Polizia Al Procuratore della Repubblica	–	Damiano Damiani
Woman Times Seven	–	Vittorio De Sica
Africa Addio	–	Jacopetti
Addio Zio Tom	–	"
The 7th Dawn	–	Lewis Gilbert
Yellow Rolls Royce	–	Anthony Asquith
Madron	–	Jerry Hopper

Bakalov

Queimada

Concerto Grosso per I New Trolls
(La Vittima Designata)

L'Amica

Non-Commercial: La Gioconda
            Apollo II ch:

Non-Commercial:
    La Notà
    Vangelo
    A Ciascuno Il Suo

Document 2: Sequenza B.
JLC, 3 ff. (all versos blank). Blue and red felt-tip pen on squared paper, 282 x 200 mm

We must now ask ourselves why Losey and the production team came to include Egisto Macchi in their project, especially since his name was not among those initially considered. According to the composer's son, Lamberto Macchi, it was actually Nino Rota, one of the composers on that very same list, who put his name forward. Since Losey was looking for music that was removed from the standard film music of the time, Rota suggested that it might be a good idea for him to listen to a lesser-known composer who was perhaps better suited to the film's particular concept. Thus meeting was set up and within a few days Macchi began working quickly with the director, trying to make up for lost time. Although Manuel De Sica was only informed about Macchi's involvement in the production of *The Assassination of Trotsky* in the letter dated 3 February 1972, the decision was likely made in the weeks before. In just one month, Losey's January 1972 frustration gave way to an immense feeling of satisfaction. A letter dated 4 February 1972 (just a day after the letter addressed to De Sica) serves as proof to this sudden change in attitude. Losey wrote a detailed memorandum to the producer Joseph Schaftel in view of their upcoming meeting, updating him on the film's progress. He touched on several matters but for this analysis the most interesting is the fourth point, which reads:

> I am delighted with Macchi as composer, arranger and conductor. I think the music will add greatly to the film, though it most certainly will not and cannot provide an exploitable theme song. He works very fast and very well and closely with me, and the sounds he is producing have extraordinary tension, richness and beauty. If the proper business arrangements are concluded with him quickly, all of the music will be finished by 19th February, and therefore ready for mixing as scheduled. Any delays in this matter would be most serious.[5]

Macchi found himself wearing different hats (as is often the case in Italian productions): not only was he a composer in the traditional sense, but also an arranger and conductor. Even though the film was an international production, the structure of the sound department was a far less rigid than similar departments in Hollywood where, on the contrary, every position was clearly defined. In his role as composer, Macchi supervised the various aspects of sound creation, from composing on paper to recording. Furthermore, the term "arranger" as used by Losey had a twofold meaning. It indicated on one hand the task of orchestration (where the timbric details were defined), and on the other the task of addressing the film's other musical needs, including – as we will see – diegetic excerpts of Mexican folklore.

We can extract a great deal of information from these circumstances and the few lines of the letters: the work's pace, which the director hoped would not exceed a month; the kind of interaction between director and composer, who worked closely together; and, above all, the notion that Macchi was not strictly confined to composition per se, as his work lied instead in creating a comprehensive sound that would affect the film's audiovisual balance broadly. Several years later, in a programme on television about film industry careers, Macchi himself – recalling this collaboration – mentioned Losey's doubts as to having a soundtrack at all. In the end, the director believed that, «if a musician exists who can invent a particular sound, this sound could probably help my film a lot in any areas where there are weak points».[6]

In the following pages we will examine the "very fast" method with which Macchi worked. Let us begin with one of the few documents that not only bears witness to the beginning of their collaboration, but that demonstrates the manner in which the composer analyses and tries to interpret a sequence's meaning through certain compositional choices. The document in question, reproduced in facsimile, comprises a series of discursive notes written by Macchi for a two-minute sequence called «Sequenza B.» that he sets to music (for the actual musical outcome, cf. Documents 22-23). He was still at the preliminary stage of composition and this document should be considered a form of "audition," carried out on paper. Instead of seeking to identify what remains of these ideas in the composer's final project, we can instead observe how, from the very start, Macchi worked on a global definition of sound by meticulously addressing matters of synchronisation.

Macchi's notes for «Sequenza B.» depict his noteworthy, dramaturgical attention in fusing the film's musical dimension with the remaining components of the work's audiovisual construction: that is, with its images and words. It is not by chance that he emphasizes certain details of the shots or that he focuses on the actors' style and vocal production. Each segment of the chosen micro-sequences is placed within the film's narrative framework; attention is paid to the characters' psychological depiction and to the story's various layers. Macchi supported the notion, for example, that certain

---

[5] Typewritten letter from Joseph Losey to Joseph Shaftel, 4 February 1972, London, British Film Institute, Joseph Losey Collection, JWL/1/19/25.

[6] Interview with Macchi in *Il cinema come si fa. La musica*, a programme realised by Giuseppe Ferrara and Giacomo Gambetti, Rai Tre, 8 November 1993, viewable on the RaiScuola portal at: http://www.raiscuola.rai.it/articoli/la-musica-il-cinema-come-si-fa/3145/default.aspx.

shots depict the characters' mental projections, as is the case for the "flash" in which Delon and Schneider are shot chatting before a fireplace. The composer interpreted this shot as a product of Trotsky's imagination: his voice, emerging from the tape recorder, continuously occupies the soundscape. Interpreting the cinematic narration does not serve as an end in itself; instead, it informs the composer's possible strategies. Even at this preliminary stage, it is clear that timbre and orchestration are chosen so as to clearly delineate the real and imaginary planes. In this phase, Macchi's approach in setting the score appears to be a purposely thematic one. In fact, he hypothesises that Trotsky's character has his own theme – and he likely thought the same way for the film's remaining characters; he also takes advantage of pre-existing melodies, such as that of the international socialist anthem, as a means of better defining the story's political-historical dimension. As the following analysis will prove, Macchi avoids citing pre-existing melodies of his own musical compositions for this film's soundtrack, much as he avoided musical instruments specifically associated to Russia, such as the balalaika. In his score for *The Assassination of Trotsky*, Macchi separates the nondiegetic cues composed from scratch – all characterised by an unconventional form of soundtrack writing – from the arrangement of pre-existing popular songs, which merely serve to create a realistic Mexican soundscape.

Different though these components may be, Macchi seemed to have a clear understanding of the strategic importance of a multi-faceted musical sound, obtained from a mixture of different elements: orchestral timbre, folk instruments, voices, effects such as a heartbeat, and the use of a synthesiser like the Synket, which in the 1960s and 70s was quite common in Italian film production.[7]

---

[7] See for an overview of the instrument Luigino Pizzaleo, *Il liutaio elettronico. Paolo Ketoff e l'invenzione del Synket*, Rome: Aracne, 2014; for a detailed analysis of its use in the field of cinema see instead Maurizio Corbella, *Paolo Ketoff e le radici cinematografiche della musica elettronica romana*, «Acoustical Art and Artifacts: Technology, Aesthetics, Communication (AAA TAC)», 6, 2009: pp. 65-75.

Transcription:	Translation:
Sequenza B. Le prime tre inquadrature serviranno come introduzione al tema di Trotzky che si svolgerà durante la dettatura al magnetofono dell'articolo contro la politica di Stalin nei confronti della arte. L'orchestrazione del tema non dovrà essere troppo carica, ma neanche troppo debole. Credo che la soluzione migliore sarebbe quella di adottare un temino tipo internazionale socialista (Trotzky fondò l'armata rossa nel 1918) ma non preso eccessivamente sul serio. Basterà forse usare un coro a bocca chiusa con un piccolo colore popolare all'unisono (fisarmonica o balalaika). In effetti le tirate di Trotzky contro Stalin degli anni precedenti (esilio 1929 e 1932) mi sembrano più che altro un fatto personale. Ciononostante l'atmosfera resta estremamente dignitosa e sempre molto piano. A 13" (interno della casa) chiuderei un poco l'orchestrazione (via fisa e archi, solo coro a bocca chiusa + c.b. pizzicati) e introdurrei il personaggio di Delon (20"). Delon interpreta il sicario la cui identità è tuttora sconosciuta. La sua recitazione è sempre molto tesa, quasi impazzita per ciò che dovrà fare, appare evidentemente vittima di un conflitto tra ideologia e missione, per cui credo che la soluzione sarebbe quella di adottare in primo piano un battito cardiaco che accelererà di ritmo (conflitto) (34" ½). Sotto questo effetto si snoderà un canone disarticolato e nevrotico di tastiere, con qualche puntata di *Synket*? Dopo 34" ½ ridurrei l'intensità per preparare il cambio di inquadratura su Trotsky che riascolta il registratore. Anche qui userei il coro a bocca chiusa (siamo all'interno) dato che la frase si rivolge contro Stalin e l'espressione del viso di Trotzky appare molto compiaciuta. Quando spegne il registratore dovrei aver terminato la prima frase del coro e passerei l'orchestrazione a balalaika + fisarmonica + archi per introdurre il flash di Delon + Schneider. Questo flash, secondo me, è una fantasia di Trotzky. Egli infatti da questo momento acquista un aspetto estremamente umano, un uomo solo, esiliato, prigioniero dei suoi stessi sostenitori (vive in una casa fortificata). A 1'34" ½, quando lo rivediamo di spalle alla finestra, continuerei la frase del flash ma lascerei solo una fisarmonica per chiudere con un pizzicato di contrabbassi sulla chiusura della finestra. 1'44". Il simbolismo della finestra credo che stia ad indicare il desiderio di Trotsky di una vita serena, un desiderio di calore umano, di sentimenti sani, spontanei, senza l'incubo di dover pesare sempre ogni parola, direi, insomma, il desiderio di godersi la pensione (Trotzky ha in questo momento 61 anni). Ma subito egli chiude la finestra, anche se a malincuore, a queste riflessioni. Ormai è troppo tardi, le scelte sono state fatte da tempo e questi lussi non sono più concessi. Subito dopo 1'47" vediamo Delon alla macchina da scrivere che sta rimuginando alibi per eventuali domande della Schneider. Il protagonista da questo momento è lui sempre teso e spaventato, preda dei propri problemi ideologici e sentimentali. Riprenderei con il battito e le dissonanze in crescendo fino a fine zoom 2'02" per lasciare un tappeto drammatico ed il battito in accelerazione per diminuire l'intensità gradualmente sull'inquadratura della finestra di Trotzky vuota, dato che questa immagine è evidentemente una proiezione del pensiero di Delon.	Sequence B. The first three shots will serve as an introduction to the Trotzky theme that will take place during the dictation of the article against Stalin's policy on art to the tape recorder. The orchestration of the theme should be neither too powerful nor too weak. I think the best solution would be to adopt an insignificant theme like the international socialist (Trotzky founded the Red Army in 1918) but it should not be too seriously. It might be enough to use a choir *a bocca chiusa* with a small, culturally appropriate instrument in unison (accordion or balalaika). In fact, Trotzky's tirades against Stalin of the previous years (exile 1929 and 1932) seem to me above all a personal matter. Nevertheless, the atmosphere is extremely dignified and always very quiet. At 13" (inside the house) I'd minimize the orchestration slightly (cut the accord. and strings, only choir with *a bocca chiusa* + double bass pizzicato) and introduce the character of Delon (20"). Delon plays the killer whose identity is still unknown. His acting is always very tense, almost deranged because of what he has to do, he clearly appears to be the victim of a conflict between ideology and mission, so I believe that the solution would be to adopt a heartbeat whose rhythm will speed up (conflict) in the foreground (34" ½). Beneath this effect a disjointed and neurotic keyboard canon will unfold, with a few episodes of Synket? After 34" I'd reduce the intensity to prepare the change of shot on Trotsky who is listening to the tape again. Here too I'd use the chorus *a bocca chiusa* (we are inside) since the words are directed against Stalin, and Trotzky has a very pleased expression on his face. When he turns off the tape-recorder I should end the first phrase of the chorus and I'd switch the orchestration to balalaika + accordion + strings to introduce the Delon + Schneider flash. This flash, in my opinion, is in Trotzky's imagination. In fact, from this moment on, he acquires an extremely human aspect, a lonely, exiled man, a prisoner of his own supporters (he lives in a fortified house). At 1'34"½, when we see him with his back to the window, I'd continue the phrase used for the flash but I'd only leave a single accordion to close with a double bass pizzicato as the window shuts. 1'44". The window I believe stands for Trotsky's desire for a peaceful life, a desire for human warmth, for wholesome spontaneous feelings, without the nightmare of always having to weigh every word, I'd say, in short, the desire to enjoy his retirement (Trotzky is 61 years old at this time). But he immediately closes the window, albeit reluctantly, on these thoughts. By now it is too late, choices have long been made and he can no longer indulge himself in such reflections. Immediately after 1'47" we see Delon at the typewriter mulling over alibis to answer Schneider's possible questions. From this moment onwards, the protagonist is always tense and scared, prey to his own ideological and sentimental problems. I'd start again with the heartbeat and dissonances in crescendo up to the end of the zoom at 2'02" to leave a dramatic drone and the quickening heartbeat to gradually decrease the intensity of the shot of Trotzky's empty window, since this image is evidently a projection of Delon's thought.

SEQUENZA B.

Le prime tre inquadrature serviranno come introduzione al Tema di TROTZKY che si svolgera' durante la dettatura al magnetofono dell'articolo contro la politica di STALIN nei confronti dell' arte. L'orchestrazione PEL TEMA non dovra' essere troppo carica, ma neanche troppo debole. Credo che la soluzione migliore sarebbe quella di adottare un Temino tipo INTERNAZIONALE SOCIALISTA (TROTZKY fondò l'armata rossa nel 1918) ma non preso eccessivamente sul serio. Bastera' forse usare un coro a bocca chiusa con un piccolo colore popolare all'unisono (FISARMONICA o BALALAIKA). In effetti le tirate di TROTZKY contro STALIN, dati i precedenti (esilio 1929 e 1932) mi sembrano più che altro un fatto personale. Nonostante l'atmosfera resta estremamente dignitosa e sempre molto piano. A (13") (interno della casa) chiuderei un poco l'orchestrazione (via FISA E ARCHI, solo coro A BOCCA CHIUSA + C.B pizzicati) e introdurrei il personaggio DELON (20"). DELON interpreta il sicario la cui identita' è tuttora sconosciuta. La sua recitazione è sempre tesa, quasi impaurita per ciò che dovra' fare, appare evidentemente vittima di conflitto interno tra ideologia e intuissassine, per cui credo che la soluzione sarebbe quelle di adottare in primo piano un battito cardiaco che accelererà di ritmo (conflitto) ~~lo~~ ~~per~~ ~~intralciare~~ ~~preparare~~ ~~la scoperta~~ ~~della piccozza~~ (34"½). Sotto questo effetto si snoderà un canone disarticolato e nevrotico di TASTIERE, con qualche puntata di SINKET? ~~Poi~~ DOPO (34"½) RIDURREI L'INTENSITÀ ~~e~~ PER PREPARARE IL CAMBIO INQUADRATURA SU TROTZKY CHE RIASCOLTA IL REGISTRATORE. Anche qui userei il CORO A BOCCA CHIUSA (SIAMO ALL'INTERNO) DATO CHE ~~TROT~~ LA FRASE SI RIVOLGE CONTRO STALIN e l'espressione del viso di TROTZKY appare molto compiaciuta. Quando spegne il registraTORE DOVREI AVER TERMINATO LA PRIMA FRASE DEL CORO E PASSEREI L'ORCHESTRAZIONE A BALALAIKA + FISARMONICA + ARCHI per introdurre il FLASH DI DELON + ~~R~~ SCHNEIDER. Questo FLASH, secondo me, è UNA FANTASIA DI TROTZKY. Egli infatti da questo momento acquista un aspetto estremamente umano, un uomo solo, esiliato, prigioniero dei suoi stessi sostenitori (vive in una casa FORTIFICATA). A (1'34"½), quando lo rivediamo di SPALLE ALLA FINESTRA, continuerei ~~con tutta~~ la frase del FLASH ma ~~solo~~ lascerei solo una fisarmonica per chiudere con un pizzicato →

di contrabassi sulla chiusura della finestra.
1'44" - il simbolismo della finestra credo che stia ad indicare il desiderio di TROTZKY di una vita più serena, un desiderio di calore umano, di sentimenti sani, spontanei, senza l'incubo di dover pesare sempre ogni parola, direi, insomma, il DESIDERIO DI GODERSI LA PENSIONE. (TROTZKY HA in questo momento 61 anni).
MA SUBITO EGLI CHIUDE LA FINESTRA, anche se a malincuore, a queste riflessioni. ORMAI E' TROPPO TARDI, le scelte sono state fatte da tempo e questi lussi non sono più concessi.
Subito dopo 1'47" VEDIAMO DELON ALLA MACCHINA DA SCRIVERE che sta rimmaginando alibi per eventuali domande della SCHNEIDER. IL PROTAGONISTA DA questo momento è lui, sempre teso e spaventato, preda dei propri problemi ideologici e sentimentali.
Riprenderà con il BATTITO e le dissonanze in crescendo FINO A FINE ZOOM 2'02" per lasciare un tocco DRAMMATICO ED IL BATTITO in ACCELERAZIONE PER DIMINUIRE L'INTENSITA' GRADUALMENTE sull'INQUADRATURA DELLA FINESTRA DI TROTZKY VUOTA, dato che questa immagine è evidentemente una proiezione del pensiero di DELON.

Document 3: Letter to Egisto Macchi from Joseph Losey, 30 March 1972
JLC, 1 f. (verso blank). Typewritten letter, 270 x 197 mm

As Macchi himself pointed out in one of the rare theoretical lectures he gave about his experience as a composer,[8] working for the silver screen is primarily a collaborative work between the musician and the technical staff of the other departments. This stance is by no means a discounted conclusion, especially if we observe what the other leading members of this field had to say at the time. For example, Vittorio Gelmetti, when he spoke at a conference organised by the journal *Filmcritica* in 1964,[9] suggested that the only way to overcome the scant regard for film music was by involving the composer in as early stages as screenwriting. Macchi, however, adopted a decidedly more pragmatic attitude. Given that a musician could likely only intervene right at the end, when editing had been completed, he argued that it was necessary to focus on the effective possibilities inherent in this intervention, as well as in controlling the final stage of organisation and management of the overall sonic balance. Much of Macchi's work was aimed at detecting the issues concerning these relationships, which strongly affect the musician's compositional prospectus, since he inevitably cannot write without considering both the visual («photographic») and sonic aspects. Recognizing the great difficulty of dialogue and collaboration with the various departments, to which the technical impossibility of intervening and juggle music-effects-dialogues was frequently added, Macchi said – on more than one occasion – that he wished for the musician to be assigned full responsibility for the soundtrack, such that he could keep an eye on these different levels "a priori", instead of having «to work without knowing the work of others, without others knowing your work, forced to give your best as if the film were made up only of effects, or music or dialogue. The meeting (far too often, the confrontation) takes place during mixing and is almost always an unpleasant eye-opener for everyone».[10]

In this respect, it is interesting to see how Macchi's perspective here coincides with that of Pierre Schaeffer, who, counter to Chion, saw the soundtrack as a unified complex. It is no coincidence that amongst the materials preserved in the Egisto Macchi Collection, we find photocopies of articles on the relationship between music and image, including an essay by Schaeffer and an article by Michel Fano, both published in the *Cahiers du cinéma* in the 1960s. Although he never abandoned a strict dialectic between the visual dimension and its narrative aspects, Macchi paid particular attention to the timbral and formal structures of soundtrack, one resting on constant interplay and balance between all sonic components.[11] He believed that it was not possible to create an acceptable soundtrack if the elements comprising it were not entrusted to one person alone, who could curate its many levels "a priori". Once the dialogues were recorded and assembled, the technician in charge of this process should proceed with the recording and editing of the effects, keeping in mind the dialogue tracks. The composer is last to intervene, and he should work with the photographic dimension, the dialogue tracks and the effects tracks in mind, so that he may decide, along with the director, the best type of soundtrack for each part of the film. Macchi's approach sought to overcome the divide between the dialogue, effects, and music tracks and to merge all the constituent components into a single soundtrack. This aegis must not be understood as an act of assuming power so as to favor the musical component over the dialogue or sound effects. In fact, it was quite the opposite. Only in this way could a composer best determine the type of piece and orchestral setting required, and, if need be, decide not to write a composition. Were a sequence saturated with sound, the composer may decide to favour the relationship between dialogue and environmental effects. Even silence itself may be considered an element of musical quality, which as a result must not undergo any further compositional intervention.

These considerations are central to the very structure of soundtrack in *The Assassination of Trotsky*, which thematises and constantly questions the traditional boundaries between music, effects, and dialogue. In the film, we witness constant changes in timbre that are not reducible to a mere binary of noise or music. We are dealing with a multi-faceted universe, comprising a wide range of sonic elements: 1) noises from visible sources; 2) musical and non-musical sounds from invisible sources, such as the band music in the beginning of the film; 3) electro-acoustically modified sounds from clearly indicated sources, as is the case with the children's chatter, heard during opening credits (cf. Document 8); 4) and finally, electronically synthesised effects – as with the Synket, for example – the timbre of which reminds us of particular environmental sounds.

Acknowledging this multi-layered complexity, it is unsurprisingly that Losey – in a letter reproduced herein – chose to entrust Macchi, with the complete authorship of the mixing operation for the Italian version of the film. The director's words clearly proves that Macchi, as early as the post-production phase of the original English

---

[8] The text is written in manuscript form without a title and without dating; for a full transcript see the Appendix 2 of the introductory essay.

[9] Vittorio Gelmetti, *Aspetti della musica nel film*, «Filmcritica», 143-144, 1964, pp. 146-147.

[10] Egisto Macchi, [Writing the score for a film], Appendix 2.

[11] See Pierre Schaeffer, *Le contrepoint du son et de l'image*, «Cahiers du cinéma», 108, pp. 7-22; Michel Fano, *Vers une dialectique du film sonore* «Cahiers du cinéma», 152, 1964, pp. 30-41.

version, had become remarkably skilled in dealing with the problems posed by Losey's film. It is thanks to this positive experience that the director engaged the composer to supervise the whole dubbing process for the Italian version in addition to the new mixing, allowing Macchi to fulfill one of his most pressing ambitions in his career for cinema, even if perhaps this was unbeknownst to Losey.

Although Macchi was in charge of the Italian version, let us not forget that another figure worked alongside both Losey and Macchi in the post-production mixing that took place at the International Recording Studios.[12] In fact, letters about *The Assassination of Trotsky* archived in the Joseph Losey Collection clearly depict the importance of Federico Savina's contribution. In a letter addressed to him on 18 March 1972, when the work on the original version of the film had already been completed, Losey wrote:

> I have known for more ten years that you are the best music recordist. I had not known the extent of your genius as a dubbing mixer. It is one of the best tracks I have had, and one of the most difficult to achieve.[13]

---

[12] See Ilario Meandri, *International Recording (1959-1969). Indagine sulle memorie orali*, Turin: Edizioni Kaplan, 2013.

[13] London, British Film Institute, Joseph Losey Collection, JWL/1/19/12.

Raphael
17 Avenue Kleber 17
Paris

March 30th, 1972

BY HAND

Maestro Egisto Macchi
Hotel Madison
Boulevard Saint-Germain
Paris

Dear Maestro Macchi,

I hereby delegate to you my full contractual authority to approve or disapprove the final dubbing and mix of the Italian version of my film THE ASSASSINATION OF TROTSKY.

I am most grateful to you for undertaking this task and I am sure that your decision will be the same as mine would have been had I been available since you are by now certainly as familiar with the picture and the mixing problems as I am myself.

My kindest regards and thanks to you and your wife.

Joseph Losey

JL:cj

cc: Mr. Joseph Shaftel ✓
    Principe Alessandro Tasca

S. A. CAPITAL 560.000 F — R. C. Seine 57 B 1907 — TÉL. : 553 07.70 — CABLES : RAPHALOTEL PARIS

Document 4: Music
JLC, 1 f. (verso blank). Blue ballpoint pen on squared paper, 221 x 160 mm

During the aforementioned television programme, Macchi explained that Losey – in engaging the composer – had requested a particular sound, but also inferred that the final result may deviate from his original audiovisual concept. Macchi recalled Losey's stance thus:

> You are a musician and I am a director, if you bring me interesting things I'll be happy to approve them, otherwise it means that the film will remain just as I had imagined it with noises and its effects and certain street music.

And it is precisely in the context of this challenge that Macchi felt free to follow constructs which were not accepted within the world of film scoring:

> Losey's position here was very interesting, very precise, and assigned great responsibility to the musician. So this was one of the few times I genuinely felt free to write as I liked, knowing that only a certain form of writing could convince a person like Joseph Losey [...] and that instead a cautious, conservative score – an ordinary one – would have certainly distanced him from me.[14]

The resulting soundtrack plays at juxtaposing diegetic and nondiegetic musical dimensions, both of which were edited by Macchi. The former – present in some way from the very start of the film's making – serves to recreate a soundscape compatible with the events set in Mexico, while the latter – the challenge set by Losey – is built from post-tonal compositional techniques.

Before analyzing the scores and reconstructing the compositional process of each musical piece, we must consider the soundtrack's numbering system broadly. The manuscript list – prepared by an anonymous collaborator and reproduced herein – served as the basis for a subsequent typewritten version submitted to Losey. In the latter, we can indeed observe the director's notes, such as the one for cue 3.M.3: «Don't like this». The cues are labelled with a progressive M. number (music), according to the labelling system used in the American film industry, wherein the digit before the letter "M" indicates a reel number and the second number serves to identify a specific cue. This kind of numbering system is quite rare in Italy, where common practice merely identifies the progressive number of each musical piece, M, without indicating the reel number.[15] Macchi instead used a slightly different numbering system to the one shown in this list where the reel number comes after the letter M; 3.M.3 becomes, for example, M. 3/3.

Although this is not the final numbering system for the film, the two versions of the list give us an overall plan of the composed music. Titles of the folkloric pieces transcribed for chorus are not specified in detail, but one piece in particular – M.1/4 – is actually missing; most probably added later, the work is mentioned – not by chance – on sheets often used for drafts. In the final editing, the piece for the opening credits is repeated in the central section of the film, and corresponds with the bullfight sequence (reel 5), much as an element from the opening credits – a magnetic tape with a buzz of voices – is used again for the closing credits.

This list, however, gives us clear evidence for the prevalence of «street music» in the first part of the film; made up of band music and Spanish choirs, it serves to articulate the story's space-time coordinates. For numbers that are totally original, the list provides essential information about their associated sequences. The list also shows us how the musical component supervised by Macchi, when compared to the overall length of the film, is actually quite short which – paradoxically – makes it all the more significant for the audiovisual framework. Moreover, the Egisto Macchi Collection contains a number of alternative versions for most of the tracks he used, allowing us to compare different musical realisations of the same piece. In so doing we gain virtual admission to Macchi's compositional workshop, and thereby can elucidate certain details about his process of audiovisual construction. Comparing different versions of a piece allows us to uncover sync points and compositional strategies as they relate to other components of the film, as well as the expressive solutions that serve to render the audiovisual scene.

---

[14] *Il cinema come si fa. La musica*: http://www.raiscuola.rai.it/articoli/la-musica-il-cinema-come-si-fa/3145/default.aspx.

[15] Meandri, *International Recording*, p. 76.

1. M. 1.	Titles
1. M. 2.	Various band sections & choruses
2 M. 1.	Guitarist
2 M. 2.	Starting on Trotsky at window - "Cancer of Revolution" down through Ruiz painting and finishing on Sheldon on top of tower.
3 M. 1.	Night scene of Ruiz painting through distribution of arms and uniforms to cars driving out.
3 M. 2.	From zoom off Jacson's eyes to return to Jacson.
3 M. 3.	From Jacson & Felipe going downstairs to firing (<u>Don't like this</u>)
5 M. 1.	Bull fight music
5 M. 2.	Death of Bull
6. M. 1.	Marimba music to continue original
7 M. 1.	From Jacson & gitl leaning over side of boat to Natalia closing door.

Document 4, Ar

Document 5: *Bandera roja,* fair copy, notes, typescript
EMC, 4 ff. (blanks Ar, Bv, Cv, Dv). A-C: pencil on staff paper, ca. 220 x 319 mm; D: typewritten, 280 x 220 mm

As we have already seen, the collaboration between Joseph Losey and Egisto Macchi was based on a rather clear agreement: Macchi would compose music for some parts of the film that had yet to convince Losey and, once the work was completed, the director would then decide whether to keep or drop these musical tracks from the soundtrack. In truth, even if Macchi's score had not been to his liking, and even if he decided not to use it for the film, Macchi's creative contribution would still have been fundamental for *The Assassination of Trotsky*. Paradoxical as this may sound, we must not forget that the film's diegetic music, much of which may seem to have been recorded live, was actually supervised by Macchi. Of course, these compositions do not bear the most obvious examples of the composer's personal style or stylistic hand, but they are nevertheless fundamental passages for the depiction of the soundscape of Mexico City. These pieces also serve to define a realistic sound environment, one that differs radically from Macchi's other pieces, thereby drawing attention to an entirely distinct horizon of audiovisual representation.

Macchi composed most of these pieces as soundtrack for the film's first sequence (in the transition after the opening credits). This sections depicts the massive popular mobilisation for the 1940 May Day demonstration. We will never know whether the extras ever actually sang any of the songs during the shooting; the camera never lingers on the faces of the demonstrators, thus there is no need for any kind of lip-synching. Even though the band music composed by Macchi was quite convincing for this context, there is no visual manifestation of it on screen; once again the composer is completely free to choose his instrumentation. At the same time, despite a lack of close synchronisation, the music unifies and authenticates the images by creating a single acoustic experience.

The whole sequence is based on a multiformity of choral songs and instrumental music that overlap each other incessantly, recreating the chaotic soundscape of the union of several processions of demonstrators converging on the capital. On a page of notes purposefully entitled «M 1/2 II parte (Cori)» (cf. 5, Cr), Macchi plans a possible temporal articulation of the choral interventions, which were then abandoned during the editing phase. Here follows the transcript:

> 0" Camera Delon
> Bandiera rossa starts in G + choir and band
> At 39", Jovem guardia starts in G + from start to finish
> (while Bandiera rossa goes to the end)
>
> [0" Camera Delon
> Inizia Bandiera rossa in sol + coro e bande
> A 39", inizia Jovem guardia in sol + da capo a fine
> (mentre Bandiera rossa va fino alla fine)]

These brief notes demonstrate that Macchi intended the choirs (and also the band music, even though it has been crossed out) to be mixed together, while also making sure that they were structured around the same key.

Especially when compared to other archived sources, it is clear that this music occupies a special place in the Macchi Collection because all of the documents – both musical and verbal – pertaining to this sequence are enclosed by a separate flyleaf entitled «Testi e musiche per cori [Texts and music for choirs]» (cf. 5, Av). Inside we find 23 sheets of paper with various kinds of text, including: typewritten documents and preparatory manuscripts with the text to be set to music; musical documentation of the choir pieces; some sketches and drafts; and the fair copies of three different pieces for an instrumental band.

The documents regarding the famous song *Bandera roja*, reproduced in facsimile, fall within the first two categories. Macchi did not create music from scratch for these songs but limited himself to re-arranging authentic, popular melodies that belonged to a specific musical culture. We have no evidence as to whether Macchi used some kind of intermediate source as reference melodies from which to transcribe these songs. Even if these sources may have been lost, we speculate that Macchi was able to use some recordings as a model, or that he already knew the songs and was therefore able to write the fair copy directly, especially since they were monodic versions. As far as the facsimile of *Bandera roja* is concerned, it is more than likely that Macchi knew the original version in Italian (*Bandiera rossa*), and thus he only needed to readapt the Spanish text, derived from a typescript of unclear origins (cf. 5, Dr). An external collaborator probably helped him to find the words in Spanish. It is possible that these texts were searched for in collaboration with a member of staff from the Mexican Embassy in Rome, since on several occasions Macchi mentioned the name of a certain Ninfa Santo, who could be contacted at this very Embassy. Research on these texts also allows us to understand how these songs were meant to be performed. For example, the typescript that preserves the text of *Ya se sienta* by Silvestre Revueltas – which is only shouted and not sung by the protesters in the film, – also reveals some information about the song's history. *Ya se sienta* was in fact performed during the 1 May 1940 events, during which the demonstrators paraded puppets with faces made to resemble political figures such as Mussolini, Hitler, and, indeed, Trotsky himself.

Once the Spanish text to be set to music had been chosen, Macchi proceeded to actually write the pieces. All the musical documents are organised in the same way: *Bandera roja* is no exception. Macchi wrote the melodic line and its corresponding text on an oblong-shaped piece of staff paper (cf. 5, Br) from the "Edizioni musicali Rete". The empty space in the bottom left-hand part of the page bears the complete text, while indications for the copyist are given in the bottom right-hand corner of the page, specifying the number of copies to be made for the pianist (1) and for the members of the choir (15). It is not entirely clear why Macchi also prescribed a copy of this part for a pianist. The choirs performed a cappella without the presence of any instruments in both the recording and in the edited version of the film. However, a pianist might have been employed during the preliminary rehearsals to help the singers memorise their parts before the track was actually recorded.

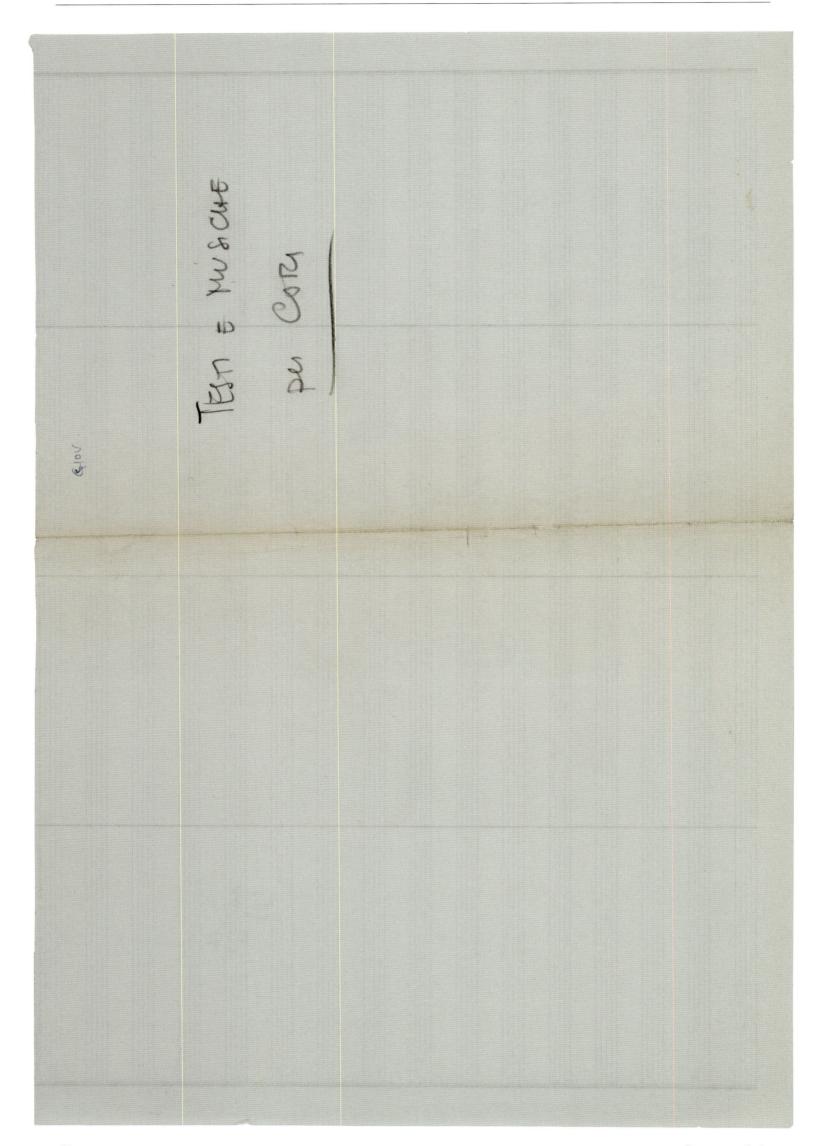

BANDERA ROJA

BANDERA RO—JA CO—LOR DE SAN—GRE ES LA MÁS GRANDE

BANDERA RO—JA COLOR DE SAN—GRE ES LA MÁS GRANDE Y TRIUNFA—RÁ

BAN—DE—RA RO—JA LA QUE TRIUNFA—RÁ BAN—DE—RA RO—JA LA QUE TRIUNFA—

BAN—DE—RA RO—JA LA QUE TRIUNFA—RÁ QUE VIVA EL CO—MU—NISMO Y LA LI—BERTAD—

BANDERA ROJA, COLOR DE SANGRE
ES LA MÁS GRANDE, ES LA MÁS GRANDE
BANDERA ROJA, COLOR DE SANGRE
ES LA MÁS GRANDE Y TRIUNFARÁ

BANDERA ROJA LA QUE TRIUNFARÁ
" " " " "
" " " " "

QUE VIVA EL COMUNISMO Y LA LIBERTAD

Edizioni musicali Rete

BANDERA ROJA

Bandera roja, color de sangre,
es la más grande, es la más grande,
Bandera roja, color de sangre,
es la más grande y triunfará.

Bandera roja la que triunfará,
bandera roja, la que triunfará,
bandera roja la que triunfará,
que viva el comunismo y la libertad.

Document 6: II Banda, draft and fair copy
EMC, 4 ff. (blanks Bv, Cv, Dv). Pencil, red and blue ballpoint pen on staff paper, ca. 220 x 319 mm

Alongside the group of scores for choir, there are three pieces of instrumental "band" pieces aimed at recreating the event's soundscape. The idea of mixing vocal and instrumental music can be deduced from one of the sheets used in preparing the vocal pieces. The typescript for *Ya se sienta* described the context in which this song was performed, specifying that it provided for the «acompañamiento de una pequeña banda de música [accompaniment of a small musical band]». Macchi thus prepared three musical interventions for the band, which however did not accompany any of the songs in particular, but developed three independent musical ideas. It is therefore not surprising that these documents lack any signs or indications on timing that suggest strategies for their synchronisation with the images or the other music tracks.

The three pieces of band music share two main features, that is: the basic instruments – 2 clarinets, 2 trumpets, 2 horns, 2 trombones and 2 drums – and the compositional technique. These are tonal pieces of a modular character, built from repeating one or more sections, in accordance with the genre of band music. From this point of view, the second composition (II Banda) can be taken as a reference model. While Macchi only gave the Spanish title for the vocal pieces, two different titling systems for the instrumental ones are found at the top of the page. The first, in pencil, identifies the three different bands that would likely play during the event (Band I, II and III); while the second is the more common system for organising tracks: with a progressive cue number in "M". When compared to the first list (cf. Document 4), the band music in this case comprises a slightly different type of numbering: M. 1/1, M. 1/2 and M. 1/3. These indications were added with a blue ballpoint pen and correspond to a second creative stage: the soundtrack recording.

The starting point for the composition is a brief sketch in which Macchi summarised the various instrumental voices in a sort of skeleton score, organised in three systems. The repeat markers in the accompaniment formula (fourth pentagram), the "da capo" signs, and the indications for the refrain all illustrate the modular nature of his composition. Its overall course had yet to be clearly defined in the draft, but it seems that Macchi had at least two main sections in mind – marked by the two parts in Roman numerals at the beginning of the second and the third systems –, as well as an alternative refrain at the end of the third, where we also find the only indication of instrumentation for the clarinets.

During the passage to the piece's fair copy, Macchi modified the general structure, changing the order of the sections, and eliminating some of the bars in the draft. He maintained the first five bars of the preliminary source, so as to move directly to the musical material he had jotted down in the third system. Next, we re-encounter the structure of the refrain with its two different conclusions, entrusted to the two clarinets. In the last section of the piece, Macchi restores the trill figuration – by means of variation – which he noted in the draft's second system (unlike the original plan); it now serves as a means of returning to the beginning until the «fine [end]».

As we will see from the examination of other sources on *The Assassination of Trotsky*, he adopted a rather different compositional approach for these musical pieces than he did for the rest of the score: not so much in terms of style – he also used a non-experimental approach for some of the other diegetic cues he composed – but rather due to the lack of close synchronization across music and images. Macchi writes music in the first sequence's score for chorus and band that is designed to be placed generically in the initial sequence, with no precise audiovisual dramaturgical function. As Losey made clear, these tracks would have been kept in the film regardless of Macchi's final role within the project as a whole. Next we will take a closer look at the phases of this creative process, which positively stimulated Losey's imagination completely erasing his initial doubts.

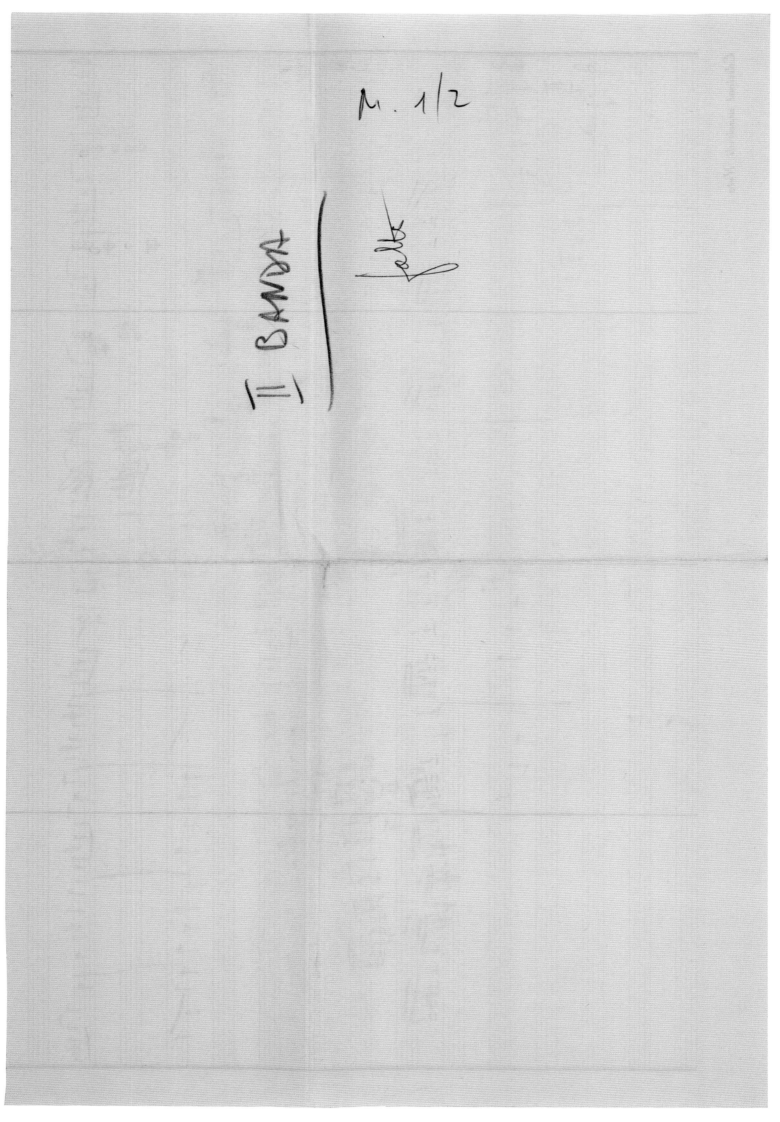

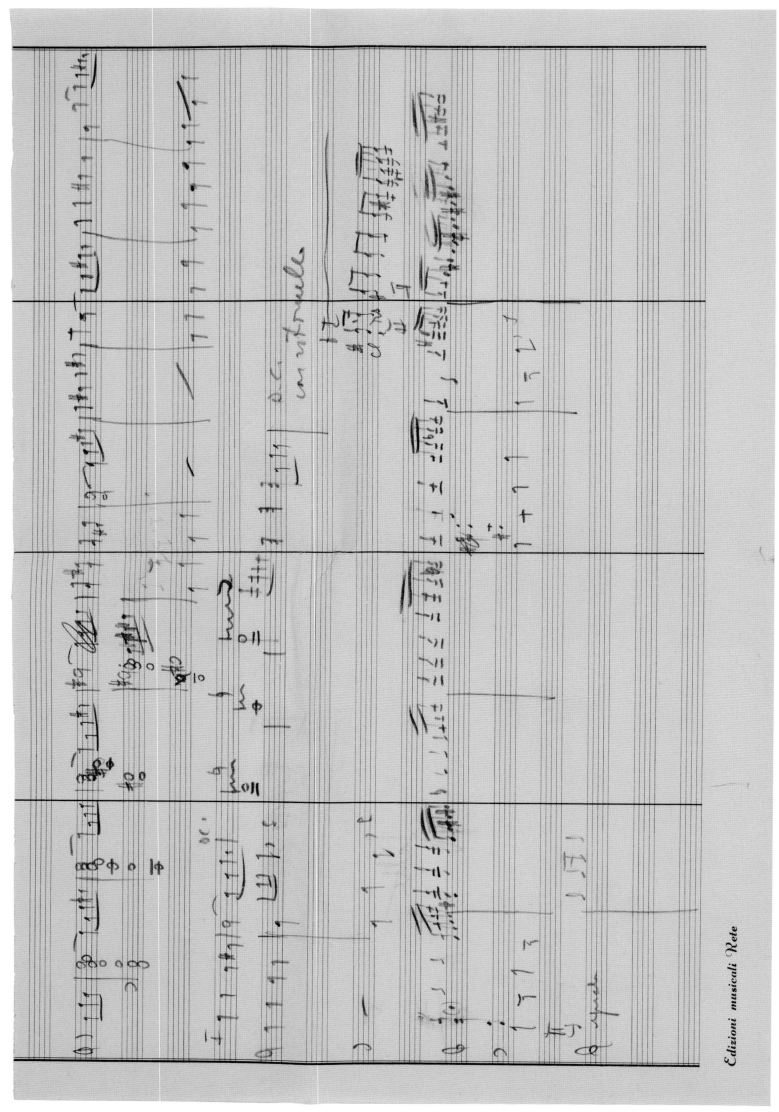

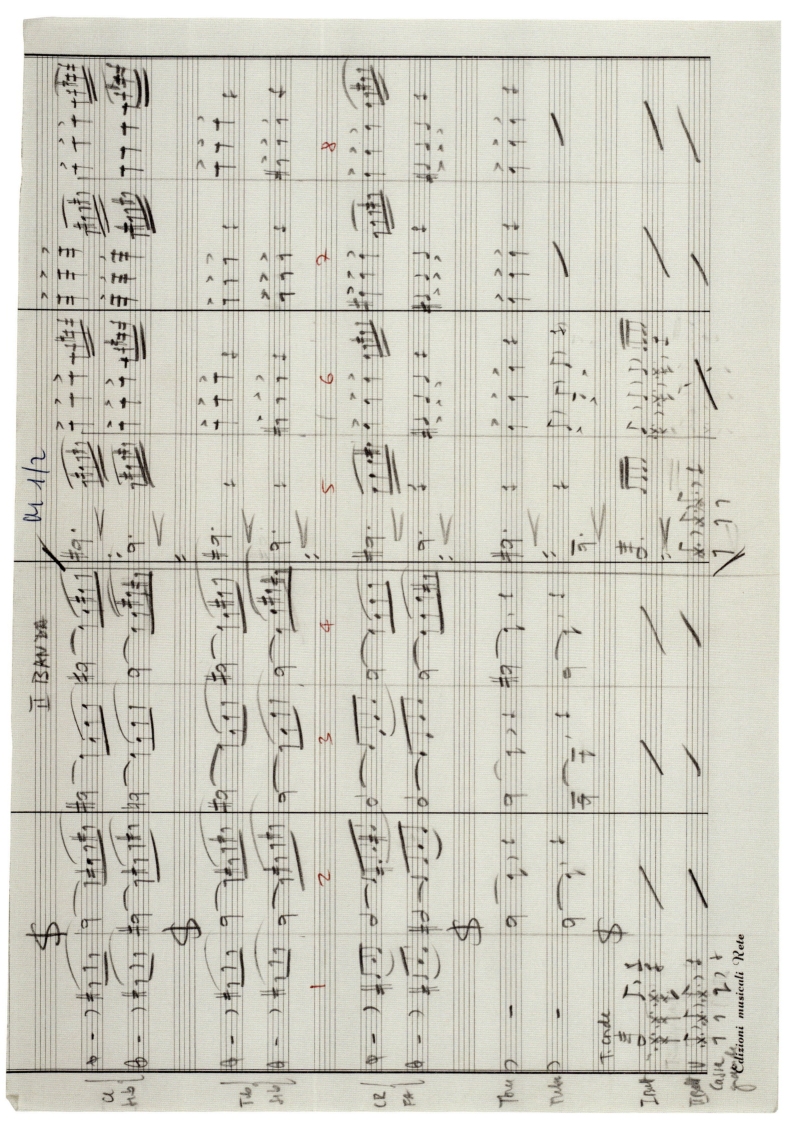

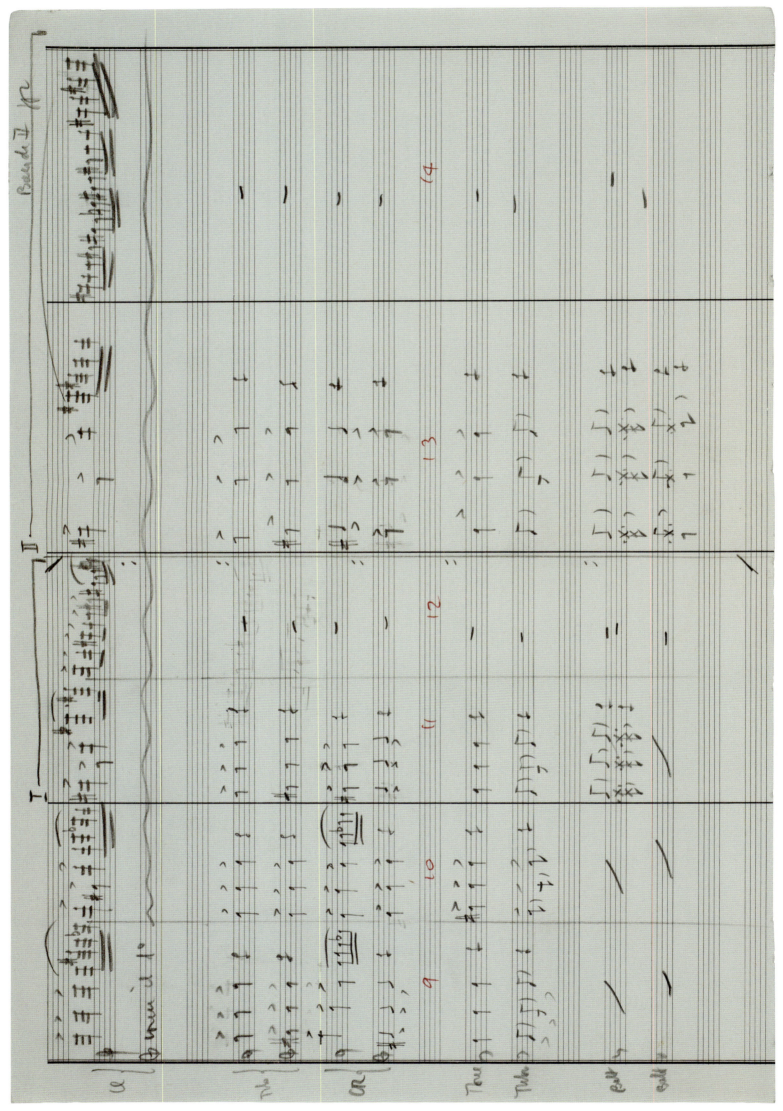

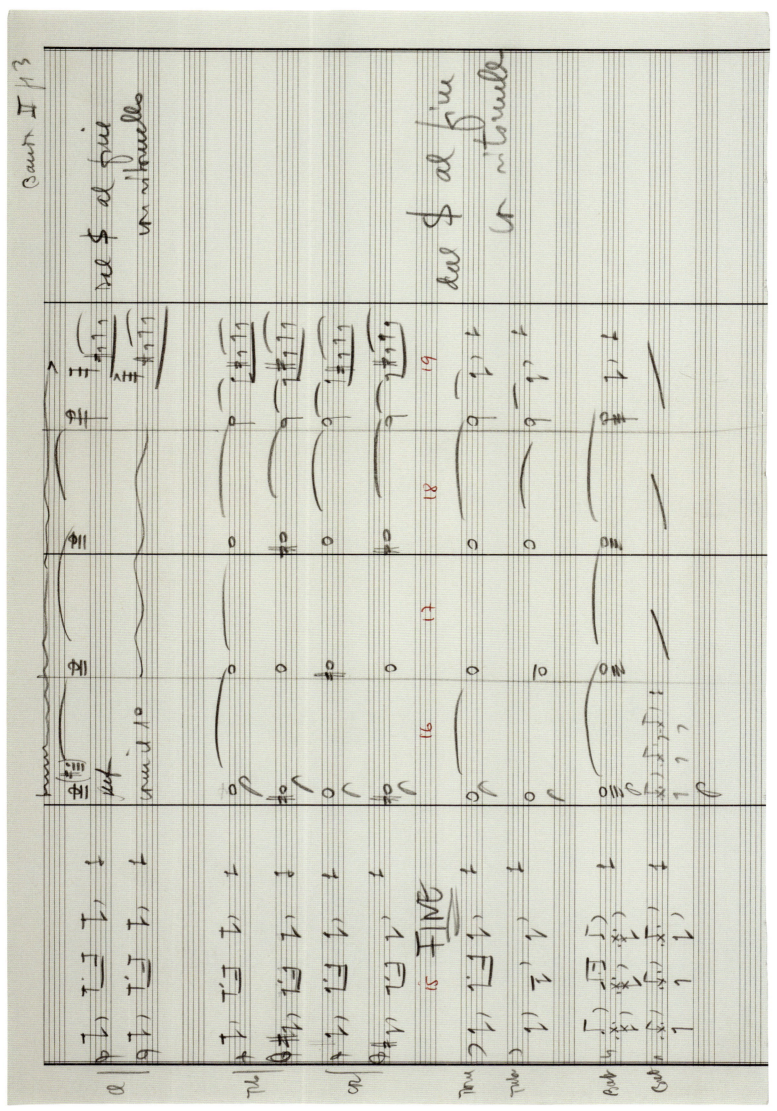

CHAPTER 11

From the opening credits to the bullfight

Document 7: Titoli, draft
EMC, 3 ff. (blanks Bv, Cv). Pencil and red ballpoint pen on staff paper, ca. 220 x 319 mm

Nearly all the fair copies of the pieces composed for the soundtrack of *The Assassination of Trotsky* are enclosed in flyleaves which mark the starting point for the various musical numbers. In terms of medium, they are oblong sheets: staff paper folded in half. Although the "Edizioni musicali Rete" logo exists on the lower-left-hand edge of the page, no link can be found between the publisher and the *Trotsky* film. Instead, this choice of paper merely serves as proof of Macchi's assiduous compositional activity in the field of documentary production from the 1960s onwards. In fact, many of the documentary scores from the 1960s and 1970s preserved in the Egisto Macchi Collection are composed on paper made by specific publishers who were the primary points of reference for documentary cinema at the time. The paper produced by Edizioni musicali Rete – plain on one side with staffs on the other – was just as suitable for organising the composer's creative process in accordance with the "very fast" method Losey admired so much.

On the verso of the flyleaf (the plain side), Macchi usually marked the "M" number in pencil. In this case, since it was a particular moment in the film's dramaturgical framework, he specifically designated that this was the musical piece that corresponded to the sequence of the opening credits: Titoli [Titles]. The verso usually contains further indications about the instruments employed in the fair copy or, as in this case, a simple preliminary note about some of the instruments that will be used in the composition (violins, violas, and cellos). Finally, Macchi indicated whether the fair copy that corresponds to the draft was indeed recorded and used for the film by writing «FATTO [DONE]» or simply the letter «F [D]», often in red ballpoint pen.

On the recto of the pages (that is, on the staff side of the original "Edizioni musicali Rete" sheets of paper), we instead find the first plans for the musical material, which is then fully elaborated in the fair copies. In this stage we usually find a continuity draft in which the general development of the piece is defined. It is a sort of skeleton score, where Macchi designated pitches for the main parts; he added timing indications for the main sync points and provided some information about the orchestration employed. Indeed, all these elements can be found in the draft of the score for the opening credits.

The draft is written over three pages which reveal two distinct phases in the creative process. At first, Macchi defined the structure organisation of the entire piece in the upper-right-hand corner of pages numbered 1 and 2 (cf. 7, Br and 7, Cr); he then decided to return to the beginning of the piece, jotting down different versions of the initial melodic line on the remaining manuscript page: the recto of the flyleaf where the piece is named (cf. 7, Ar). Let us start with the two numbered pages. Both are set out in the same way, with the musical material subdivided into two systems made up of five staves per sheet, for a total time of 3', 07". Different time intervals, regardless of the rhythmic values of the notes, are indicated above every bar line. Although the entire draft – metrically speaking – is organised according to an implicit 4/4, there is no regular metronomic indication: the semibreve-unit lasts between a minimum of 4 and a maximum of 8 seconds. Macchi only defines two particularly important sync points, circling the chronometric indication at 1', 16" and at 1', 36", which correspond respectively to the sequence of title cards containing the opening credits and the title of the film.

The skeleton of the piece is essentially structured according to two main sound layers: the first – a chordal layer assigned to the first and second violins, violas, cellos, and first organ – saturates the entire diatonic collection (for the organ, Macchi calls for all keys – ranging from E1 to F4 – to be pressed simultaneously by means of a long line); and the second – entrusted to the sopranos, a children's choir, and second organ, plus first violins (1', 24") – presents instead a single melodic line that hovers over this texture. These two layers are supplemented by another level with an undefined pitch called «brusio [buzzing]» (1', 04") and then by an additional sound level built on three notes assigned to the Synket, indicated as being the sound of crickets (1', 16"). In drawing up the first page, Macchi seems decisive in his intent. The work plan is quite orderly and there are already some dynamic indications, such as the crescendo hairpin that marks the reappearance of the melodic incipit assigned to the sopranos and children's choir, marked «S. R.». We can however observe a series of variations in the melodic line – noted under the main staves, or inserted inside them in brackets – from the last two bars of the first page and throughout the second. These are mostly notes indicating turns or passages in chromatic figurations that modify the melodic profile, without radically altering the pitch content.

As mentioned before, there is a series of possible melodic incipits in the remaining, unnumbered page. It seems that, once Macchi had finished the continuity draft, he chose to return to the beginning of the piece; experimenting with alternative solutions, he avoids the literal repetition of the sopranos' and organ II's first five bars. He noted six different versions which can be divided into three different "groups". The first group is noted on the second staff of the page; the second group includes the next three versions written on the sixth, seventh, and tenth staves: the first cancelled out, the second reworked according to that model, and the third transposed a semitone higher; finally, the third group includes the two melodic lines noted on the twelfth and thirteenth staves of the page, and – in this case – the former is interrupted, while the latter is developed according to that model up to 1', 16"(the point at which the melodic incipit is repeated in the continuity draft).

Finally, in the last two staves, Macchi added a pitch group that saturated the same soundscape, as defined at the beginning of the continuity draft, by merely altering the G sharp from the originally planned diatonic collection.

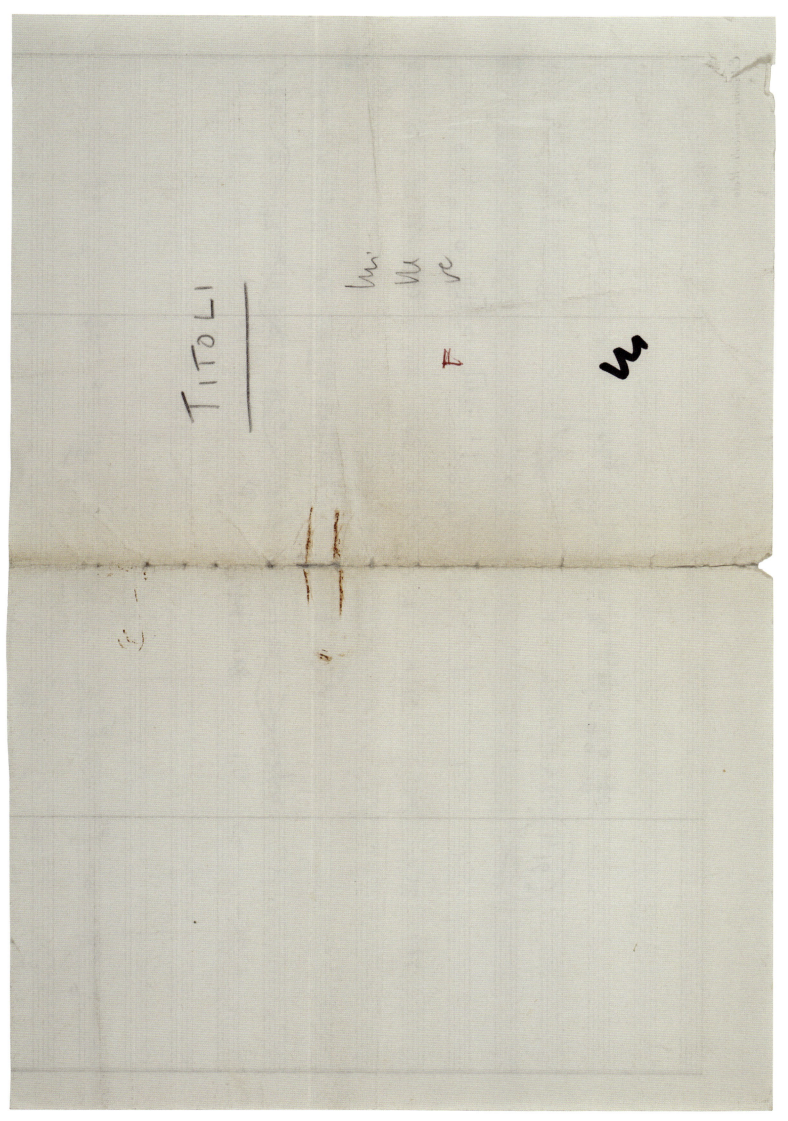

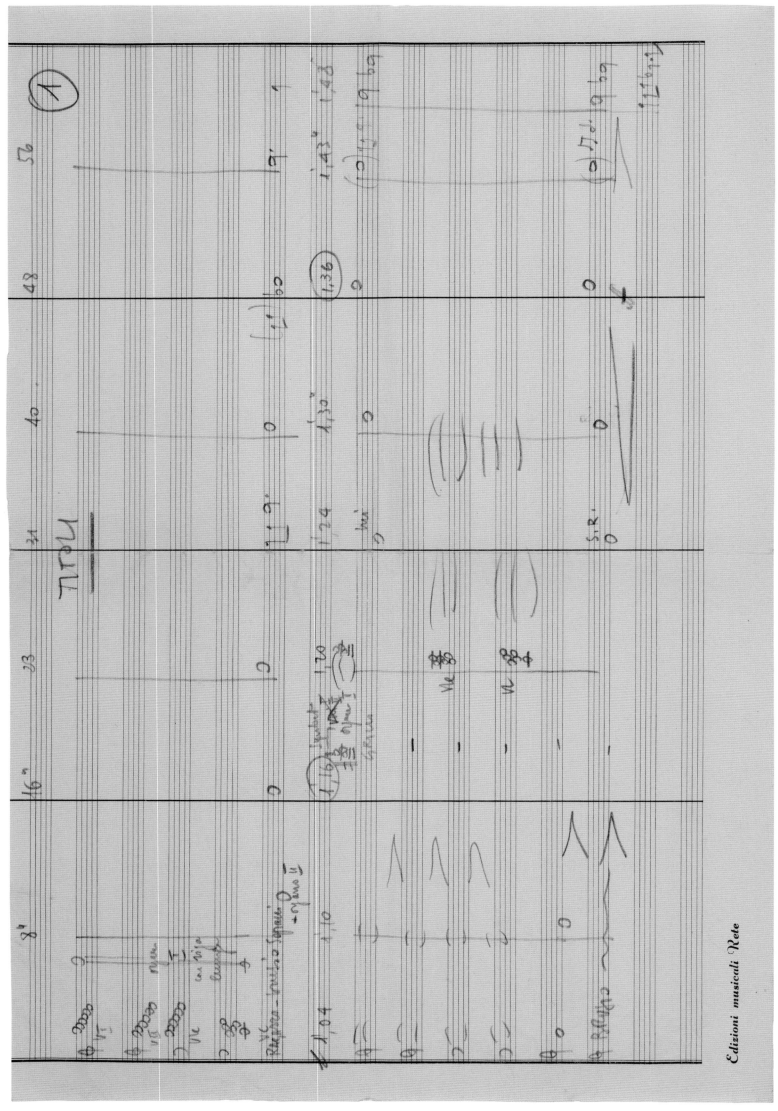

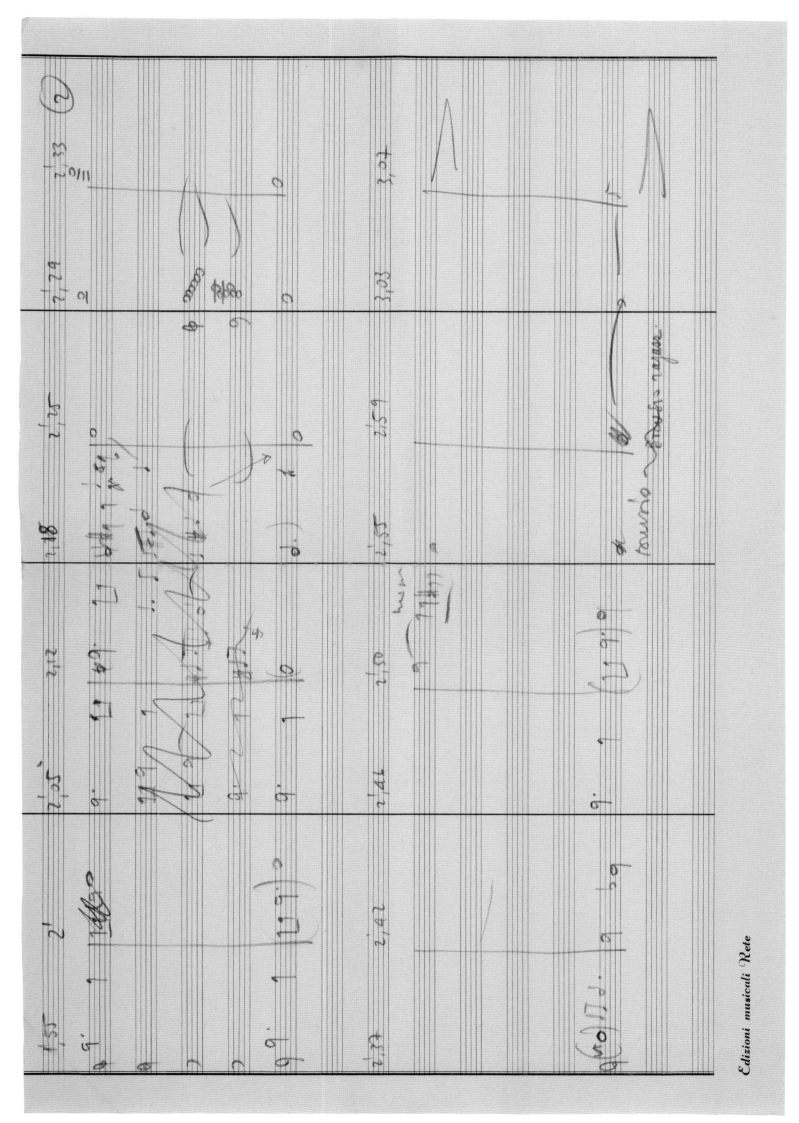

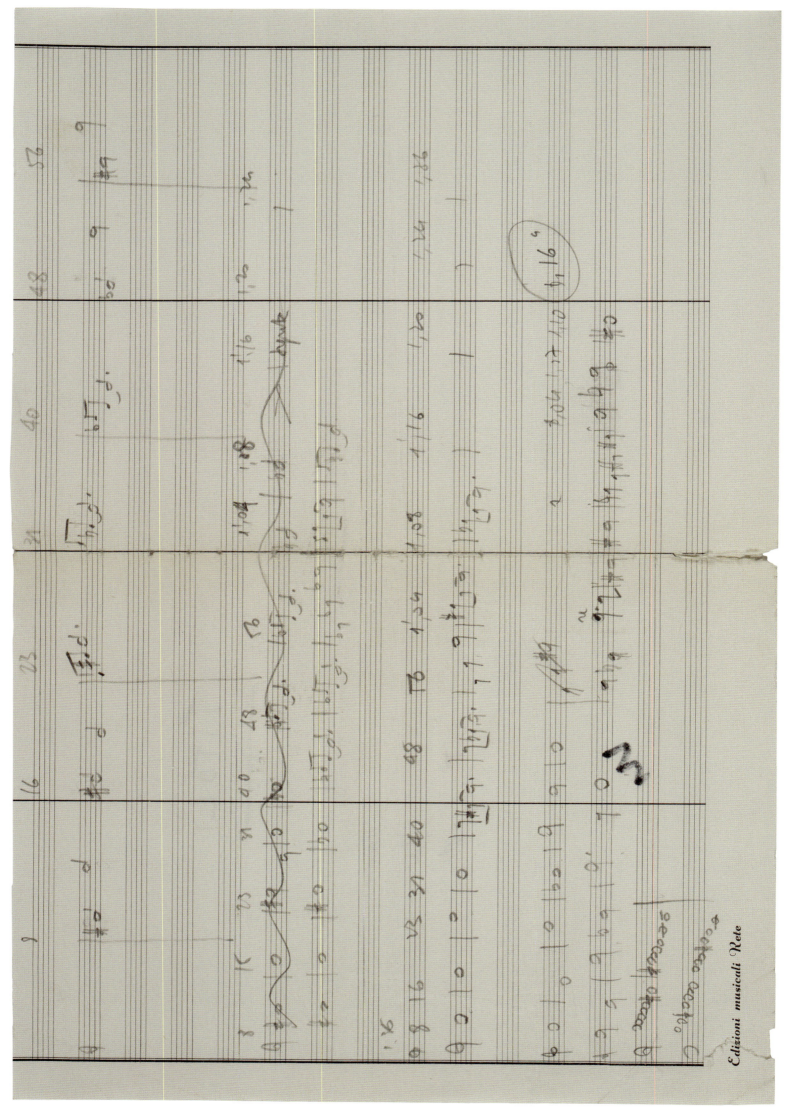

Document 8: Titoli, fair copy
EMC, 3 ff. (all versos blank). Pencil and black felt-tip pen on staff paper, 470 x 325 mm

The music for the opening credits is the *The Assassination of Trotsky*'s calling card and it deliberately showcases the great variety of sound elements that are employed during the film. As the previous document shows, Macchi had already planned for this heterogeneity in the draft, in the final version it becomes even more clearly defined. The orchestra is made up of 2 organs tuned a quarter tone apart, 8 sopranos, a children's choir, the Synket, 3 first violins, 3 second violins, 6 violas, and 6 cellos. Clearly, this composition was conceived by a process of addition, through a layering technique that superimposed distinct sound layers, each with its characteristic timbre. This process can undoubtedly be traced back to Macchi's experience with electronic music, especially in the way he uses the Synket, employed primarily as a sustained sound. However, Macchi perhaps employed this procedure simply because – as a conductor of his own music – he assiduously participated in the recording sessions: the addition of individual instrumental tracks, which were then assembled together in the final mixing stage, was standard practice.

The transition from the draft to the final version usually followed a rather linear process: Macchi fixed all the musical and extramusical parameters – orchestrating the piece and redefining the different sync points – before moving onto the recording sessions. The fair copy demonstrates the process of reworking that has been applied to the melodic incipit of the draft. Macchi combined the two aforementioned different phases of realisation and opted for the melodic variant noted on the recto of the flyleaf, thereby avoiding the repetition of the originally intended melodic fragment. Though the fair copy allows us to see how the composition developed between the draft and the final version, it also gives us the chance to explore the more specifically performative phases that characterise a musical text for cinema. The different layers of manuscripts disclose at least two other creative phases that took place during the work in the recording studio. In the first compositional stage, Macchi used a pencil to write the actual music and to note the sync points on the thirteenth and fourteenth staves, corresponding to the changes in framing on the screen. Another layer – also written in pencil – is added at this level; the composer changed some details regarding instruments in the second and third pages, giving the sopranos' part to the organ and bringing the buzzing track forward by one beat at the end of the piece; he then adjusted some sync points and provided tempo indications (such as «veloce [fast]», «accelera [accelerate]»), which serve to establish a successful relationship between the development of the music and the images. Lastly, the timing of the sync points was corrected in black marker, making them clearly visible during the conducting and recording session of the music.

The piece was initially composed to mark the sequence of the opening credits, which is divided into two segments. The first segment – corresponding to the first page – presents a series of photographs alongside captions that retrace Trotsky's life, from his childhood to the period of his exile. This series of photographs is coordinated with beat changes, approximately every eight seconds. This piece is based on a static and immobile sound mass, above which a melodic movement unfolds through long notes assigned to the sopranos. This sound mass is static only in pitch. In fact, all the strings and the first organ create a complex sound that saturates the chromatic scale from E1 to F4. The pitches involved cover the entire range of white keys except for G, which is always present in the altered form of G sharp, according to the variant noted on the draft's unnumbered page.[16] This first timbric layer, entrusted to the strings alone, exploits each of the instruments separately to obtain an extremely wide and dense sound layer, which unfolds the heptachord in ascending order. Above this musical layer – with its steady pitch and uniform timbre – it is not a coincidence that Macchi gives explicit indications to avoid vibrato – another similarly steady sound element stands out. This is the cue he called the buzzing; a studio reworking of several indistinct children's voices, it is impossible to make out what they are saying.[17] Though the multiformity of voices creates light aural ripples from a timbric perspective, the principle of sound continuity is maintained. These three sound layers, all based on the immobility of tempo, are "assembled" one on top of the other, thus giving rise to a sound mass that remains globally static but that changes timbrically, making use of acoustic (strings), electronic (organ), and human (murmuring voices) sounds.

A melodic line on an OE diphthong is inserted in this triple sound layer, performed an octave apart from the sopranos and the organ; it is based on the concatenation of ascending and descending leaps of a perfect and a diminished fifth which establishes a continuous circular development.

The opening exposition of the melodic line therefore coincides with the first segment of the initial sequence like a perfect mirror between the visual and musical dimensions. The next page considers the opening credits, which present the film's technical crew and its cast through a series of white signs on a brown background.

---

[16] This is heptachord 7-32, attributable to a dominant Phrygian scale starting from E.

[17] This is the only sound element at the end of the film. Macchi used a similar effect, always based on children's voices pronouncing single syntactic units, in *Padre Padrone* (*Father and Master*, dir. Paolo and Vittorio Taviani, 1977).

Macchi emphasised the caesura by circling the sync point set at 1 minute and 16 seconds, corresponding with the card that presents the producer (Shaftel) and assigning an entire beat to the sound of a solo Synket: three notes which are a semitone apart (D sharp-E-F) in the instrument's highest range alongside the sound of crickets.

The synthesiser designed by Paolo Ketoff plays a central role in the organisation of the film's sound levels. The Synket enjoyed great success in both the film industry and in Rome's free improvisation movement because its three keyboards made it so simple to use and because it could reproduce a large variety of timbre. The type of sounds that mimicked nature were precisely the ones often exploited in the film industry, almost as if they were an expansion of the orchestral sound. In this case the choice of «grilli [crickets]» sounds creates a strong link with the sound environment that surrounds the film. In fact, on more than one occasion, the Synket is used to create this sound of insects, which not only recalls the incessant chirping around Trotsky's fortified house, but which – since the sounds are sustained in such a high register – is also an indirect reference to the sound of the alarm-siren that protects the statesman's residence. Soundscape and musical imagery in this way infiltrate each other. As in the first part, the interval between one card and the next in this section almost always corresponds to the interval of a bar, except for the card with the protagonists' names – Richard Burton, Alain Delon and Romy Schneider. They set the stage for the title, *The Assassination of Trotsky*; circled by Macchi on the score it corresponds to the apex of the voices' opening arpeggio. All the musical layers can be heard in this second section, where the Synket adds another immobile musical level to the static sound mass consisting strings, organ, and the murmuring voices.

In the remainder of the fair copy, Macchi did not make any further observations about the opening credits, except for the director's name which he highlighted with two arrows at the end. At first, his name was emphasised by the attack of an electro-acoustically reworked track of the children's chatter. However, during the final editing, the sync point is brought forward to 2 minutes and 55 seconds; a synchronization that relates to the film's soundtrack, rather than to the card about the producer (Norman Prigeen), it is likely a later addition since a voice over comes in with words from Trotsky's *History of the Russian Revolution*: «In revolution there is no compulsion, only circumstantial. Revolution occurs only when there is no other way out».[18]

At first conception, Macchi viewed the music of the opening credits music as exclusive to that part of the film, as is evident in Document 4. In the final editing, however, the piece was also used for the bullfight sequence, which is central to the film's dramatic development. The opening credits music therefore enables us to establish a link with one of the film's key sequences. Though the score for the Titoli had initially been conceived as a soundtrack for the opening credits – having precise sync points with its cards –, I believe it is useful to consider the music's other functions inside the film itself – not only because it is the only piece within the entire soundtrack that is repeated literally, but also because Macchi's own words about the matter can indirectly elucidate his interpretative process, even when, as in this case, it is based on "pre-existing" music.

In fact, the archival materials contain a draft of an article he had written to be used at an unspecified conference that was dedicated to the relationship between music and cinema.[19] After reflecting on the status of music "for" – and not "from" –[20] films, Macchi takes examples from his compositional production to discuss, «three fundamental ways of looking at the scene»: with empathetic sound, anempathetic sound, and didactic counterpoint. The composer evidently adopted the terms introduced by Michel Chion to classify music that: 1) «can directly express its participation in the feeling of the scene, by taking on the scene's rhythm, tone, and phrasing»; 2) «can also exhibit conspicuous indifference to the situation, by progressing in a steady, undaunted, and ineluctable manner»;[21] 3) «is useful in providing meaning to a concept, to a complementary idea».[22] He chose an excerpt from *The Assassination of Trotsky* to illustrate the second category; specifically, he chose the central sequence of the bullfight. It is interesting to observe that, in his notes, Macchi had originally called for the audience to watch the sequence first without any sound, and later with the audio restored. He said:

> bull and bullfighter look like fish in an aquarium. The music isolates them, freezes them in the distance, ignores them and makes the drama more brutal. [...] Start real bullfighting effects + children's chatter. Then just my music without real effects. When the bull dies (Trotzky) [sic] the real effects return.[23]

---

[18] Quote from the third volume of *History of the Russian Revolution*, at the beginning of the chapter *The Art of Insurrection*; see Leon Trotsky, *History of the Russian Revolution*, trans. by Max Eastman, Chicago: Haymarket Books, 2008, p. 740.

[19] Published in Daniela Tortora, *Nuova Consonanza 1989-1994*, Lucca: Lim, 1994, pp. 159-162.

[20] In this excerpt, Macchi insisted on the fact that there is no such thing as inherently cinematographic music but only music conceived for cinema, Ivi, p. 159; given that Macchi and Sergio Miceli were close friends, it is reasonable to think that such an interpretation was derived from the argumentation Miceli had presented on this subject in several of his studies.

[21] Michel Chion, *Audio-vision. Sound on Screen*, New York: Columbia University Press, 1994, pp. 8-9.

[22] Michel Chion, *La musique au cinéma*, Paris: Fayard, 1995, pp. 122-124.

[23] Tortora, *Nuova Consonanza 1989-1994*, p. 161. In this case too, a possible derivation from Chion's theoretical apparatus is quite feasible. He suggested using precisely *the*

The sequence is an important constituent in the hitman's psychological development as Losey sketches it. On one hand, it serves to mirror Alain Delon – who plays Frank, sent to kill the Russian statesman – and the bullfighter, as well as Trotsky and the dying bull in the arena. The delicate relationship between victim and executioner is reexamined according to the cultural tradition of bullfighting, where the strong sense of a spectator's involvement is accentuated by the continual alternation of shots that show us the public and the protagonists in the arena from opposite perspectives. Frank's feelings of guilt and emotional instability become increasingly evident, just as we can see the clear discomfort of the girl close to the statesman – played by Romy Schneider – who in turn is used by the hitman to reach his murderous goal. From a visual point of view, the whole segment is delimited by the same visual movement that opens and closes the scene: the sequence opens with an obvious zooming forward – a characteristic trait of the American director – which frames a bronze statue of a bull and a bullfighter, his face covered by his *capote*;[24] this shot is then echoed by one of Delon, who, at the end of the spectacle is visibly upset, his face covered by his hands. From a musical point of view, the sequence is set to the piece of the opening credits alongside some diegetic music of trumpet and drums – composed separately by Macchi – which marks the different phases of the bullfight. This is followed by cue M. 5/2 composed for the death of the bull, however, the present analysis will only consider the reutilisation of the music for the opening credits.

As in the opening credits, it is also possible to distinguish two micro-sequences based on different sound equilibrium in the reutilisation of this music. In fact, in the first part, the two actors observe the bullfight in silence, while the dialogue becomes progressively more animated in the next segment. Unlike the opening credits, where the vocal track is immediately and clearly perceptible (since there are no other elements in the soundtrack), the bullfighting sequence presents a slightly modified mixing balance at first. The transition from crowd noises to the musical intervention is carried out gradually and focuses on the morphemic continuity of the spoken words, while the vocal track sung by the children's choir is perceived only gradually.

Once the first section of the music finishes, the empty beat of the Synket once again serves as a form of transitional section. It is synchronised with a full shot of the crowd; the noises of the public are eliminated: only the music and the voices of the two protagonists remain. The track with the chattering voices permanently replaces the arena noises and this time we begin to hear all the sound elements of the Titoli distinctly, without any alternations in the mix. The melodic profile sung by the sopranos is thus made to correspond to the preparation of the bullfight's second phase. In fact, the second section of the opening credits' track marks the crucial moment of the *lidia*, when the matador confronts the bull directly, his cape and sword hidden behind his back. This is the phase in which we perceive all the musical layers: when the Synket is added to the static sound mass of the strings, the organ, and the chatter. It is once again the electronic layer that functions as a transition, leading us to the piece numbered M. 5/2 for the last phase of the bullfight: the killing of the bull.

---

masking method to better analyse the audiovisual structures of a sequence; see Chion, *Audio-vision. Sound on Screen*, p. 187.

[24] The cape of rigid cloth with which the bullfighter incites the bull to charge during the first stages of the bullfight.

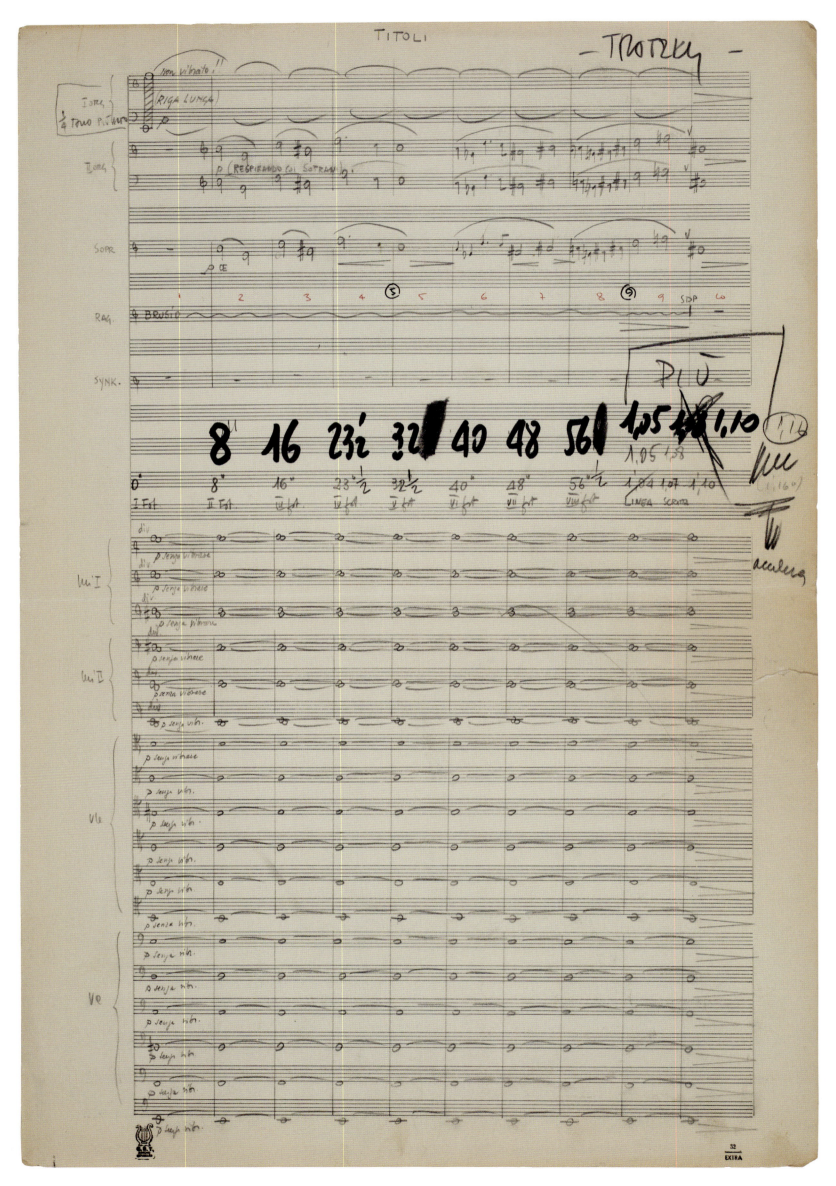

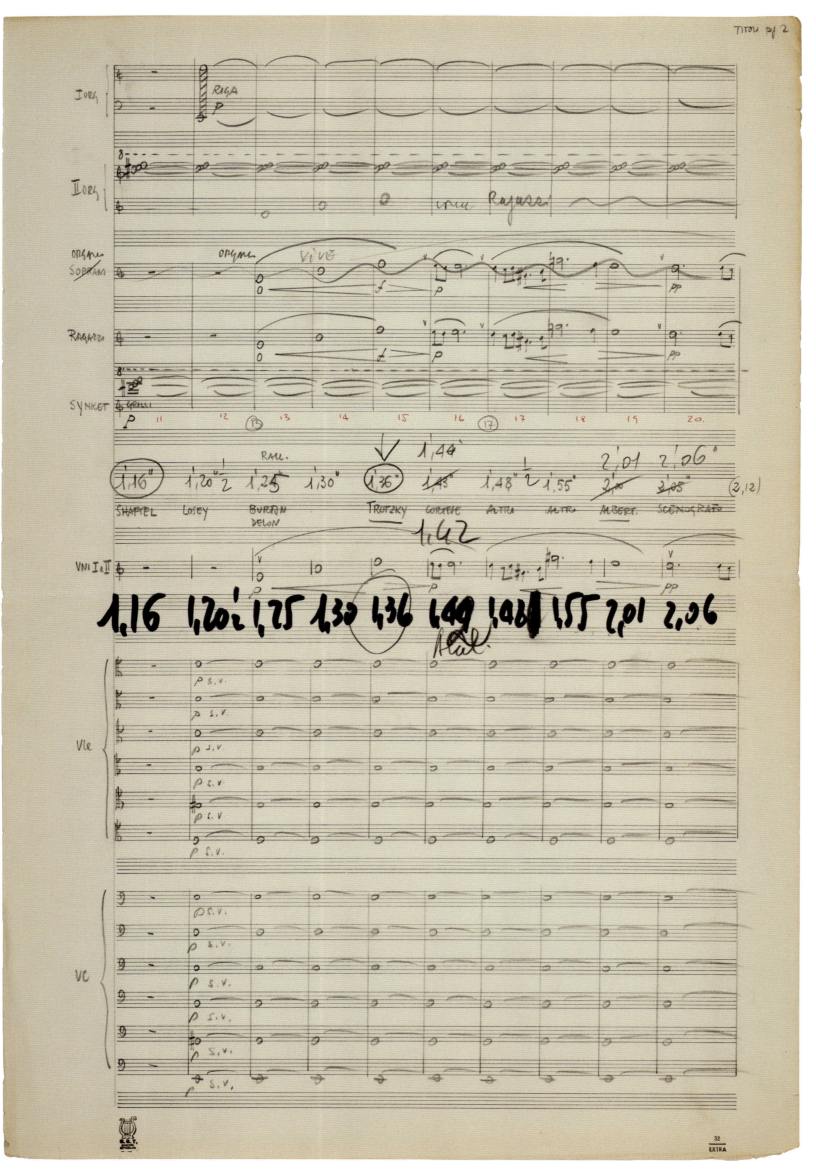

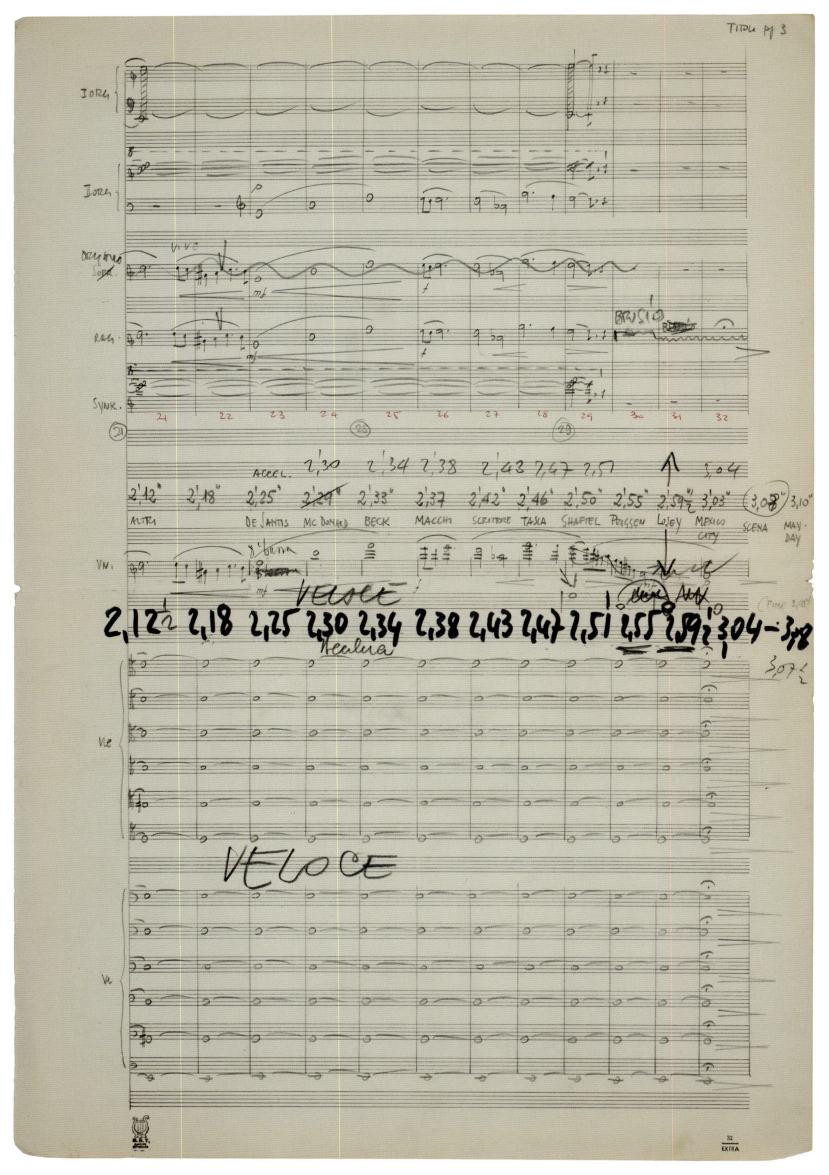

Document 9: M. 5/2 I versione, sketch

EMC, 1 f. Pencil, red pencil, red ballpoint pen on staff paper, ca. 220 x 319 mm

Now let us consider the final segment of the bullfight sequence. We have already noted that, after reusing the music from the opening credits, Macchi composed a new piece for the last part of the bullfight. M. 5/2 is particularly interesting because several versions of the piece exist, each with their relative sketches and drafts. They help us not only to reconstruct the creative process of composing music on paper, but also to observe its transformation during studio mixing. In fact, two different versions of the piece are preserved – called «I e II versione [I and II version]» – that Macchi used in drafting the final version. Although the three versions of the piece differ in terms of instrumentation and overall pitch handling, they are nonetheless characterised by a clear definition of the points of intersection between the audio and visual dimensions.

The sketch of the first version represents Macchi's first attempt at a musical realisation of the piece. The verso of the paper offers some information that helps us to establish how the work was planned and its genetic path: in fact, Macchi labeled it in pencil as «M. 5/2 I VERS.». This suggests that right from the beginning, he was well aware that he would probably have to make at least one other version. As we will see in the third chapter, this process was repeated for many of the musical numbers in the score: proof that Macchi decided, probably alongside the director, to plan for alternative musical versions which would then be evaluated during editing. There are also other traces of writing on the page that provide evidence that can help us establish further links between documents. In the facsimile, we can see how the notes in red ballpoint pen were added at a later time, proving that the first version was then merged into a «D[efinitiva] [Final]» version (cf. Document 13). Instead, the first plan of the musical material appears on the recto of the page.

The composition begins on the recto of the paper and is reproduced here. In this document we witness a rather embryonic stage and it is precisely for this reason that it should be seen more as a sketch, rather than as a real draft. In fact, there are no clear indications for instrumentation at the beginning of the various noted staves, but Macchi clearly thought about using several voices to articulate the sound space: on the left-hand side of the page we find sequences of six pitches in an ascending chromatic scale (staves 3 and 5) and then a descending one (staves 9 and 10), saturating all 12 chromatic pitches. At the centre of the page (staves 7 and 8), the concept of chromatic descent is condensed between two pitches a perfect fourth apart, indicating the chromatic descent in writing with the formula «CROM.», and specifying precisely for it to be performed on the first or second string (according to the abbreviation «I corda» and «II corda»). The only information about the possible instruments is given in the upper and lower margins: Synket and organs – specifying a typically tuned Farfisa organ and a Baldwin organ tuned a quarter tone sharp.

In curly brackets on the right-hand side, Macchi marked a descending chromatic sequence that initially oscillates between several voices in the top part of the page and then develops into a series of gradual entrances. However, this sequence seems to be read «al contrario [back to front]», as the indications written alongside it suggest. Three sync points have been indicated: 11 seconds, 12 seconds and 19 and a half seconds. If we compare this source with its subsequent versions, it is clear that these indications have yet to be finalised, especially since only one second transpires between the first two. However, two moments of strong caesura can be identified, the first at 11 seconds – corresponding with the last fragment of the descending scale – and then at 19 and a half seconds where the sketch is interrupted, by a straight line.

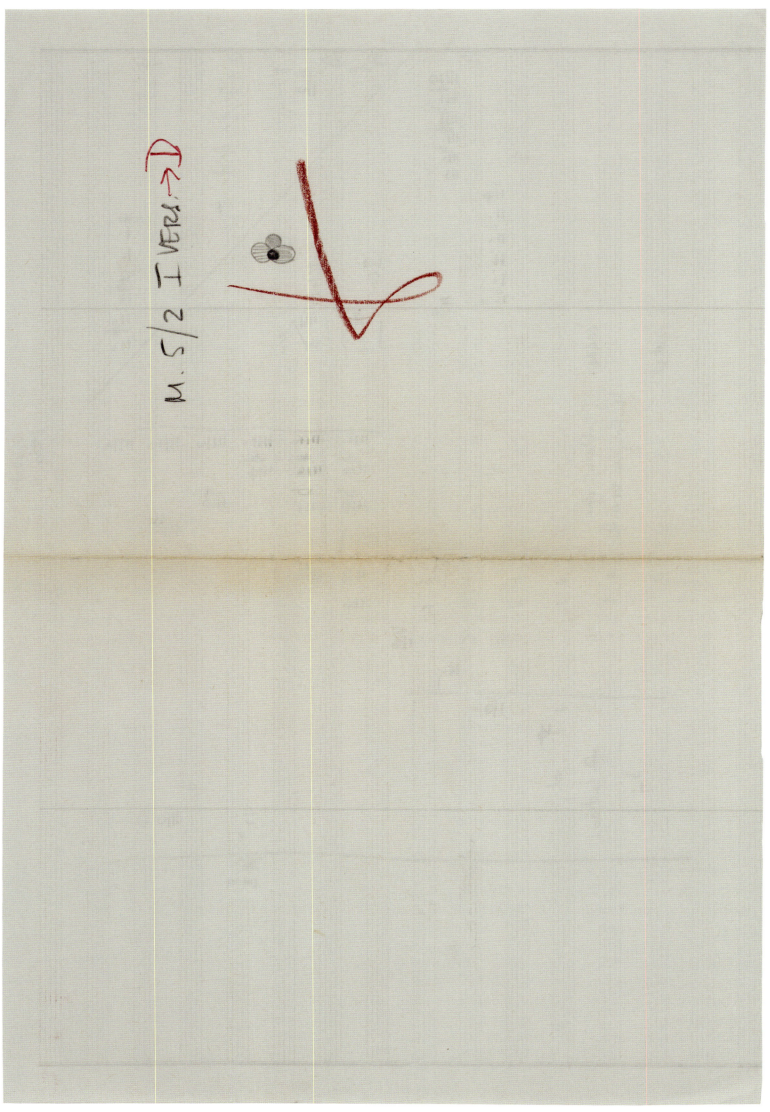

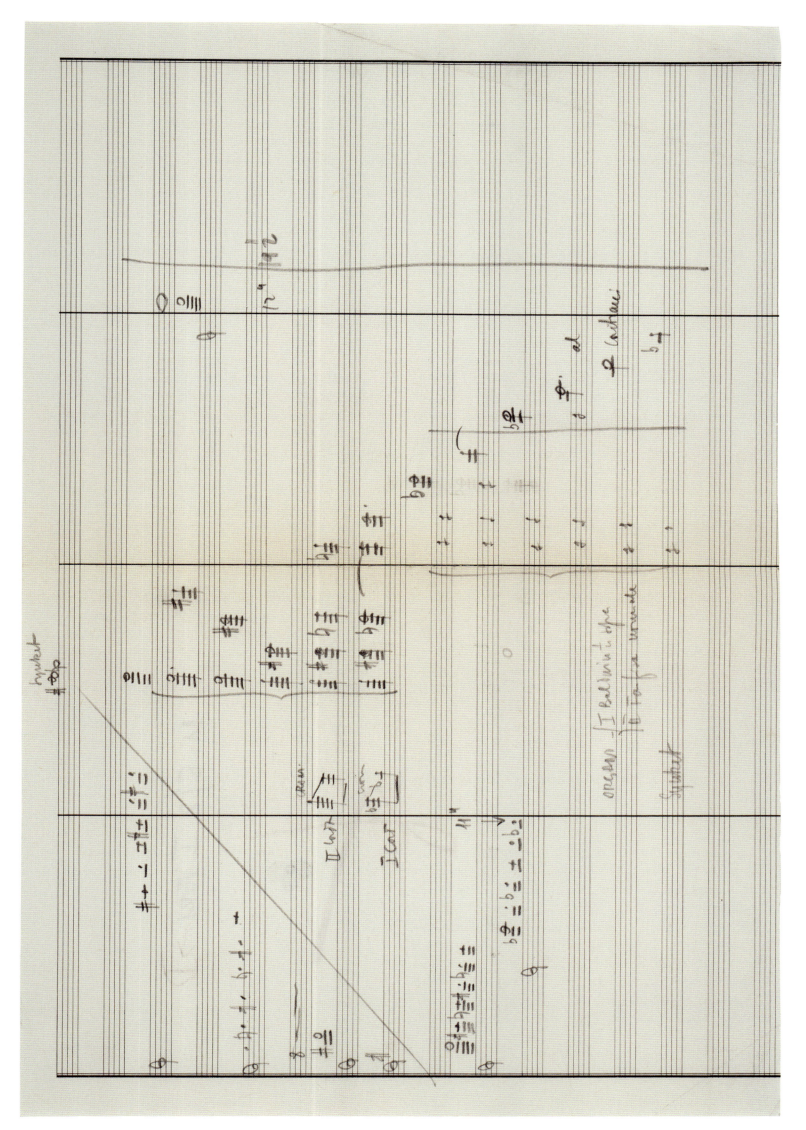

Document 10: M. 5/2 I versione, fair copy

EMC, 1 f. (verso blank). Pencil, red ballpoint on staff paper, 470 x 325 mm

Using the sketch reproduced in the previous document, Macchi went on to extensively develop the piece into its first version in every last detail: pitch distribution, orchestration, dynamic indications, and timing. All the elements observed previously have now been completely defined according to the contents of the reference sequence. Cue M. 5/2 corresponds to the last segment of the bullfighting sequence and is introduced immediately after the opening credits. The images of the wounded bull as it collapses alternate with shots of the two protagonists, who engage in what turns into a heated discussion. Although they only seem to argue about the bullfight itself, their quarrel in fact reveals the obvious anxiety of Delon's assassin about his impending task. From a visual point of view, we have a tripartite sequence – a shot of the bull; and two shots of the actors; two still shots of the bull – one that also corresponds to the sonic balance with which Macchi's music must interact: the death rattle of the bull and the sound of its hooves coming from the arena corresponding with shots of the animal – which are alternated with the two characters' voices as they watch the scene. These elements of audiovisual syntax set the stage for the definition of the micro-formal turning points of the piece. Even though the three versions differ in terms of instrumentation and in terms of overall pitch management, they all exhibit a clear audiovisual organisation. All three versions have alternating groups in 4/4 and in 5/4, and Macchi indicated precise durations in seconds, always setting the sync points at 10", 19 ½" and 23", plus a secondary point placed just over 21". Instead he used a red pen to number the 6 bars comprising the total length of the cue.

In the first section which corresponds to the first 10", he reworked the ascending and descending scale fragments found in the sketch. These are the starting points for organising the two string sections: six violas and six cellos. Each of the two groups of strings employs a single chromatic hexachord (6-1), the notes of which are distributed horizontally, following the normal course of the bar; vertically, the various notes of the hexachord are assigned to the six-stringed instruments as a starting point. In this way, the first cello and the first viola play all six notes as a quarter note, while the other voices progressively follow the ascending profile, according to the initial note. The sound space is thus increasingly saturated from a chromatic point of view, by means of an ascending profile alone. The principle of descending pitch organisation, present in the sketch on several occasions, is instead used in a symmetrical manner for the section lasting from 19 ½" to 23". However, while the duration of the first section was marked second by second, this time the execution time is nearly halved. In the central section, there is a long stasis that lasts from 10" to 19 ½". It is obvious that the piece is designed to be synchronised with the sequence by means of timing and not by the duration of beats. It is equally evident that the stasis section corresponds to the central moment when the actors engage in a lively discussion, while the ascending and descending chromatic saturations served to mark the various phases of the bull's death.

The evolution of sketch to fair copy reveals not only a more defined musical development: what emerges most clearly is the sonic construction of the piece, which is entirely designed in high registers. The two string sections are based entirely on the harmonics of the violas and cellos. In keeping with the characteristic colour of the string harmonics, the electronic instruments are used in their highest register and serve to create a more static type of layer. Once again, we find the previously indicated pair of electric organs alongside a Synket, in addition to a chord composed of A, G sharp, and G (pitches that are semitones apart), shared between a synthesiser, organ I, two flutes, and a clarinet. It is particularly interesting to note that, here too, the Synket is played in the timbre of the crickets, once again, acting as a sonic bridge between the track of the opening credits and the bullfight's final segment.

The dynamic hairpin markings that establish the different sound layers' intensity are equally decisive in this first version. Macchi also accentuated the ascending chromatic scale by means of a gradual crescendo: from the initial *pianissimo* until *fortissimo* is reached at 10". The inverse chromatic segment does not have a diminuendo hairpin; rather a crescendo is repeated at the end of bar 5. Instead, a general decrescendo is observed after the sync point set at 23", which marks the return to the sound environment of images with noises coming from the arena. It is interesting to observe how Macchi in his role as conductor-composer altered the arrival point slightly to 23", crossing out the crescendo hairpins of the three wind instruments with a black ballpoint pen, and replacing them with just as many hairpins in diminuendo, written in pencil. It seems that the final passage of the strings risked being overshadowed by the flutes and clarinets in the balance of the overall ensemble.

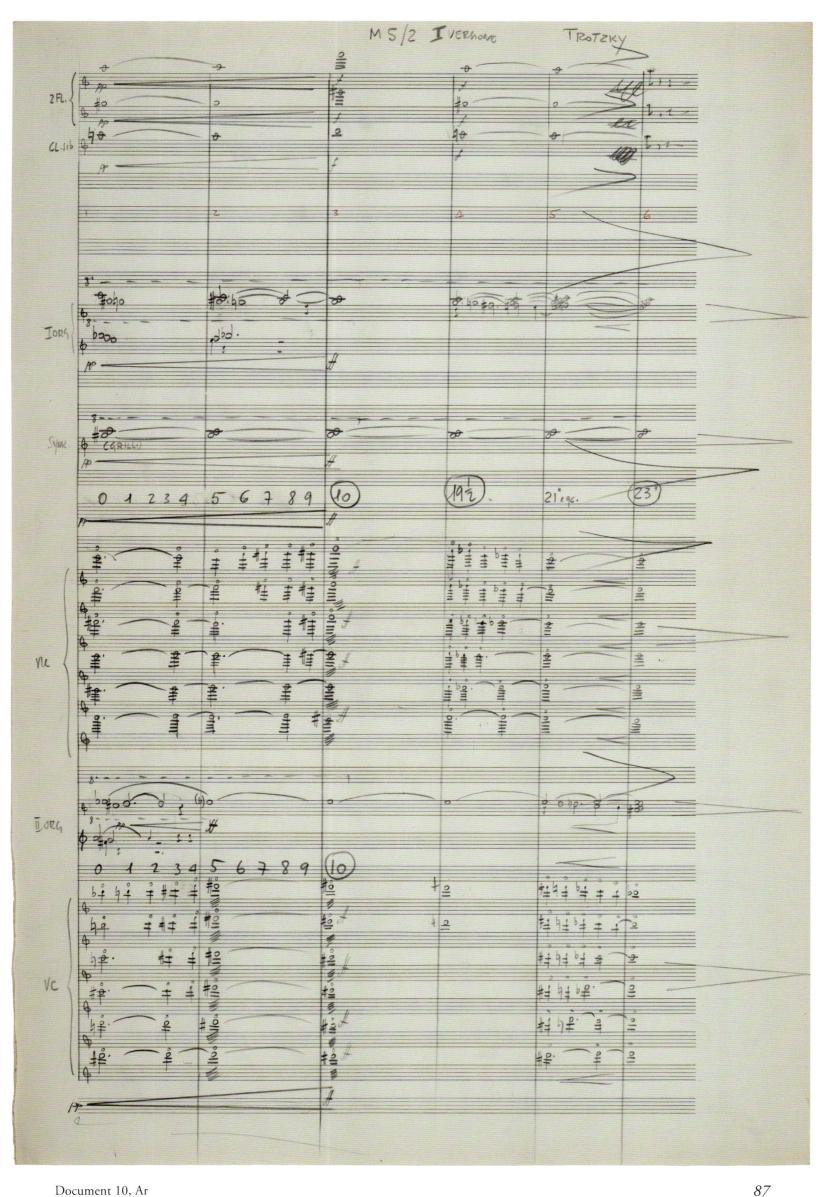

Document 11: M. 5/2 II versione, draft
EMC, 1 f. Pencil and black ballpoint pen on staff paper, ca. 220 x 319 mm

The death of the bull represents a crucial moment in the bullfighting sequence, and thus it is plausible to suspect that Macchi and Losey explored various ways of achieving the most effective musical solution for it. It is no surprise that, though this excerpt is quite short – only about 26" –, Macchi prepared many different versions, as he experimented with the balance of the audiovisual effect. Just like the draft for the first version, this second version also called version B on the verso of the draft flyleaf – calls for three precise sync points: set at 10", 19 ½", and 23". However, unlike the previous example, the structure of the piece is more thoroughly planned in the first stage of the composition. We can thus interpret the document reproduced herein as a real draft, whereas the sketch and the fair copy of the first version (cf. Documents 9-10) can be interpreted, retrospectively, as preparatory materials for the new elaboration of the piece.

There is in fact a certain degree of continuity between the first and second versions. As far as the pitch organisation is concerned, the ascending and descending chromatic movement is eliminated, and the key element becomes a chord constructed on three notes (a semitone apart) that previously worked as a background element. This chord is now transposed a semitone higher; we now have a piece built only on G sharp, A, and B flat. Another element of continuity is that of the orchestration. In the draft, Macchi redistributed the pitch content over three layers: including the flutes, another group of violins, the Synket and organ I, and another group of cellos and organ II. In addition, a new eight-part sound level has been added, with pitches assigned to the aerophones, but which have not been precisely indicated. With the generic suggestion of "aerophones", Macchi was thinking of one in particular: a bull-roarer, an instrument made of a flat piece of wood or bone fastened to a piece of string, which when spun around one's head makes a strong and deep sound, similar to a bull's roar. The instrument is widely used in ethnic traditions throughout the world and often has a strong symbolic value, with ties to religion and rites of initiation. This decision by Macchi can be seen as part of an acoustic investigation connected to the specific audiovisual context, that activates a cultural dimension not only connected to the ritual that the bullfight represents, but also to the psychological development of the characters. And as we have already seen in part, with the characteristic timbre of the Synket represented in the register of the crickets, Macchi's choice of instruments moves to eliminate the traditional boundaries between the film's musical dimension and its sound effects. The draft in question allows us to see that, even when faced with what are ostensibly simple compositional choices, this solution makes the soundtrack of *The Assassination of Trotsky* – in the classic tripartition of music, dialogue, and sound effects – a complex aggregate that is uniform yet problematic at the same time.

The piece is broadly organised by alternating moments of saturation and silence, the latter indicated by the term "stop". Once again, the central segment that goes from 10 to 19 ½ seconds has been structured to ensure that the actors' voices predominate in the soundtrack. Amid the silence of other instruments, only the sound of the aerophones remains. The moments leading to the bull's final collapse at 23" are also scored in this draft with a crescendo, which subsequently leaves only the layer of the second stave to return the audiovisual narrative to the sound of the images depicted on screen.

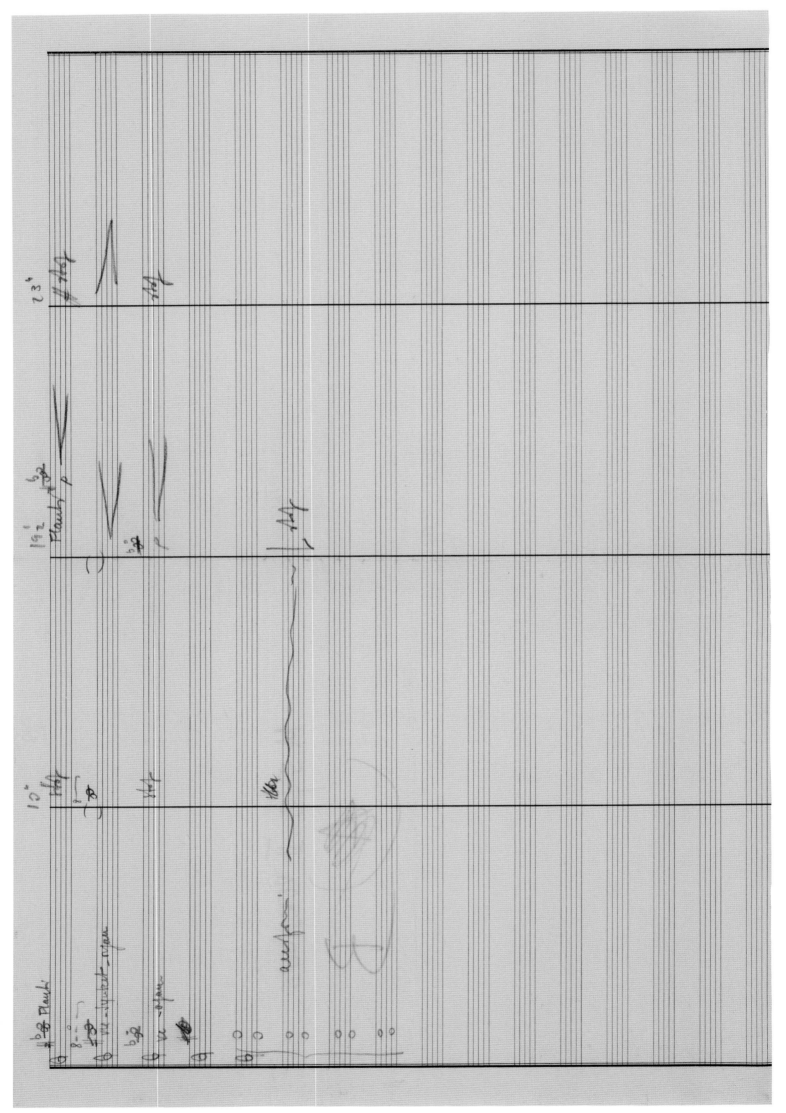

Document 12: M. 5/2 II versione, fair copy

EMC, 1 f. (verso blank). Pencil, red pencil, red ballpoint pen on staff paper, 470 x 325 mm

In this document, Macchi followed a more linear path in the transition from draft to fair copy than he did in the first version. The second iteration of cue M. 5/2 went through two writing phases: one in grey pencil and another in red pencil, as he added or modified some details. In the first phase, the different layers that were condensed in the draft have now been "opened up," and the three key notes of the entire piece have been assigned to the instrumental parts. The notes entrusted to the strings – most likely 6 violas and 6 violins (though not specified) – here too exploit the particular colour of first string harmonics, with the exception of the second violas which play harmonics on the second string. In this draft, Macchi programs and defines the appearance of the soprano aerophones in the first two bars. The clarinet is the only instrument that is not explicitly required in the draft and – as in the previous version – it is paired up with the two flutes. Contrary to what was initially planned, only the winds are silenced in the second bar, while the cello and organ II continue to sound the bichord. Another small difference between the draft and the final version is the addition (at least in the initial stage in pencil) of the notes repeated by the violas and cellos in the second bar, which correspond to the rests in the wind section.

Overall, M. 5/2 becomes a static piece – constructed on just three notes (G sharp-A-B flat) – where the three temporal caesuras are differentiated from a purely timbric-sonic point of view. Though the piece is extremely simple, there are some elements that allow the caesuras (indicated by circled seconds across the bar) to be identified at an auditory level. As we have previously observed, Macchi established an element of discontinuity by means of timbric subtraction; he altered the density of the layers of instrumentation, assigning two rests to the woodwind pedal. From a sonic perspective, he thus saturated the two segments which serve as the soundtrack for the wounded bull's movements. With respect to the draft, the strings then produce two different sounds with the bow, from the well-known notes of the first bar to the repeated ones in the next. Finally, the most distinctive feature was achieved through his use of dynamic hairpins, which serve to modulate the sound intensity of the harmonic agglomerate in correspondence to the wounded bull depicted on screen.

The most distinctive feature of M. 5/2's second version is the existence of two writing phases, both of which determine how certain details in the piece are altered and which probably occurred during the recording session, when the volume of dialogs and sound effects were directly compared. Macchi edited the second version by "recording" another layer modifying the balance between the initially planned instrumental parts. At the top of the document, the two instances of winds separated by pauses have been completely eliminated and replaced with aerophones. The new passage was marked with an unmistakably new pair of "stop"s. Further down, Macchi also eliminated the repetition, which is the only other element that interrupts the sound of strings. This gave rise to a piece which is substantially homogeneous throughout its duration, where the dynamic hairpins characterise the caesuras in sync with the images. The crescendos remain at the first and third bars, as does the decrescendo on the fourth. However, a diminuendo peak was added in the middle of the second bar corresponding to the 9 ½ seconds of dialogue between Alain Delon and Romy Schneider. The changes he made in red pencil did not alter the content of the piece in terms of pitch, but only affected the dynamics of the various instrumental voices. It is as if Macchi were operating in a sort of virtual mixer, testing the different channels at the console: once the most convincing solutions were found in performance during the rehearsals, he then went on to "engrave" them on paper and, obviously, on tape.

A final difference is the letter «F» added in red ballpoint pen under the title. As we saw previously, Macchi used this abbreviation to indicate which tracks were actually included in the editing of the film if there were multiple versions of the same piece. However, as we will see in the next document (cf. Document 13), the second version of the piece M. 5/2 is not the definitive one. To understand why he used it here, we need to consult the official disc recording.[25] This record contains the music Macchi created for both *The Assassination of Trotsky* and for the 1973 film *Il delitto Matteotti* by Florestano Vancini. The first seven tracks refer to Losey's film and comprise a number of musical cues arranged in succession, with identifying titles that refer to key moments of the film. In this case, however, the actual title is misleading because the musical pieces related to the bull's death are grouped under «*L'attentato nella notte* [Night attack]». The fourth track does not refer to the sequence of the assault on Trotsky's villa (cf. Documents 18-21), but to a montage of all three versions of M. 5/2: starting with the second version, followed by the first and then the final one. Crosschecking paper and sound documents thus reveals another dimension of Macchi's compositional process. We are obviously outside the boundaries of the film project, but it nevertheless shows the process of how a piece that was initially conceived for an audiovisual setting was then adapted to fit a discographic one. Apart from this change in destination, and therefore of use, this "constructed" recording provides further insight into Macchi's (and Losey's) creative workshop. In fact, the

---

[25] Egisto Macchi, *L'Assassinio di Trotsky – Il Delitto Matteotti*, Beat Records – CDCR 15, 1990.

crosschecking of apparently discarded paper documents with sound sources is the only way we can reconstruct the diverse nuances of a compositional and performative process.

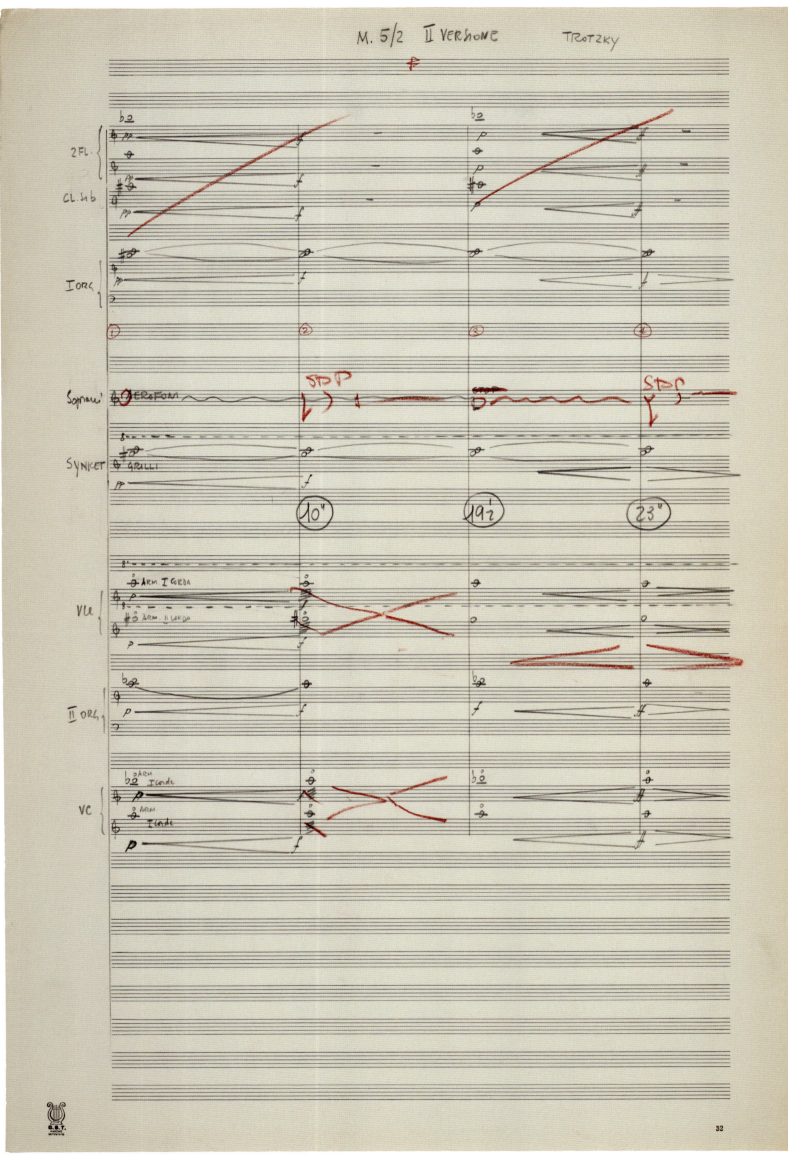

Document 13: M. 5/2 versione definitiva, fair copy

EMC, 1 f. (verso blank). Pencil and red ballpoint pen on staff paper, 470 x 325 mm

Only the fair copy of the definitive version of M. 5/2 survives in the composer's archives today. In the light of the sources just examined, it is clear that the previous versions contributed to determining the final shape of the piece, making a draft copy unnecessary. Here too, just as we saw in the transition from first to second version, the various attempts can all be reinterpreted as preparatory sources for the final compositional stage. As was the case in Document 9, the first version served as the principal model for the definitive one, as Macchi himself suggested with the arrow followed by the letter «D» on the verso of the draft flyleaf. In fact, at first glance, the final version reveals a structure that is more akin to the first, thanks to the instrumentation and the pitch dynamics. However, a closer look shows us how the composer made use of elements that were tried and tested during both the composition and execution of the second version.

Cue M. 5/2 was mainly organised by combining the instruments used in the two previous versions – the Synket, two electric organs, violas and cellos, aerophones – along with 12 additional violins to expand the sound aggregate built on strings harmonics. The main sync points were handled in the same way, except for one crucial difference: the last caesura set at 23" is no longer a mere endpoint that leads within a few seconds – in diminuendo – to the conclusion; it now becomes a turning point that basically divides the piece in half. The six bars of articulation of the cue now become twelve, for a total duration of 47 seconds. Before taking a closer look at how Macchi dramatised the last block of the number, let us see what happens to the "tried-and-tested" sections.

In terms of pitch distribution, the opening of the piece seems to be more in line with the second version. Up to 19 ½ seconds, we have a completely static mass, dynamised only by the crescendo and diminuendo hairpins, which at the second bar reproduce the drop in sound intensity that was experimented with during the recording sessions of the second version. The type of sound balance in compositions of this kind is crucial for the correct interpretation not only of the pure musical level, but also for its future assembly with the images and sounds of the film during editing. Not surprisingly, at the end of the page, Macchi told the copyist to «ripetere le indicazioni di dinamica su tutte le parti! [repeat the dynamic indications for all parts!]».

The descending chromatic movement, already observed in the first version, was developed in different ways in the second part of the piece (bars 5 and 6). The segment that goes from 19 ½" to 23" corresponds to the collapse of the wounded bull during the last part of the bullfight, and Macchi seems to have created a sort of musical isomorphism through the descending profile of the cellos. This also happened in the first version, which came to an end on the target note of the scalar fragment. This time, however, Macchi decided to assign a perhaps even more strategic role to the last moments of the animal's life as it lay on the ground. The sync point set at 23" is no longer a simple coda meant to dissipate the musical sound; it has now become a new finishing point. It is both the composition's apex in terms of dynamics (*fortissimissimo*), and also the point of greatest chromatic density: all the twelve tones are saturated. This is followed by a progressive diminuendo that extends for more than twenty seconds and varies in pitch every two. During the recording phase, Macchi added several arrows that served to guide him visually in conducting the piece. These underlined the fact that the strings oscillate over five pitches (D, D sharp, G, G sharp and A), which, in turn, form the group of reference notes for the first two bars of the piece. The music follows a circular path in which aural ripples marking the death throes of the animal are now in contrast with the initial stillness of the piece.

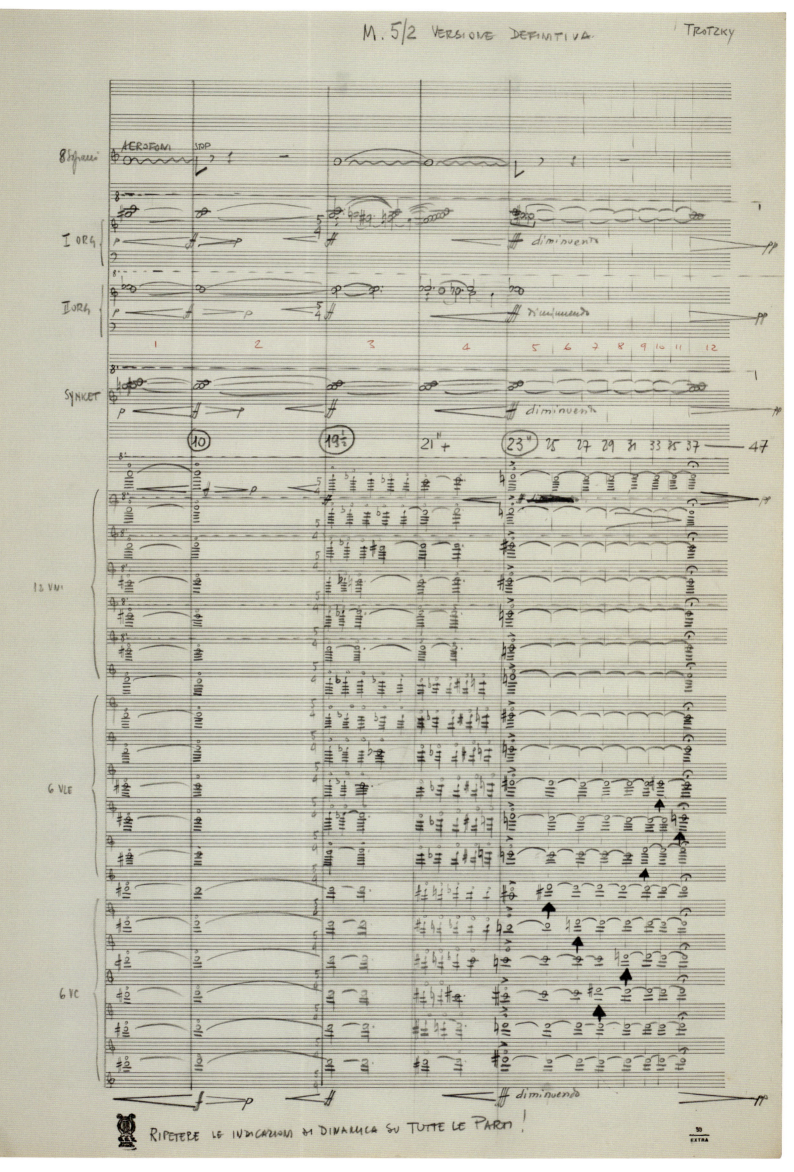

Document 14: M. 6/1, draft
EMC, 1 f. Pencil and blue pen on staff paper, ca. 220 x 319 mm

The bullfight sequence does not formally end with the death of the bull. When the bull's tremors cease –, in perfect synchrony with the conclusion of M. 5/2 –, the noises of the arena take over again for a few seconds. The soundscape is saturated by the voices and whistles of the crowd celebrating the end of the bullfight. Delon jumps up and walks away from the arena, promptly followed by Schneider. The two characters walk quickly through an exit aisle, while the noises of the crowd gradually dissolve away, and the sound of the man's anxious footsteps takes over, loud and clear. The music composed by Macchi gradually returns and almost occupies the whole scene with a clear sync point connected to a frame change, which shows us a group of men dragging the animal's carcass out of the arena. The cue for piece M. 6/1 coincides with this cut; the first draft, which Macchi used to then compose the final version, is conserved amongst his papers.

The recto of the sheet shows the draft of cue M. 6/1. It is organised into two systems – the first with three staves and the second with four – which define the overall structure of the piece, to be developed later in the fair copy. At this stage, Macchi defined the main pitch content, associating it with certain instrumental groups, and finally indicated, as he usually does, the duration in seconds, corresponding to each change of beat. As in the sketch and in the first version of the previous piece (cf. Documents 9-10), Macchi also proceeded by accumulating six-tone aggregates. The first three entrances, respectively assigned to cellos, violas, and violins, are based on the hexatonic scale on the two levels of transposition. The fourth aggregate, entrusted to the first violins, interrupts the strictly hexatonic logic, as it is missing a single note. The four entrances occur in tempo and establish 3-second intervals per bar. These intervals were originally set at four seconds and then corrected, as the original indications in pencil demonstrate. The twelfth second originally foresaw the entrance of the bichord G-C by the Synket, changing the temporal unit of each beat to just one second. Beneath the sustained sound of the Synket, the four instrumental strings groups dissolve, until a new turning point at 19 seconds.

The second system depends on a principle of chromatic aggregates in the highest register, with a series of progressive entrances that reach their apex at 25 seconds, highlighted with a circle. It seems that Macchi had at first intended to continue the sound of the Synket up to this sync point, seeing as how he wrote but later canceled out «STOP Synket».

In the following bars, Macchi returned to the hexatonic collection, once again combining the two levels of transposition between the four instrumental groups, and then ending the piece with a change of articulation by means of a trill. From the last temporal indication in seconds (41") onwards, the «fermo senza trillo [steady without thrill]» sound of the violas and cellos persists as a form of echo.

This peculiar quality of the conclusion is also represented on the verso of the sheet, where we find a diagram that summarises the development of the piece. It is impossible to ascertain whether this diagram was created *ex novo* and then translated into the pitch designations we find on the recto of the draft, or whether it is a sort of visual summary noted down only after Macchi had defined the structure of the piece. Naturally, it is clear that Macchi only specified instrumentation – violins, violas and cellos – once the draft had been defined, much as he often does on the verso of other drafts. The logic of the relation between the diagram and the actual draft is less obvious. It is reasonable to suppose that the draft marks the first moment of creation, in which only some of the characteristic elements of the piece have been defined: a peak halfway through the piece, followed by a progressive thinning of the sound. In fact, the articulation of the first and equally important part of the piece – constructed through the accumulation of events – is missing entirely. It is equally significant that, from the very beginning, Macchi anticipated a moment of discontinuity in the sound at the end of the piece, expressed in musical terms through the change in articulation to the trills of the strings.

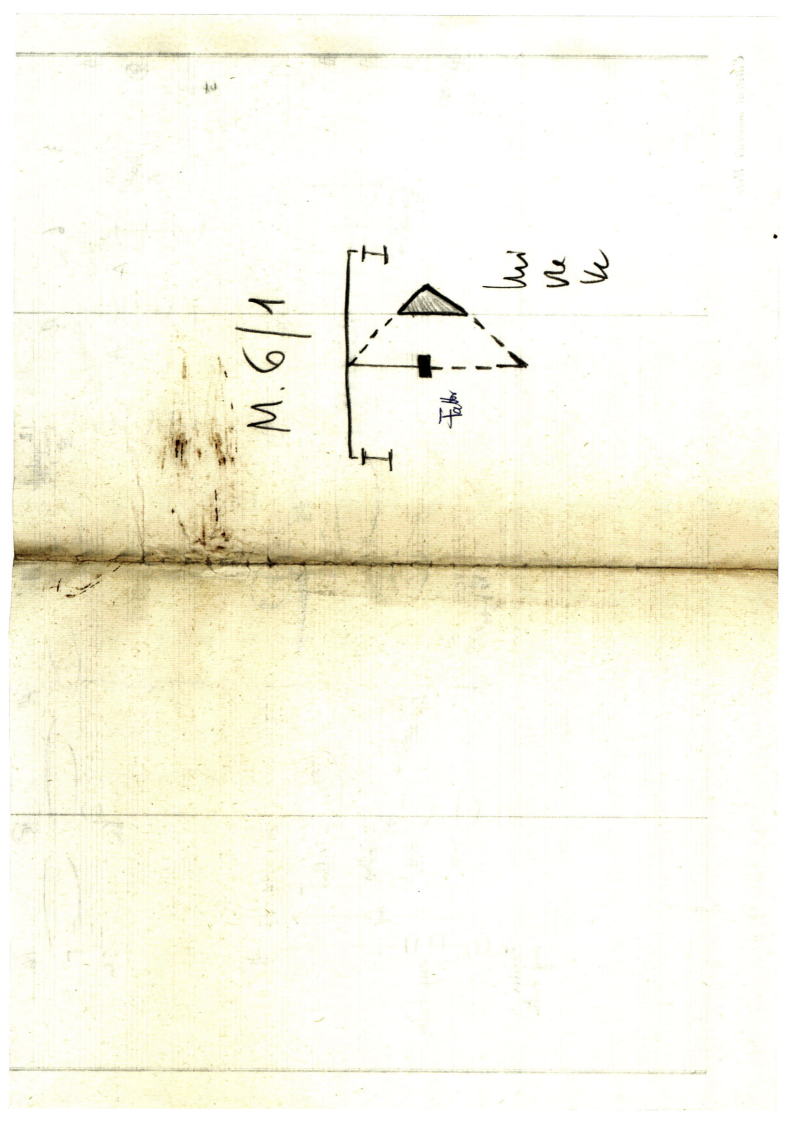

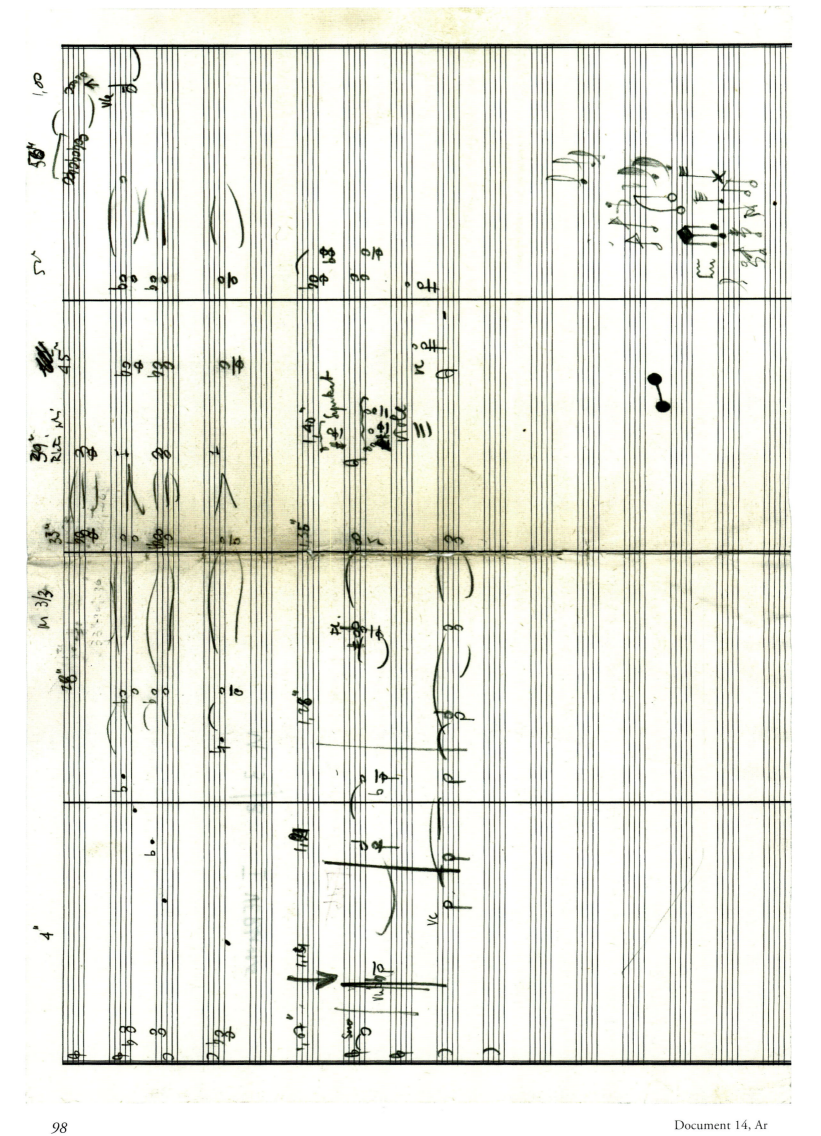

Document 15: M. 6/1, fair copy
EMC, 2 ff. (all versos blank). Pencil and red ballpoint pen on staff paper, 470 x 325 mm

As he progressed from draft to fair copy, Macchi followed a rather linear path aimed at redistributing the sound aggregates across the various instruments: cellos, violas, second violins, and first violins. However, compared to the first design phase, Macchi also expanded the orchestral ensemble in the fair copy, creating a close link with the previous piece, M. 5/2. In fact, here too, the composer writes for two organs and the aerophones (the latter assigned to 8 sopranos).

Before analysing the definitive version of M. 6/1, it is important to note how these details on instrumentation can help us understand Macchi's *modus operandi* during the working phases of the scoring for *The Assassination of Trotsky*. As often happens with composers of film music, the first phase of work begins at the moviola when some essential elements are established, looking at and listening to an almost final cut of the film. This is a crucial moment in planning for the musical creative process, but it inevitably involves rather rapid processing times, as we can see from the writing in the drafts. It is no coincidence that Macchi worked on smaller pieces of paper which made it easier to jot down synthetic models quickly. The next stage was the less frenetic elaboration of the musical pieces, after which the drafts were "tested" in the recording studio and modified where necessary. However, one question remains: during each session at the moviola, did Macchi work on different sequences and write several sketches one after the other, or did he instead concentrate on a single track at each sitting, completing the fair copy before moving on to next one? Differences found in the comparing the instrumentation between the final versions of M. 5/2 and M. 6/1 favour the latter hypothesis. In fact, the four groups of strings that first appear in the fair copy of the definitive version of M. 5/2 were already indicated in the draft. Above all, the relationship between the two pieces is also established thanks to the expanded orchestral ensemble mentioned above.

From an audiovisual perspective, there is clearly a close link between the two pieces. The sequence corresponding to M. 6/1 continues to establish a close relationship between the bullfight and Frank Jackson's unease, accentuated by the animal's death. As far as the overall organisation of the piece is concerned, we can observe how, in passing to the fair copy, Macchi identified some additional sync points, highlighted by the circled indication in seconds. The first nine bars of the piece are direct transcriptions of the corresponding bars in the draft, without any substantial modifications. The fair copy marks the entrance of the Synket and specifies the timbre to be used, which once again is that of the crickets. As is customary in the orchestration phase, this is the moment in which the dynamic planes are better defined: though not a strictly musical process in itself, it serves to define how the musical track is best integrated with the soundtrack's remaining elements, and more generally with the film's audiovisual structure. Here, for example – marked by a generally soft dynamic level and followed by a crescendo that reaches its first peak at the fifth bar – the beginning serves different purposes. Musically speaking, it allows the sound mass of the strings to grow progressively; in terms of sound, it facilitates the gradual transition from the sound effects – characterised by the arena noises and especially by the sounds of the men's footsteps and the horses' hooves as they drag the bull's body – to the musical soundtrack; in audiovisual terms, the crescendo of the strings harmonizes with the cinematography: the piece is synchronised with a change in frame where the static camera, placed at the end of leading out of the arena, shows us the arrival of the lifeless bull.

All the different pivot points marked (by a circled number of seconds) are always connected to the frame changes in the crosscut between Frank and Gita leaving the arena and the bull's carcass being dragged away to slaughter, or are otherwise connected to particular camera movements. The Synket's entrance in bar 5 corresponds to the cut where Frank and Gita quickly walk down the steps outside the arena. The sync point set at 19 seconds is even more significant. In fact, at bar 10, Macchi added a new unscheduled musical layer to the draft at exactly 19 seconds, also marked with a circle. Along with the originally planned strings, he now included the aerophones and – above all – the two organs, which in turn saturate the chromatic whole with four chords, comprised of three notes a semitone apart. The high and highest registers of the organ amplify the string harmonics, marking a strong moment of discontinuity with the previous bars. What is a strictly musical shift in logic is once again driven by the film's visual dimension. The sync point set in the score at 19 seconds corresponds to an interesting camera movement: the camera pans away from the two actors and focuses on a set of bronze statues placed on the roof of the adjacent building that represent the bulls. It is a panoramic view of the statues from left to right, synchronised with the gradual addition of chromatic blocks assigned to strings and organs. The clear connection between the assassin and the killing of the bull in the bullfight – a ritual that, as already mentioned, foretells the killing of the Russian statesman – fully integrates the film's audiovisual construction.

The second page of the fair copy reaffirms the strategic sync point set at 25 seconds, the moment when the strings gradually reassume the articulation defined in the beginning. The dynamic levels are better defined, with crescendo hairpins that go from the *mezzoforte* to the section punctuated by trills, which however must be performed with a sudden *piano*. Bar 18 is considerably different, since it ends at around 41 seconds into the draft. In this case, the two organs are inserted in bar 18 alongside the diminuendo of the cellos, and they present the transposition levels of the hexatonic collection, divided into three sub-sets. A final harmonic complex entrusted to the strings follows, bringing the overall duration of the piece to 51 ½ seconds.

In compiling the fair copy of M. 6/1, Macchi wrote an additional layer, again in pencil, but with a more distinct hand, granting him more control over the temporal sequence of the piece in terms of the visual editing, and also drawing more attention to the general timbre required from the orchestra. It is no coincidence that the entrance of the organs at 19 seconds is underscored, just as the attack of the aerophones – an element that was not initially included in the draft – is also underlined. At bar 14, we can also read the indication «striduli [shrill]», which clarifies the desired timbral effect, with particular reference to the tempo of the aerophones played the sopranos. Finally, again at bar 14 and shortly after bar 16, the additions he made in pencil during the recording sessions call for a temporal extension almost as long as a fermata. We should in fact remember that here, as in other numbers of the score composed by Macchi, there is no precise relationship between actual durations and musical values. The real chronometric duration is in the hands of the conductor, who follows the sync relationships established with the visual montage directly in the recording studio. This is why the fair copy contains additional written notes: they aid in controlling these relationships during the execution of the piece, and exemplify the twofold nature of Macchi's creative role. The document shows us both the creative work of an artist who composed the sound of the score, and that of a conductor who translated the project into a performative act. For example, Macchi wrote «lunga [long]» and «LLL [*lunghissimissima*]» at 25 and 30 ½ seconds respectively, transcribing an instruction that is both paratextual and textual in the draft. On one level, these indications had a clear mnemonic purpose, to remind Macchi-the-conductor to lengthen the duration so that the music would be synchronised correctly with the images. On another level, however, they determine the very structure of a piece which has its *raison d'être* in the technologically dependent moment of recording.

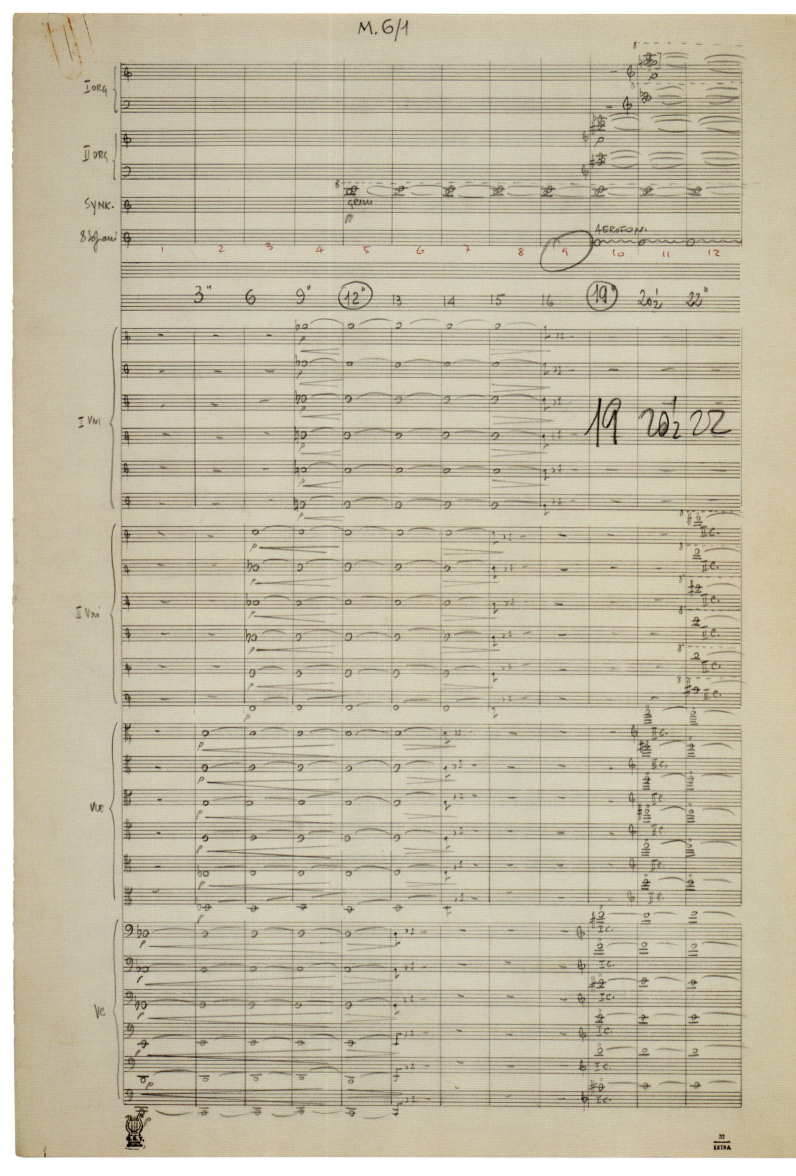

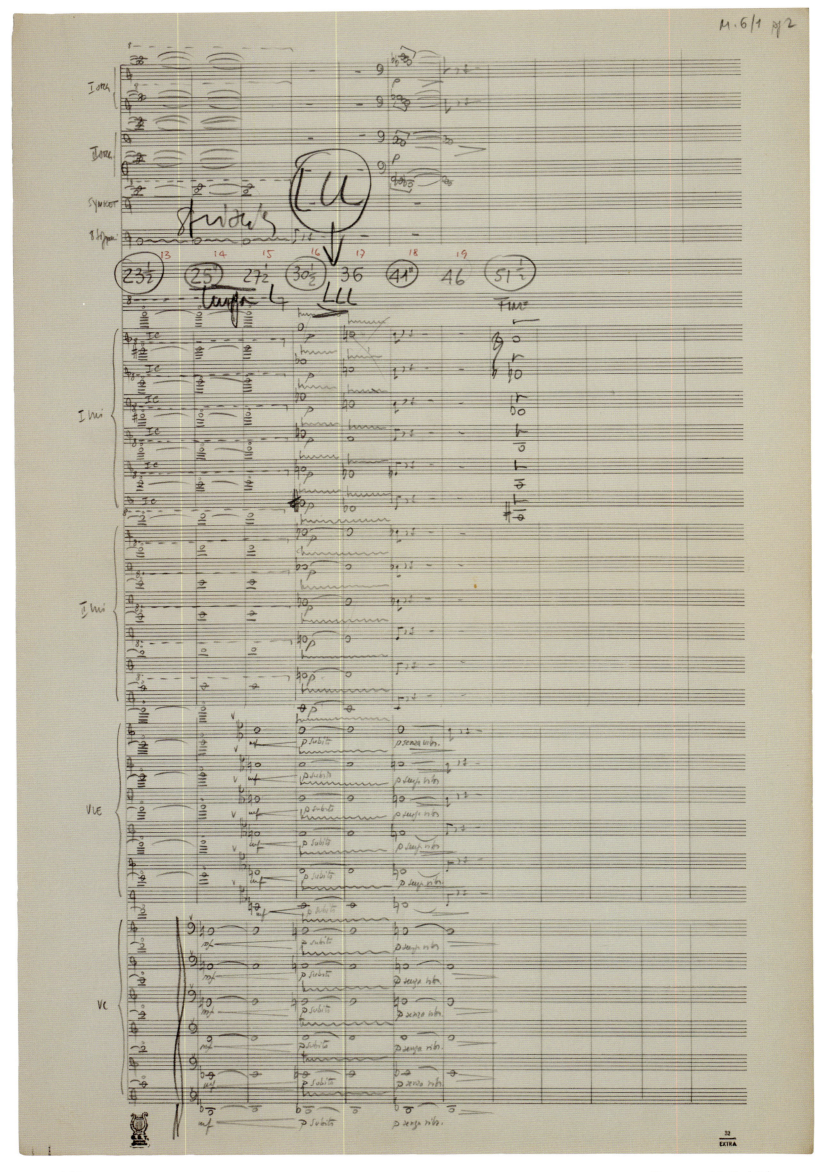

CHAPTER III

Alternative routes

Document 16: M. 3/2, sketch

EMC, 1 f. Pencil and red ballpoint pen on staff paper, ca. 220 x 319 mm

In writing a film score, the composer usually starts by taking notes at the moviola so as to extract certain indications and details from the director's suggestions, which are then "translated" into musical terms. However, no such documents exist amongst the working papers for *The Assassination of Trotsky*, except for the one found in the Joseph Losey Collection described above (cf. Document 2). We are therefore not able to establish whether Macchi simply did not keep track of this initial stage, considering it useful to preserve only the musical documents, or even if he chose to follow this creative process or not. In any case, it is important to analyse how often this gap occurs within the Egisto Macchi Collection.[26] To investigate the creative process behind the Macchi film scores, one must approach the surviving sources with different strategies so as to obtain additional information. In the case of *Trotsky*, a good approach lies in comparing the alternative versions of the same piece of music. As with the sources pertaining to the bull's death (cf. Documents 7-13), comparing different musical realisations allows us to establish which elements of the audiovisual scene Macchi favoured in the actual compositional act; we assume therefore that these were fundamental points as discussed with the director or, at least, strategic ones for the musical conception of the sequence. Macchi often adopted this approach, creating two or three alternative versions and only deciding which was the most effective one after the recording phase.

M. 3/2 with its three different versions lends itself well to this comparative method. As usual, the first stage is characterised by smaller-size sheets used for the first few notes. In this case, it is more of a sketch than a real draft, given the fragmentary nature of Macchi's indications. The verso of the sheet reveals the final stage of the drafting process, since it is also the flyleaf which encloses the various drafts. At the bottom, we find the complete orchestral ensemble, regardless of differences there may be in instrumentation between the three tracks: 2 flutes, 1 B-flat clarinet, 3 horns in F, 6 violas, 6 cellos, 8 sopranos, two organs, and the Synket. The top of the sheet contains indications about the individual parts for the copyist:

1) always specify the key
2) the dashed lines count as bar lines
3) MAKE PHOTOCOPIES OF THE SCORES

[1) mettere sempre le chiavi
2) le linee tratteggiate valgono come divisione di battuta
3) FARE FOTOCOPIE delle PARTITURE]

The number of versions he composed is shown at centre page: three, all of which have been recorded as indicated by the letter «F» in red pen. As was the case for M. 5/2, though only one version was used in the film, the other two were included in the released recording. Track seven of the disc, entitled «Il giardino di Trotsky [Trotsky's garden]», contains the three versions of M. 3/2 and the piece M. 6/1 all in succession. The title could not be more misleading, since none of the three pieces has anything to do with Trotsky's house in Mexico. We have already seen that M. 6/1 was linked to the last segment of the sequence at the bullfight, while the three versions of M. 3/2 were composed for a short segment of the meeting between Frank Jackson and one of the coordinators of Trotsky's murder. The dialogue between the two is rather enigmatic, alluding to a first attempt by a group of Mexicans; the audience can intuitively understand that Frank himself will be involved in a second attack should the first one fail (as it later does). The conversation between the two takes place inside a building where the walls are entirely covered with murals; Frank's interlocutor comments on how the painter has a «marvellous control of violence, colour, form». The man who painted them, he adds, is a man of action. Although not an explicitly historical film, Losey's alludes to the figure of David Siqueiros, a painter who played a key role in leading the first attack in Trotsky's villa. The piece M. 3/2 intervenes when the man to whom Frank is talking lifts up his sunglasses and asks: «what goes on behind those quite blue eyes?». The camera closes in on Delon's face and then pans to a detail of the mural: a group of men staring at a sort of cash register, into which a stream of coins is poured with the words «moneda buena [good money]». A cut leads to a full shot of the library, with Schneider in the foreground sitting at a table, while a portrait of Karl Marx stands out in the background. Another cut follows, this time with a descending camera movement that takes us from the mural back to Delon's face. The music stops and Frank then answers the man's questions about how much the girl can be trusted to assist them in entering Trotsky's house.

Macchi conceives three different versions for this short segment. He does not seem to have made any kind of sketch for the first version, but indications for the second

---

[26] The only exception is a notebook conserved amongst the materials related to the film *Bronte: cronaca di un massacro che i libri di storia non hanno raccontato* by Florestano Vancini (1972). For more on this see Marco Cosci, *Vancini, Macchi and the Voices for the (Hi)story of Bronte*, «Archival Notes», 2017: http://onlinepublishing.cini.it/index.php/arno/article/view/63.

and third ones can be found on the recto of the sheet. The second version occupies the first five staves and is characterised by four entrances in which Macchi opposes two augmented triads with 2 bichords of a perfect fourth and fifth. The instrumentation is also indicated: flute and organ for the E flat-G-B triad; horn and organ for that of F-A-C sharp; and then the cellos and violas for the two bichords. Finally, Macchi indicates a temporal sequence, linking the four musical events, respectively, at the beginning of the piece, at 2 ½", 7 ½", and finally at 14 ½". The relationship is also strengthened by some dotted lines that act as a guide whenever the actual bar lines are missing. The piece closes with an indication for an «eco [echo]» placed at 17 ½", and a decrescendo which extends to the end of the piece set at 22".

The third version of the piece is even more concise than the previous one. In this case we no longer have any triads or bichords, but single notes divided amongst the violas and cellos, which on the whole can be traced back to a diminished seventh chord. No clear measurements are given in seconds, but the piece follows the temporal course of the other version, as it was written in exactly the same way in the staves that follow.

Alternative routes

ooooo

1) mettere sempre le chiavi
2) le linee tratteggiate valgon una divisione di battuta
3) FARE FOTOCOPIE della PARTITURE

M. 3/2

I VERS
II VERS
III VERS.

2 Flauti
1 CLARIN Sib
3 CORNI in FA
6 VIOLE
6 VC.
8 SOPRANI
I ORGANO
II ORGANO
SYNKET

Document 16, Av

Document 17: M. 3/2 I versione, II versione, III versione, fair copies
EMC, 3 ff. (all versos blank). Pencil, red pencil, red and black ballpoint pen on staff paper, 432 x 319 mm (A), 470 x 325 mm (B, C)

The fair copies of cue M. 3/2 contain three different versions (also referred to as A, B and C). Version A is composed on "Edizioni musicali Rete" paper, normally only used for drafts and flyleaves. During the transition from the sketches to the actual composition, the order has been inverted, indicated by a correction in black pen: the sketch for the second version becomes the fair copy for the third, and vice versa (the sketch of the third is developed into the second version). Comparing these two fair copies, we observe that the two pieces were planned in parallel to each other. In fact, both versions have the same time measurements as the sketch, with the two main sync points set at 11 ½ and 17 ½ seconds. Contrary to Macchi's usual approach, the different versions of cue M. 3/2 also indicate film length (expressed in feet, and marked in red), to allow for greater control over the temporal sequence. Able to be inferred in part from the sketches, the musical organisation in the second and third versions is based on a gradual and regular overlapping of sound layers up to the fifth bar, followed by a partially empty soundscape for two bars (bb. 5-6), leading to the coda at bar 7. This process is particularly evident in the third version (C), both with regards to the instrumental soundscape – 2 flutes, B flat-clarinet, 3 horns, 2 organs, Synket, violas, and cellos – and to the density of selected pitches, as in the previous sketch. The empty sound space at the sync point 11 ½ seconds is also marked by the diminuendo hairpin with the indication «sparire [vanish]» immediately before it, further accentuating this clear-cut interruption to the sound. The same principle can be observed in the second version (B), although in this case fewer instruments are used – in fact, the three horns and the clarinet are missing – and the pitch organisation is based entirely on single overlapping sounds, and no longer on complex chords. In this version, Macchi also specified the tuning system for the Synket, indicating that the «I-II-III drawers [should be] tuned as before [I-II-III cassettino accordati come prima]». However, this information is missing from the other fair copies of the M. 3/2 and can only be deduced by referring to another piece from the soundtrack of *The Assassination of Trotsky*, M. 8/1 I versione (cf. Document 23), where Macchi explained the tuning system of the three drawers [cassettini] of the Synket. This instrument was equipped with three-manual keyboards, which could easily be tuned to quarter tones.[27] Indeed, not only do we find the same sustained note (G) in M. 8/1, but Macchi gave even more precise instructions for the tuning system, indicating that the first drawer [cassettino] must be tuned a ¼ of a tone sharp, the second as normal, and the third a ¼ of a tone flat. Apart from these details, the relationship between the two pieces shows that the order of composition and recording did not follow the M-number sequence.

By comparing the two versions of M. 3/2, we observe the different strategies that were used to create the empty soundscape in the fifth and sixth bars. In both cases, the sound peak in the two previous bars is decisive. This apex is not only obtained from an accumulation of sound events, but mainly through a polarisation of the registers: in fact, the E performed by the flutes, organ I, and violas in bar 3 stands out in the second version and is linked to the G in the next bar. On the contrary, the sound peak in version C is reached by means of a reversed trajectory: through the exploration of the low registers, through the entry of the cellos in opposition to the wind instruments and the organ in the previous bars.

Generally speaking, the two versions of M. 3/2 have the same length of 22 seconds total. For the first four bars, the time interval is set at 2 ½", then 3 seconds in the fifth and sixth, and finally a coda of 4 ½ seconds. We must remember that note values – in this case semibreves – are not absolute measurements in seconds but are modulated on the basis of synchronisation with the images. Despite differences in sound, the two versions share the same strategies for scoring the images, especially with regard to camera movements and editing cuts. The first four bars mark the camera movement that pans from Delon's eyes to the mural behind him, establishing a direct relationship between the continuity of the movement and the progressive saturation of the soundscape. The sound culminates with the closeup shot of the mural. The fifth line is synchronised with the cut that shows us Romy Schneider in the library, and the bar of musical stasis establishes the parenthetical nature of this shot. Finally, the sixth and seventh bars follow the reverse audiovisual path from the mural to Delon's face.

The first version of M. 3/2 (the one actually used in the film) is quite different. By comparing it with the other two versions, we observe certain discrepancies in the general organisation of the piece, as well as some elements of continuity, all of which allow us to understand the audiovisual strategies Macchi adopted. The orchestral ensemble is larger than in version C – including, for example, sopranos who sing *a bocca chiusa*; Macchi also provided additional details about the instruments common to the other versions. Like many of the pieces that comprise the soundtrack, the number of violas and cellos is fixed at 6 per section and Macchi indicated the type of keyboard tuning in the staves for organ I (a ¼ of a tone sharper than organ II), as we saw previously in the sketch for M. 5/2 (cf. Document 9). But what immediately stands out is the way the composer indicated the length of the footage in red pencil, allowing

---
[27] Pizzaleo, *Il liutaio elettronico. Paolo Ketoff e l'invenzione del Synket*, pp. 54-55.

us to observe the different pivot points set at 9, 18, 27, and 33 feet, which correspond respectively to 6", 12", 18", and 22". This version is peculiar because some of the previous sync points have been readjusted by about half a second. Unlike the drafts examined above, Macchi subdivided this one into just four bars, even though the formula of progressively accumulating musical layers remains. What changes is the directionality of the piece, which now peaks at 12" alongside the cut of the shot with Schneider. The first section of the piece, which corresponds to the first two bars, is in fact organised on the concatenation of an augmented fourth (A flat-D), assigned to cellos, and a diminished fifth (A-E flat), assigned to organ II, and violas. Macchi then proceeds from the lower registers to the higher ones, keeping the sound as steady as possible by indicating «senza vibrare [no vibrato]». Once again, we see how Macchi adopted compositional strategies aimed at replicating the continuous, yet ascending, movement of the camera. However, while in previous realisations the apex of the sequence coincided with the closeup on the mural, the climax in this first version of M. 3/2 (A) coincides with the "imagined" shot of the woman. After the phased string entrances, the whole orchestra intervenes with a sound mass built on a single transposition level of the hexatonic collection (C-D-E-G flat-A flat-B flat), which imparts a completely new sound to the piece. The effect of directionality towards this apex is not only thanks to the ascending profile of the strings, but also – and perhaps above all – to the dominant relationship created by the descending leap of a perfect fourth on the violas (E flat-B flat), an effect which is particularly evident in the dynamic balance of the score and in the resulting recording. The last bar, corresponding to 18", becomes a mere «echo» of that apex, which by means of a general decrescendo marks the camera's return to Delon's face.

By comparing the three versions, we are able to more clearly understand the audiovisual strategies Macchi implemented in the process of composing a brief micro-sequence based exclusively on visual elements. Note that the film segment Macchi set to music has no other sounds, such as noises or dialogues. All the versions relate exclusively to the film's visual component and in fact show a common strategy in scoring the camera's initial movement: a series of regularly phased musical entrances. What changes is the establishment of the climax (or lack thereof), and thus the way in which the shot in the library is handled. While in the second and third versions the way the shot was framed seems somehow suspended in its impertinence to the conversation between the two men, in the first version it is directly connected to Delon's gaze. Underneath the musical process, which establishes a clear audiovisual connection between the assassin's unperturbed gaze and what could be interpreted as his mental projection, we are able to observe what actually «goes on behind those quite blue eyes».

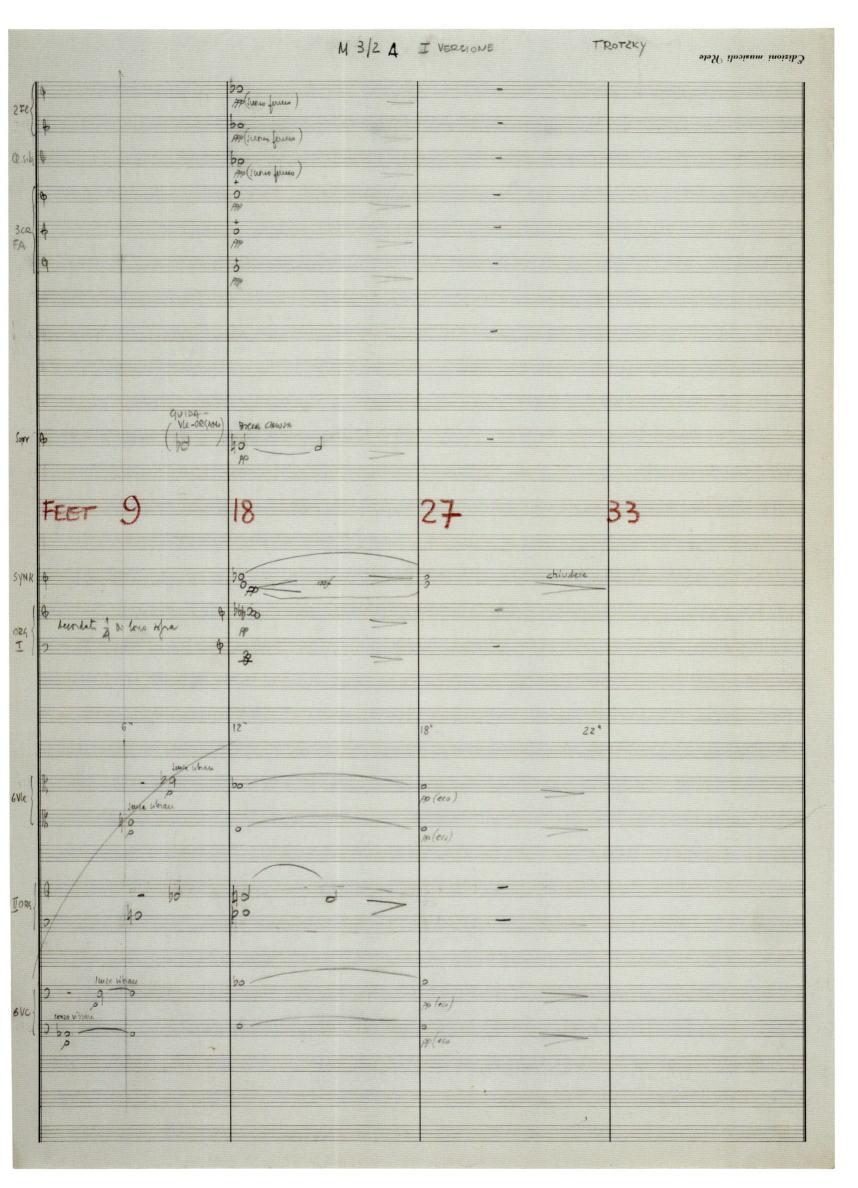

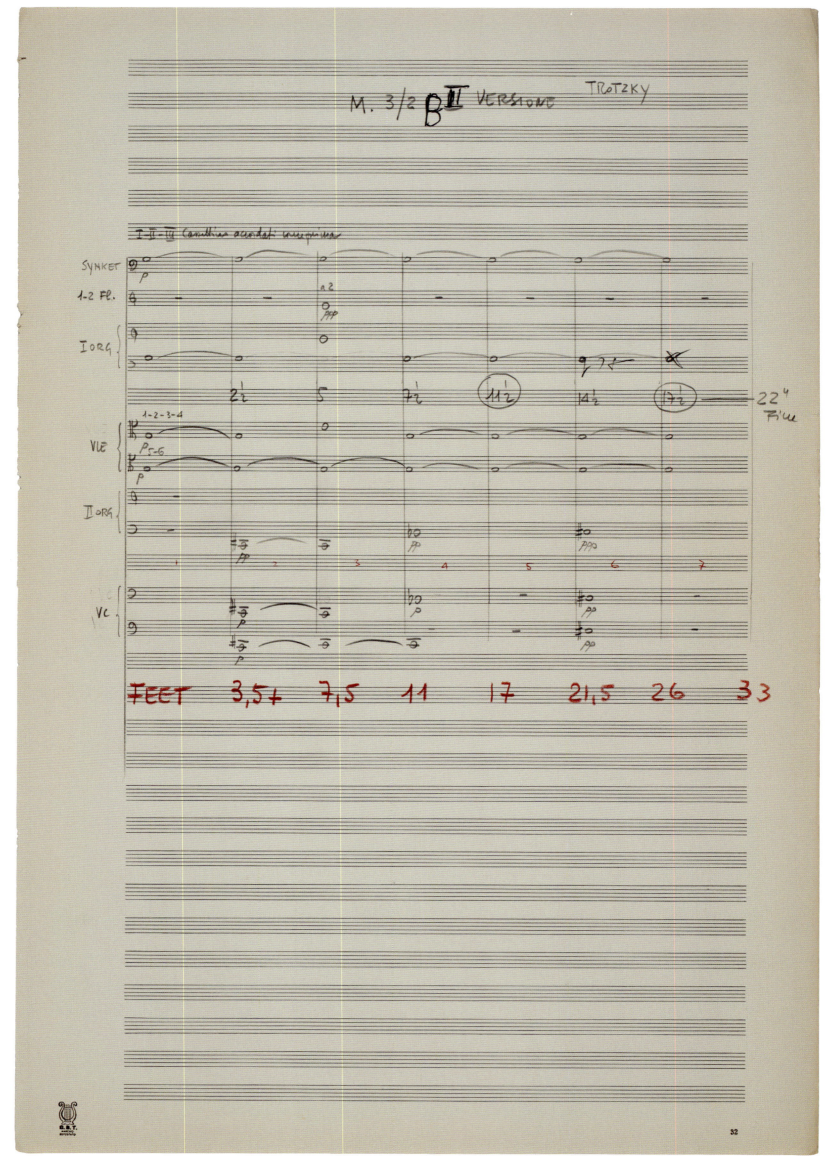

Document 18: M. 3/3 I versione, draft
EMC, 1 f. Pencil and red ballpoint pen on staff paper, ca. 220 x 319 mm

Now that we have examined the creative process behind an extremely short sequence, let us observe how Macchi approached a more complex one, both in terms of length – about two and a half minutes – and content – thanks to the presence of noise elements within the soundtrack. Like before, the two different versions of this piece provide us with a key to the composer's workshop. Cue M. 3/3 corresponds to the entire sequence of the first attack on Trotsky and it traces the different phases of the raid carried out by a group of Mexicans on his fortified house. The beginning of the musical cue is synchronised with the end of the conversation (analysed previously) between Delon and the man, corresponding to a closeup shot of the mural which portrays a series of men during a gunfight; and it ends with the gunshots directed at the statesman's home.

The draft of the first version of the M. 3/3 is written on the recto of the flyleaf; «Fatto [Done]» in red ballpoint pen already makes it clear that this is the version used in the film. This draft is summarised on a single page, which describes the general development of the music, distributed in two groups of systems: the first occupies the first four staves, while the second spans the sixth to the ninth pentagram. There are no clear bar designations; they are practically absent, and the subdivision sketched on the staff paper is of no value to the piece. The temporal sequence as indicated in seconds, however, is more evident. Arrows point to what appear to be two particularly important moments: at 1 minute and at 1 minute and 14 seconds. On the right-hand side of the page, we find some notes jotted-down (mainly acciaccaturas) which however have nothing to do with the piece. They likely bear no musical value, as they refer to other moments of the production process.

Although all the notes on the recto of the sheet are written in pencil, we can identify at least three stages in the draft's making: the first came to an end almost immediately, as can be seen from the erasure marks in the first two staves at the centre of the page; the second stage, instead, defines the whole development of the piece; and the third one is where Macchi revised some of the sync points using a pencil to correct the number of seconds. As often happened in the drafts for *The Assassination of Trotsky*, the core orchestral ensemble was not indicated at the beginning of the system. But over the course of the draft, Macchi specified some of the instruments that would execute certain musical events: at the end of the second staff, for example, we find the indication for violas («vle»), cellos («VC»), flute («Fl.») and Synket. In any case, though the orchestral ensemble was not precisely defined, it is clear that Macchi wrote the draft having already thought of how to layer the instrumentation. This distribution is particularly evident in the first system of the draft, where we can see a total of four different musical levels – made up of bichords or triads – corresponding to the first four staves on the page.

The beginning of the piece is punctuated by an overlapping of semibreves, grouped into three bichords with the same interval structure (a diminished fifth and two augmented fourths). Starting from 4", Macchi indicated six notes with staggered entrances; they are derived from chromatic shifts starting from those bichords, which determine a new vertical structure at 28", still composed of three sound layers, but now with a perfect fifth and two diminished fifths. Another level is added at 33", which helps to redefine the overall sound, now organised around the hexatonic collection, divided into exactly four layers. At 45", the three levels return – through a new concatenation of bichords, obtained by a shift of a tone and semitone – and Macchi returns to the harmonic complex established at 28", based still on a low perfect fifth and an overlapping of two diminished fifths. The new hexatonic collection appears at 56" but is now concentrated in a single instrumental block. From the very first minute, the musical discourse changes in a rather significant way, and no longer proceeds in chord blocks, but through a gradual re-composition thanks to the entrance of single instrumental voices – violins and cellos – towards the low registers. The interspersed nature of the bichords changes, until reaching a perfect fifth combined with a major sixth, at 1', 28". The last musical interventions are all bichords a semitone apart, distributed between the flute, the Synket, and the violas with harmonics (the C natural is cancelled out, leaving only C sharp-D). The temporal sequence starting from 1', 40" becomes more ambiguous, with two last notes assigned to a solo cello and the reappearance of a concatenation of two bichords.

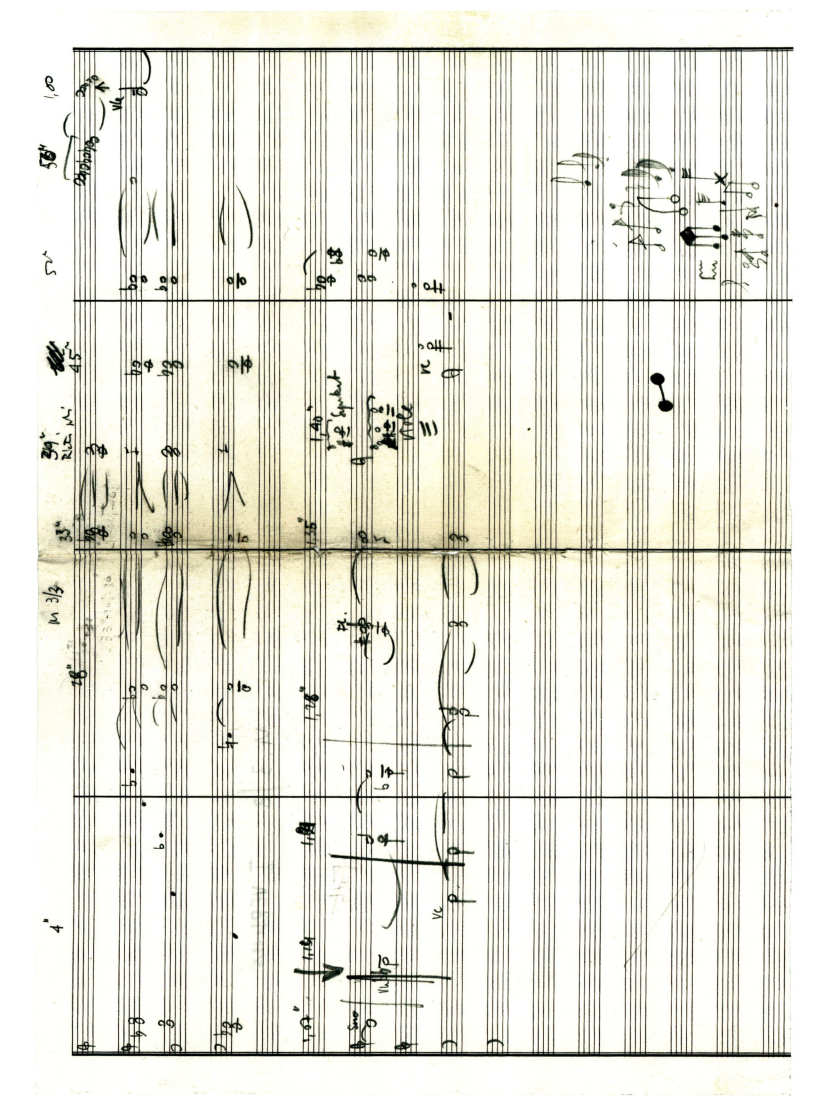

Document 19: M. 3/3 I versione, fair copy
EMC, 3 ff. (all versos blank). Pencil and red ballpoint pen on staff paper, 470 x 325 mm

Once he had established the overall structure of the piece, Macchi started to define the necessary details for the audiovisual merger of the sequence in question. The core orchestral ensemble remains the same as in the previous musical number: there is a clear polarisation between winds plus organ I and the strings plus organ II. The keyboards use the same tuning system (a ¼-tone apart) as in other parts of the score. The six violas and the six cellos are grouped in pairs, in two three-part systems, and are tasked with executing the three bichords of the draft, reorganised here into two chords assigned to violas and cellos. The static beginning, already discernible in the draft, is reaffirmed by a type of sound that is now better defined: *piano* and, above all, devoid of vibrato.

As he progressed from draft to fair copy, Macchi exercised a certain freedom in the way he drew the bar lines – in fact, he used dotted lines on the first and second pages; this choice does not imply however any fluidity in the chronometric sequencing of the musical events. The bar numbers are still written in pencil and red ballpoint pen. Indeed, the very beginning of the piece in the draft's final version is structured according to a series of additional time-points, which fill the wide interval of time between the first two key circled sync points at 4" and 25" (thus no longer at 28" as in the draft). Within these 21 seconds, the ascending sequence of notes is maintained, noted in the draft in solid black. For the string section, however, he specified that these notes derive from the initial chord structure. While the notes in the draft indicate that organ II performs them in an ascending sequence, the violas and cellos play the same notes with a series of internal chromatic shifts starting from the first chord structure. The compositional effect achieved through the addition of layers is therefore weakened from a perceptual point of view, and the new chord complex of the seventh bar is reached through an internal movement of the parts. This movement is also underlined visually by an arrow and a circled number that make it easier to cue the entrances in the recording phase, once again demonstrating the crucial link between the compositional and performative phases.

Though it may seem that the beginning of the music for the assassination attempt was organised in the same way as the entrance of the first version of M. 3/3, the sound contours and – above all – the sound impact underwent substantial changes in the transition to fair copy. Considering the attention Macchi paid to the details of visual construction, before we proceed to analyse the fair copy it is important to observe how these first eight bars interact with the images in the film. As mentioned earlier, the beginning of the piece serves as a link between the end of the sequence (showing Delon with one of the organisers of the attacks) and the actual sequence of the assassination attempt. The first chordal structure is synchronised with the closeup of the mural and serves to introduce the sequence. In fact, this structure is left out in the bar count and is merely replaced by the indication «A» in red ballpoint pen. At 4" there is an editing cut which allows us to observe the different phases of the night attack. The music takes over the soundtrack, almost eliminating the ambient sound, and marks the stasis of waiting which is represented visually by three fixed shots showing the outside of Trotsky's house and the inner garden. Although we cannot really say that the musical parts suggest any true directionality in their movement, we can nevertheless perceive a superficial change in the soundscape that leads to a pivot set at 25 seconds: on screen, a car stops in front of the house. The soundscape is frozen for seven seconds – at 25" we have a long fermata – and the music and noise are altered, thanks to a diminuendo hairpin that, on a musical level, creates a certain balance within the mixing of the soundtrack that brings the noise of the car's engine to the foreground. We have already seen how there was a radical sound change in the draft at 33", with the addition of a new musical layer and Macchi's exploration of the hexatonic collection. This strategic point was also highlighted in the final version of the draft (now set at 32"), but above all it has been dramatised with the expansion of the core orchestral ensemble thanks to the winds' and organ I's entrance. The desired tonal effect is always aimed at exploring a static sound mass throughout, indicated by «suono fermo [steady sound]». This all corresponds to the entrance of the leader of the Mexican group (the aforementioned painter), who gets out of the car with some of his companions. Once again, the diminuendo hairpin of the strings makes it easier for the audience to hear the footsteps of the man and his companions – all dressed in uniform – as they approach the sentry post outside the house. In perfect synchronisation with the exchange of greetings between the leader of the group of assassins and the guard (who suspects nothing on account of their military uniforms), the music proceeds on to a new section of the piece (45") at the page turn.

Just as he did for the beginning of the fair copy, as he elaborated the draft, Macchi reorganised the concatenation of the three bichords into two chords assigned to the viola and cello section. Here, however, the resulting sound is completely different, thanks to the crescendo hairpin which grants the music a certain directionality, also emphasised by the change of chord structure at 52" (that is, when the guard is attacked, and the would-be assassins enter the villa). The return of the hexatonic collection at the second 56, which is as usual assigned to winds and organ I, marks the last phase outside the house, since it is synchronised with

117

the attack on the other guard and, above all, with the signal from the "mole" inside Trotsky's home. Besides directing our gaze to the decisive events in the plot, the increasing intensity of the strings and the entrance of the wind instruments also serve to modify the balance between the different components of the soundtrack. The whole sequence is based on a subtle game of musical immersion and noise emergence, in a balance of levels mostly managed by the musical composition. In this case, for example, the culmination of sound at 56" serves to cancel out all the other elements from the sound effects track. It is no coincidence that we do not hear the noises of the struggle between the men, or even the sound of the bell rung by a woman to signal the man inside the house to open the door. Following this logic, we understand why Macchi attenuates the sound mass on a single *pianissimo* note starting from the first minute – to which the human timbre of the eight sopranos *a bocca chiusa* is also added –, which sets the stage for the transition to the inside of the house, where we see (and hear, this time) the noises that the boy makes as he opens the door from the inside (1', 07"), allowing the rest of the group to complete the attack.

As far as pitch height is concerned, the section stretching from bars 14 to 19 retraces the draft's model. The only variant is a rhythmic one: the semibreve is kept as a reference duration value. This is obviously a relative value, modified on the basis of the sync relationships with the images and determined by timing. On the one hand, this moment of discontinuous sound serves to accentuate the noises inside the house; on the other, it gives a distinctive sound to the last phase of the attack. The scene of the men entering Trotsky's home confirms a compositional strategy found throughout M. 3/3 that avoids linking the musical processes to particular camera movements or editing cuts – as we found for example in M. 3/1 – and instead tries to make them correspond with the movements and in the actions of the actors captured on screen. The soundscape enlargement, starting from bar 15, goes hand in hand with the men's incursion into the house, just as the appearance of the A sharp-D bichord on the flutes and organ I is synchronised with the movement of the group leader who carries the rifle.

Let us now examine the last section of the piece which was rather ambiguous in the draft. Starting from the sync point at 1', 40", the violas and Synket play a C sharp-D bichord in the highest register, alongside the added organ I, for which Macchi indicated the appropriate registers. It is interesting to note that both the Synket and the strings are instructed to sound «come grilli [like crickets]»: that is, the desired timbre should be obtained with both acoustic and electronic instruments. The cricket layer remains steady «senza diminuire [without decreasing]» for the whole duration of the piece set at 2', 34". The word «striscia [strip]» written in capitals seems to allude to the continuous nature of this last entrance, the aim of which is to establish a relationship between the musical sound and the noise landscape: the high pitch of the «striscia [strip]» is clearly perceptible to the listener, much like the chirping of crickets spreading through the air around the house. Tension is thus created even before the volley of rifle shots aimed at the various rooms of the house, accentuated by five isolated moments of cello harmonics that emerge and are reabsorbed by the soundscape. Every note in *pianissimo* was marked with a crescendo and a diminuendo hairpin, which, as soon as they were written on paper, contributed to defining a fluctuating sound. This musical decision was present in the draft; it was only repeated twice, and it will assume a central role in the temporal evolution of this last segment of the sequence, thanks to the dynamic parameters and the sync points that were chosen in the final version.

Both the film's visual and sound elements contribute to prolong the wait before the shots are fired: the closeups on the Mexicans and the interior/exterior shots of the house on one hand, and Macchi's music on the other. The unpredictability of what is going to happen – or rather, the unpredictability of the precise moment at which the attack will take place – is instinctively expressed by the oscillating entrance of the cellos, combined with the «striscia [strip]» of the crickets. The harmonic homogeneity of the violas, Synket, and organ offer no clear temporal marks; and the cellos do not enter at regular intervals. Not only do they enter at irregular intervals – 8, 9 and 11 seconds –, they are entirely devoid of clearly defined attacks or exits. Their timbre merges with and gets mixed up in that of the crickets and the dynamic hairpins help to smooth out the contours, effectively undermining the viewer's sense of control and ability to anticipate the flow of events.

M.3/3 I VERSIONE — L'anaminio di Trotzki

Document 19, Ar

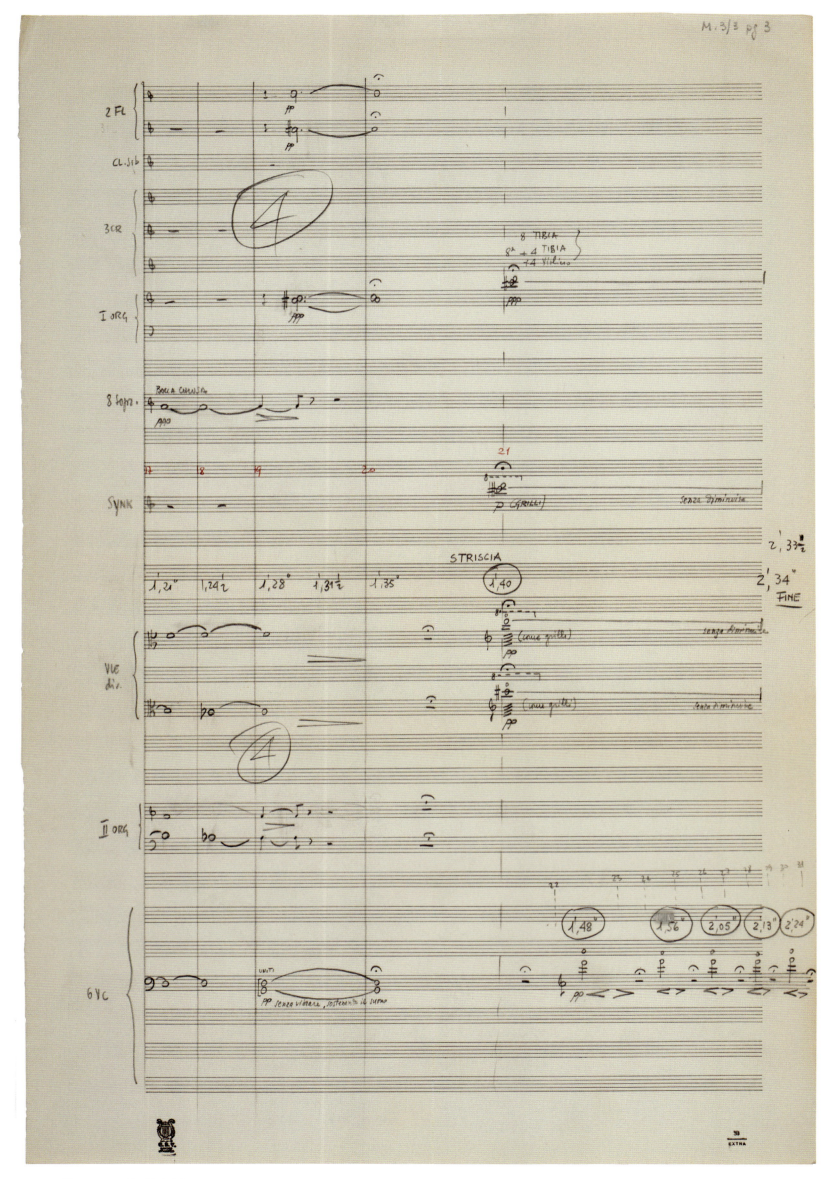

Document 20: M. 3/3 II versione, draft
EMC, 3 ff. (blanks Bv, Cv). Pencil on staff paper, ca. 220 x 319 mm

After he composed the first version of M. 3/3, Macchi considered alternative routes for the sound dimension during the sequence of the first assassination attempt. This does not signify the decoupling of the time points marking the musical interventions, but rather his intention to impart a different reading of the piece that favoured other elements of the audiovisual structure. The words «non fatto [not done]» written in pencil on the verso of the draft of the second version divulge its destiny: it would not be included in either the film or on the recording. However, it is worth taking a closer look at the elements of continuity and discontinuity in the planning and implementation phases of such a crucial sequence in the dramaturgical evolution of the film. Likewise, it is interesting to enhance our understanding of the audiovisual experience that Macchi tried to infuse each time through his compositional process. Rather unusually for Macchi's practice in this film, the structure of the draft of this second version reveals at least two phases. Two versions of the draft are preserved in the composer's archive: an incomplete (and unused) version, and a second one on which the final version is based.

On the verso of the flyleaf displaying the title of the piece, we find a first attempt at approaching the sequence. The draft is organised in two systems of three parts apiece, with Macchi's usual notes for the instrumentation. As noted above, the timing references of this first formulation suggest that it was incomplete. In fact, we have seen that the first version of M. 3/3 lasts 2', 34", with a noticeable interruption at 1', 40"; and the draft of the first version, although it does not include the last section, actually goes as far as this sync point. On the first page of the draft of the second version Macchi seems to have stopped planning the piece much earlier, at 1' and 12". This could be interpreted in two possible ways. The first and perhaps most obvious one is that Macchi, unconvinced of the path he had taken, halted his creative process during the draft and decided to start again from scratch. Not surprisingly, on the other two sheets we find a draft that has been elaborated up to the established point of 1' 40". However, another interpretation cannot be ruled out, namely that Macchi was weighing the possibility of setting only the first visual segment of the assassination attempt – corresponding to the arrival of the group of Mexicans outside the house – to music, leaving only ambient sounds for the rest of the sequence, with the chirping of crickets clearly in the foreground. Moreover, around 1' 12", the obvious visual change of perspective when the door opens from the inside, would have justified this type of decision. In any case, at least at first, Macchi undoubtedly considered this draft as one that could possibly be developed; he paid particular attention to the organisation of the material, specifying the pitch durations and some dynamic levels, and giving precise performative indications, such as in the fourth bar where he noted that the violins should «premere molto l'arco [press the bow hard]». An analysis of this document makes clear that, also in this case, Macchi decided to organise the audiovisual narration according to some key points that are similarly found in the first version. In fact, the first chord, corresponding to the zoom-in on the mural reappears, along with the first clear interruption of timbre at 4" with the change in the camera angle. It is interesting to note that, rather than a gradual build-up of sound, from the fourth second onwards we find a note repeated by the violas combined with the Synket. It therefore appears that Macchi started from the same musical idea that he previously used to close the sequence – a static soundtrack which combined instrumental and electronic timbres. Macchi divided the musical sequence between the two opposite registers of the sound space at the precise moment that the car carrying the Mexican group leader appears (24"). This comes after a gap in the sound achieved via decrescendo, which also serves to foreground the noise of the car engine. Immediately after this, at 40" – the moment when the sequence passes to the guards being taken out – we witness the entry of a new sound level noted on the first staff, which proposes a different arrangement of the hexatonic collection in descending order at each bar change.

Notwithstanding our consideration of this version as a draft in its own right, Macchi undoubtedly used it as a model when he developed the second draft. Generally speaking, both versions share a noticeable use of the hexatonic collection, often associated with an entire family of instruments. However the genetic link between the drafts is indeed proven by the presence of the same chord constructed in perfect fourths (C sharp-F sharp-B-E-A-D) at 14" in the first draft, and at 19" in the second.

Let us now take a look at the draft he actually elaborated when he laid out the second version of piece M. 3/3. The first page contains almost all of the musical material organised into three systems, while the second sheet has only two chord structures in the upper left-hand margin of the page. Overall, Macchi organised the piece on the basis of the bar lines printed on the staff paper, alternating figures in semibreves and minims. He only added some other subdivisions into bars in pencil in the lower right-hand part of the page, probably as an attempt to finish the draft on the same page and to make room for any writing. In any case, the focal point of the timing given in minutes is noted above each of the three systems. The chronometric indications are partly the same as the ones of previous drafts and final versions, or they differ by only a second. But largest change surrounds the identification of the structural points around which the formal course of the piece is constructed. Take for example the incipit of the musical number. As in the previous cases, the first time indicated is at 4", but we can immediately notice that the articulation points have been handled differently. Macchi chose not to interrupt the music. On the contrary he handled the whole first part up to 19 ½" with a certain uniformity, building it entirely on the hexatonic collection, on the two levels of transposition, associated with the violas, winds and organ I. The pitch organisation changes in correspondence with the quartal chord entrusted to the cellos (19 ½") combined with a minor triad on the violas, where Macchi then built the next section through a series of chromatic slides. A new apex has been set at 52". Macchi progressively raised the pitch by a semitone up to the E flat-D bichord with two chromatic hexachords at 1' 3". This is followed by a line with nothing but an F sharp assigned to the two flutes and organ I, which acts as a sound bridge to the last section. The last four bars of the page are constructed on three staves that correspond to the three instrumental levels indicated in the draft: violas, winds and an unspecified third. However, what is particularly striking here is the way in which he indicated the timing variations for the violas above and below the staff. In this case Macchi contemplated two timing levels separated from each other by just a few seconds. All the corrections and crossings-out demonstrate that Macchi was evidently evaluating different sync points for each of the bars noted. The final part of the draft is clearer and seems to follow the final section of the first version of M. 3/3: a final sound layer in the upper register to provide sound to the moments before the gunfire erupts.

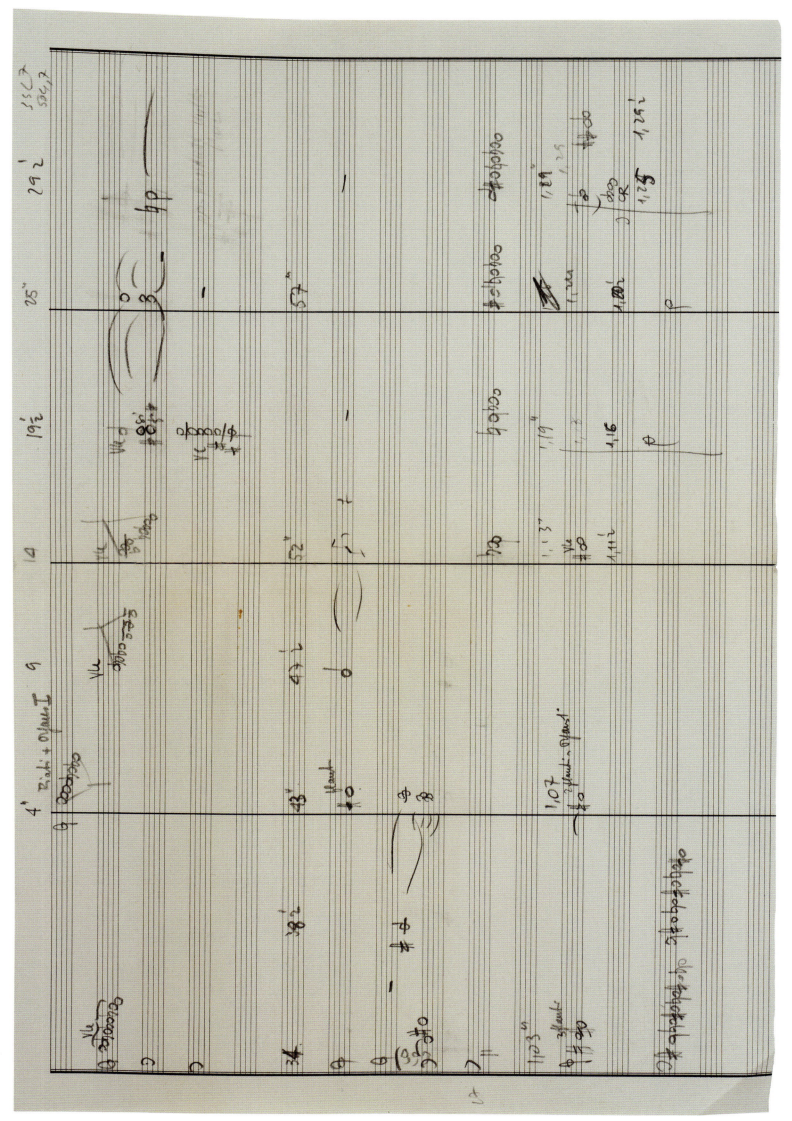

Document 21: M. 3/3 II versione, fair copy
EMC, 3 ff. (all versos blank). Pencil and red ballpoint pen on staff paper, 470 x 325 mm

One glance at the fair copy of the second version of M. 3/3 already gives us obvious indications as to which of the two drafts Macchi modeled it after. The overall timing indications alone demonstrate that, even for the second version, he eventually decided to provide sound for the whole sequence based on the model from the longer draft, as we saw in the previous document. The fair copy exists on three pages that roughly trace the structure of the first version for a total duration of 2' 34". Compared to the latter version, here there are only three sync points marked with a circle and these all occur in the last section, starting from the point in the sequence where the Mexican group enters Trotsky's house.

The core ensemble in the orchestration is the same as in the first version: 2 flutes, B-flat clarinet, 3 horns, 2 electric organs, 6 violas, 6 cellos, the Synket, and finally the 8 sopranos. In the fair copy, Macchi subdivided the various instrumental parts that had been grouped on a single level in the first draft, indicating, as usual, the dynamic planes and the type of sound articulation required from the performers. When assigning the orchestral parts, Macchi associated each note of the hexatonic collection with a single instrument according to the dynamic balance he elaborated in the previous creative phase. The two opposing parts of woodwinds and violas are made up of 6 instrumental parts, which in fact easily lends them to pitch distribution. Likewise, the two organs, having three notes for each of the two staves, also pose no problem for pitch subdivision. Essentially, the entire first page is without any major differences; the only variant is the entrance of organ I which, at bar 4, doubles the hexatonic collection played by the violas.

Following a lack of indication for the presence of vocalists in the draft, here Macchi's use of the sopranos provides a certain element of novelty. In the final version, human voices enter in the second bar along with the hexatonic sound of the wind instruments and the organ. The eight singers are divided into 4 sections and they no longer have to sing individual notes *a bocca chiusa* – as they did in the first section – but are asked to produce sounds at undefined pitches on some consonants using Italian pronunciation: CH, SC, F, T. The adopted a mode of vocal emission can be compared to the *Sprechgesang* from a notational point of view. This same emission mode is resumed at bar 6, varying the consonants (V, L, N, J) and the standard register, which – according to Macchi's written indications – is now polarised between the medium and the lowest one (according to the formula «sonoro registro medio [medium sound register]» and «sonoro registro grave [low sound register]». It then then continues, starting from bar 7, with a variation in the type of sound emitted via «leggerissima oscillazione [very slight oscillation]» indicated in the score. Although it seems that he only added the voices when the fair copy was being drawn up, a preliminary indication of this sound layer can be spotted on the other page of the embryonic draft we saw in Document 20. At four seconds, this musical document shows us that Macchi had already planned the repetition of a note at an unspecified pitch using a very similar notational form. In the second version of M. 3/3 the voices take on a structural role in defining the boundaries of the first part of the sequence. In fact, they intervene at the second bar in correspondence to the camera cut that takes us from the mural to the exterior of Trotsky's house and then, most importantly, when the car enters at 25". If the peculiarity of the timbric effect in the former case is dictated by the visual syntax, in the latter it is evident that the driving force of the new timbre is the appearance of the car on screen, and hence the noise of the engine that becomes clearly perceptible. Although the same strategic point at 25" has been maintained in both versions, the way Macchi handled the sound of this key point is quite different. Macchi abstained from inserting new musical events in the first version, opting to synchronise the entrance of the car with an overall crescendo, combining the two sound levels – music and noise – so that they did not interfere with one another. He pursued quite the opposite effect in this alternative version: a new sound event determined an encounter and clash between the two sound levels.

Effectively, the compositional strategy he adopted in the second version of M. 3/3 seems to be aimed at testing a complete reversal of the musical processes. While in the first version the beginning of the piece plays on the gradual build-up of sound through the internal movements of the parts, in the second one, it is based on clear chordal blocks that intervene at every bar change. Moreover, the segment coinciding with the camera panning slightly to the right just before the attackers gain entry to the house, where the sound tapers off to a single note in the first version, is characterised in the alternative version (bb. 12-17) by a progressive chromatic saturation in the cello section.

Beginning at 1', 07" – a circled structural sync point also in the second version – the development of the piece seems instead to adhere more closely to the tried and tested sound profile of the first version, based on a two-part division of violas and cellos. The subtle difference between the two versions is the time interval of each musical event. In this case, Macchi did not synchronise the musical events with particular visual elements, but instead followed the uninterrupted movement of the camera which follows the assassins' entry into the house, going from a 3 ½" interval to a 4 ½" one without any editing cuts. With regard to the timing, Macchi followed the second chronometric sequence noted down in the draft. In the end, also in this version, the entire last part of the sequence revolves around the «striscia [strip]», which replicates the timbre of the crickets using the Synket and the harmonics of the violas, together with the intervention of the combined cellos. The latter are no longer fixed according to specific references in the score, instead, it is clear that the conductor will coordinate their performance. Therefore it is quite likely that Macchi sought to adopt the same solution as the previous version, no longer requiring that the timing of the interventions be fixed from a chronometric point of view.

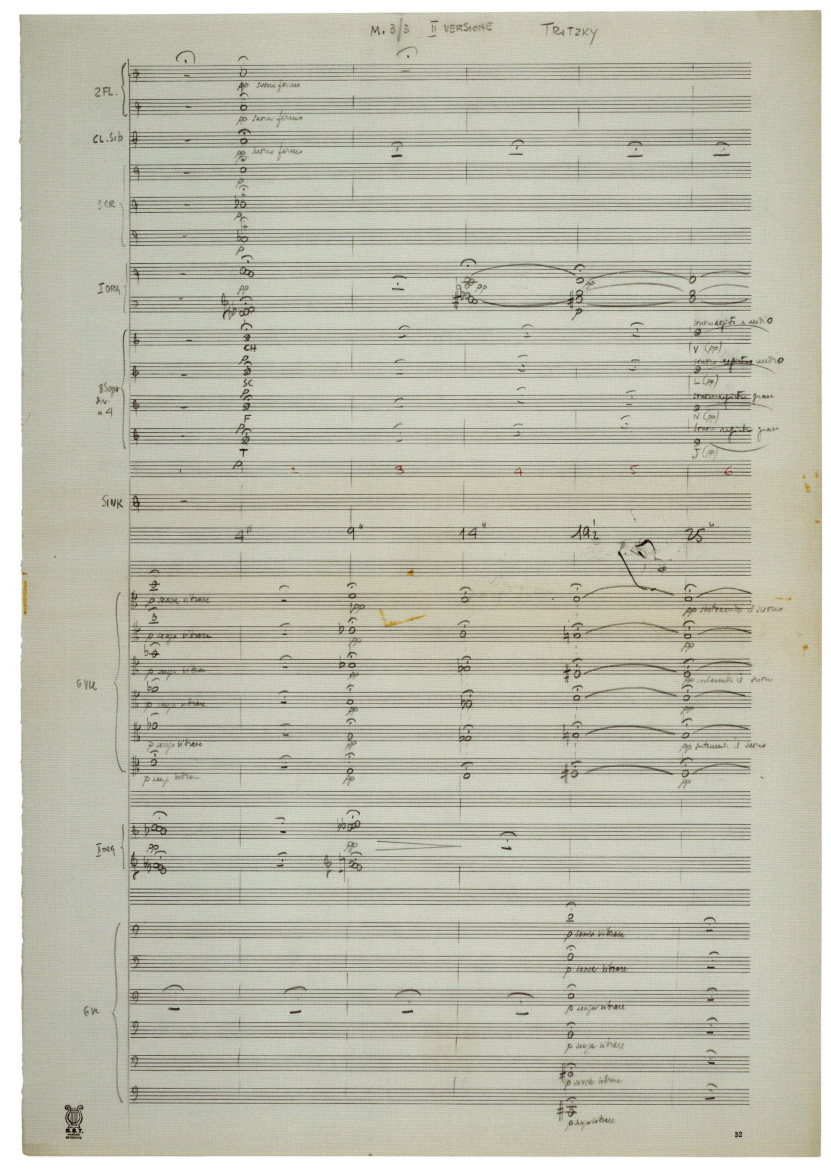

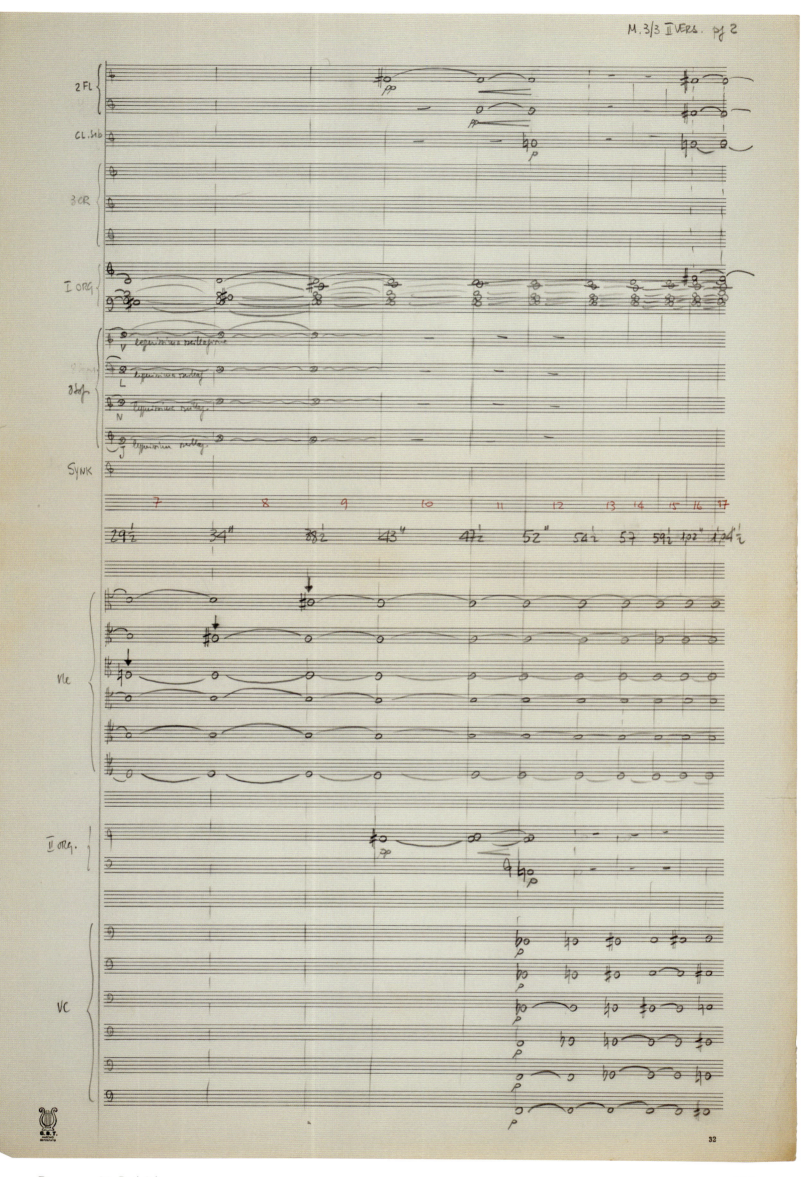

Document 21, Br («2»)

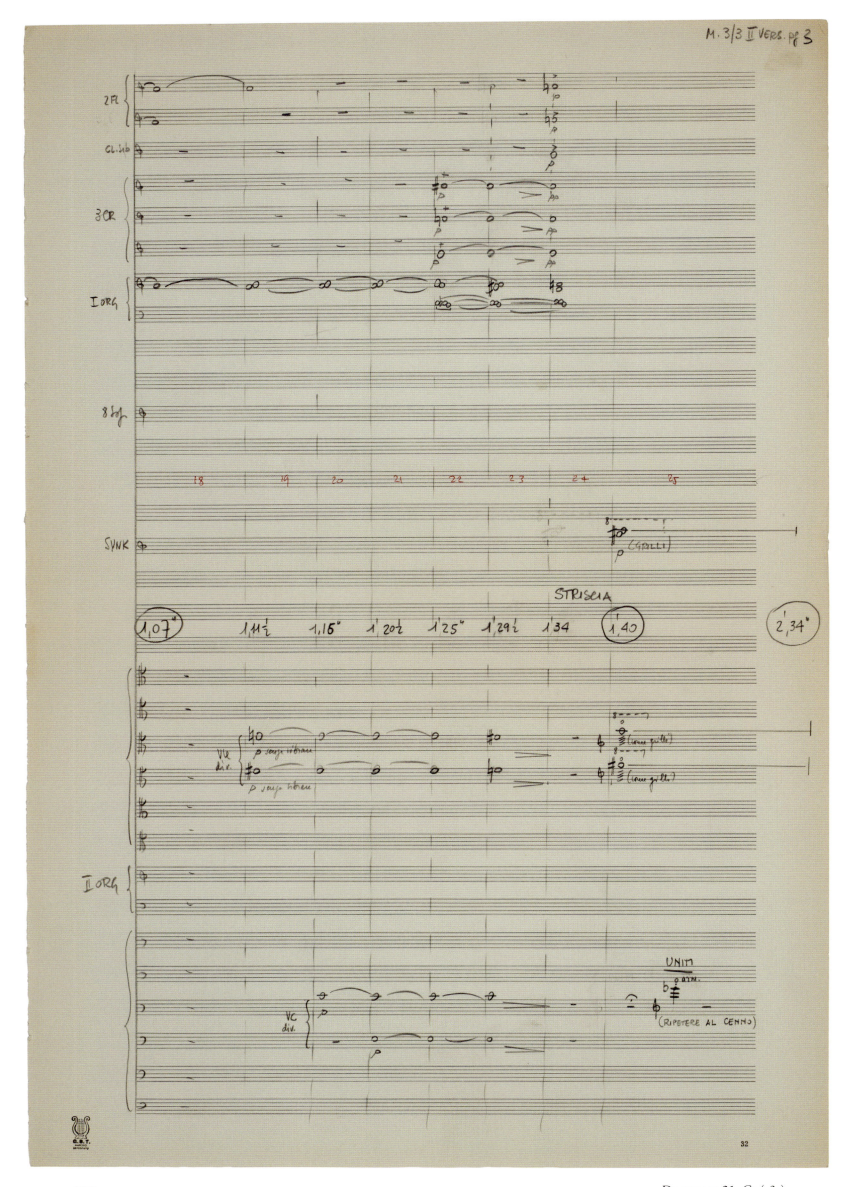

Document 22: M. 8/1 I versione, draft
EMC, 1 f. Pencil on staff paper, ca. 220 x 319 mm

In the first chapter we examined notes regarding – «Sequenza B.» – a particular sequence from the film in which Macchi verbally described a possible musical materialisation for the soundtrack of *The Assassination of Trotsky* (Document 2). Based on the description, it is plausible to presume that these notes refer to the sequence that corresponds to cue M. 8/1. Two different versions also exist for this piece, along with the theoretical one he initially described in Sequenza B. As was standard for his alternative versions, Macchi specified on the verso of the flyleaf which one was actually produced, marking the first version of M. 8/1 as «Fatta [Done]»; instead the recto has a continuity draft showing the structure of the piece. The musical material is organised as a short score in three systems of four staves each.

Macchi's indications for the instrumentation of the core ensemble, and the kind of writing he uses within the single staves, make it apparent that the type of musical formulation planned in this draft is far removed from the sound hypothesis summarised in his preliminary notes. In fact, there is no accordion or balalaika, nor is it possible to recognise any theme recalling the Socialist International. Only the Synket and the strings remain from his original notes. Just like the instruments indicated in the draft (organ I and II, flutes, horn), they are in line with the instrumentation employed in most of the score for Trotsky.

Overall, the first two systems of the draft present a rather linear creative process: only the penultimate bar of the first system assigned to the flutes (32") has been erased and then rewritten. In terms of timing, Macchi only adjusted a few indications – «56 ½» and «1, 23» – in addition to replacing the 38 at the beginning of the second system, likely a mistake, with a 44. The last system is a different story, since, after completing the draft, Macchi decided to modify the organisation of the pitches of some of the instruments. Unlike his erasures in the first system, here we can clearly read the first written layer crossed out in pencil. In the first version Macchi sketched out the last part of the draft, lengthening the chord construction starting from the C sharp at 1', 08". This chord, assigned to the cellos and violas, was kept as a stable sound layer in the medium-low register, above which a new level was added in the high register, formed by three notes a semitone apart: D flat-C-B (in the first pentagram), to be performed on the organs or on the Synket, resuming the figuration executed by the flutes at the end of the first system. In the second draft, Macchi returned to these two levels and decided to cancel them with neat pencil lines, opting this time for a musical discourse that was polarised on individual pitches, and contrasted by a new intervention of the horns at 1', 36". The new pitches are marked like this, or altered in cases when they have not been completely crossed out, as is the case with the C sharp at 1', 42" or the B flat that becomes natural in the following bar. In the latter case, the alteration serves to avoid an exact repetition of the same chord structure that is gradually deployed between 1, 08" and 1', 23". Starting from 1', 42", Macchi opted to change the pitch arrangement, which, through a musical gesture similar to the one in the previous system, ends the draft with another chord. Aside from the changes he made to the last system, it seems as though Macchi chose to leave the key sync points unchanged at 19", 56 ½" and 1' 42", for a total duration of 2', 22".

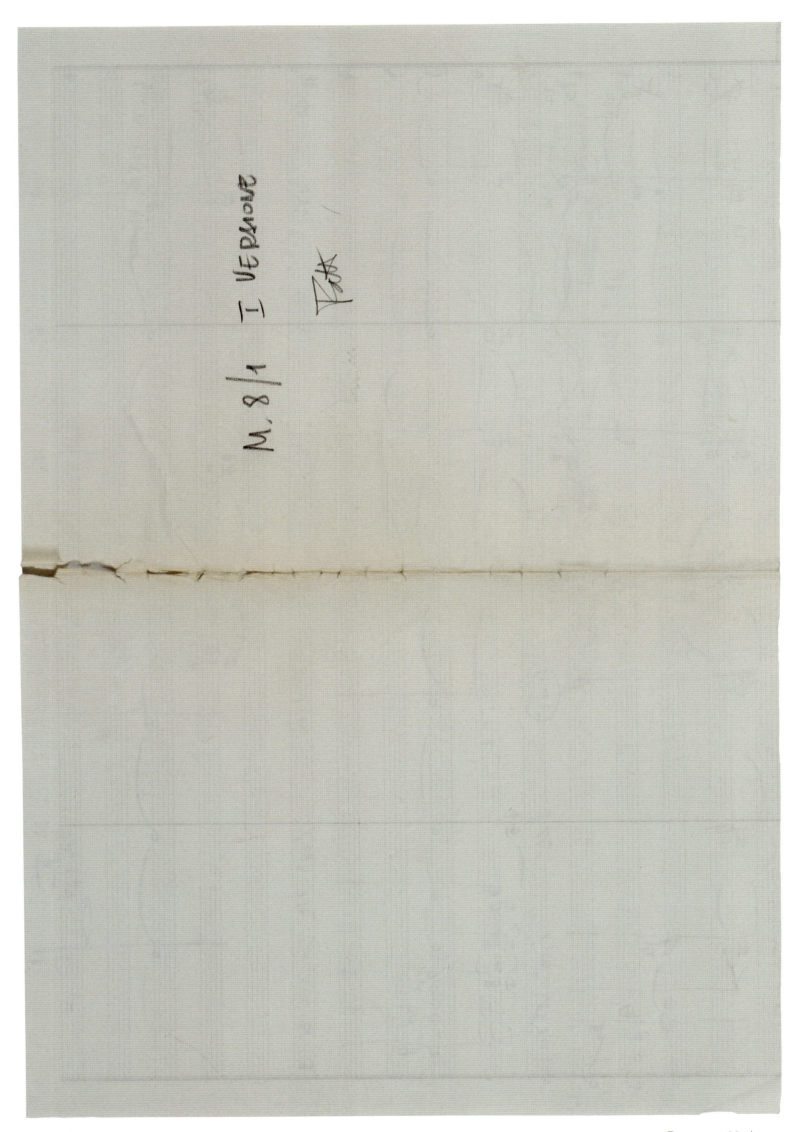

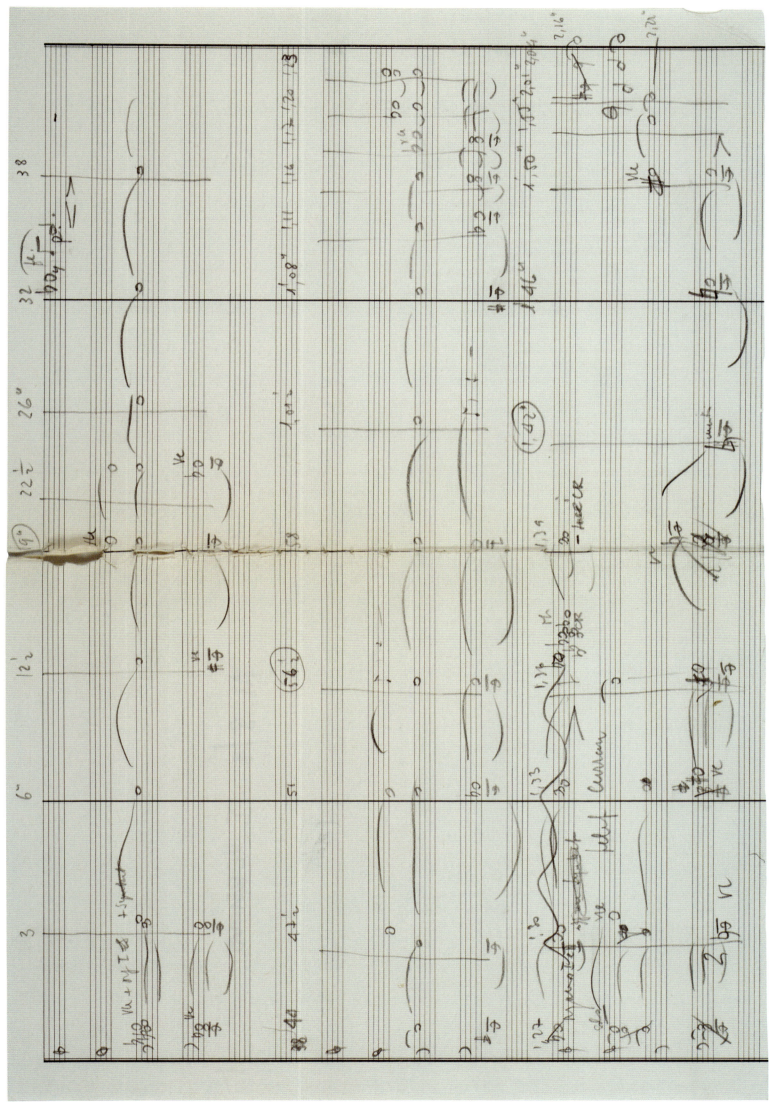

Document 23: M. 8/1 I versione, fair copy
EMC, 3 ff. (all versos blank). Pencil, red and blue ballpoint pen on staff paper, 470 x 325 mm

As evidenced by the previous document, the first version of M. 8/1 contains the music actually used for the soundtrack of the sequence described in Document 2. If the draft had already laid bare a different musical imagery, the final version confirms that, in the composition phase, Macchi nearly abandoned the notes he took in the preliminary phase all together. From the point of view of style, the piece is aligned with the rest of the score, which in the meantime has taken a different path, one that avoids any kind of thematic profile. At the same time, these written notes offer us an interesting window into the composer's workshop allowing us to verify the musical strategies he used. Apart from the contrasting musical outcome, the cinematographic elements of the sequence around which Macchi developed the score remain roughly the same as the ones he established in those pages of notes. They can also be correlated to the annotations on timing present in the score, which help to determine the sync points designed as cornerstones of the soundtrack. In fact, when compared to the original three in the continuity draft, in the final version Macchi circled some additional timing indications, giving him greater control over the details of the temporal course, especially in the phase of synchronisation with the images during recording sessions.

As for instrumentation, the fair copy of the first version of M. 8/1 includes the B-flat clarinet and the eight sopranos in the wind section. The female voices are no longer assigned «un temino tipo internazionale socialista [a minor theme of the international socialist type]» however they are deployed in three strategic points of the score, exploiting different modes of emission. Beginning with the first page, in the first vocal intervention (bb. 1-2) Macchi integrated the voices within the instrumental mass, entrusting the two pivotal notes – A flat and G – to the sopranos to be sung on the consonant "v". The opening of the piece presents a static global mass based on an overlapping of perfect fourths on the cellos (C-F-B flat), combined with an overlapping of perfect fifths on the violas (D flat-E flat-A flat), which is eventually "resolved" on the general G-natural. The directionality given by the descending chromatic movement is particularly evident when listening to the piece, thanks to the human timbre of the voices that stand out from the rest of the group. Although the first two bars are simplistic, they still serve as a sort of introduction even in this distinct sound variation, before Trotsky's voice enters dictating a speech on a tape-recorder. These lines are synchronised with three shots that provide a series of details focusing on a mural depicting a protest, and then on pickaxes raised by protesters, evidently foreshadowing the weapon the hitman will use to assassinate the Russian statesman. Rather than introducing the Trotsky theme – as Macchi had considered in his written notes – these two bars sustained by Trotsky's voice bring into play what will become the tonal sound of his speech. A single note on which the organ I, the Synket and the violas converge characterises the dictation being recorded and its subsequent playback by Trotsky. Macchi was quite precise about the type of G he sought to obtain from the instruments: the violas together exploit the timbre of the open G string (the 3rd string, precisely) while the synthesiser adopts three different tuning systems a ¼ of a tone apart, so as to create an «oscillazione continua, quasi impercettibile, intorno alla nota del II cassettino [continuous almost imperceptible oscillation, around the note of the II keyboard] [i.e. the one with normal tuning]».

Macchi thus chose to associate Burton's voice, and later Schneider's acousmatic one, with the G pedal, following the aforementioned principle of hierarchical organisation between the various layers of the soundtrack. Especially in this opening sequence, the musical dimension must not interfere with the intelligibility of the words. Not surprisingly, at the end of the two spoken interventions by the actors, Macchi underlined the exit of this sound level with an arrow and the word «tace [silence]» (bb. 19 and 27). It is important to also consider the visual component when we seek to understand the sync points circled on the first page at 6", 19" and 26", and the other musical interventions in the score. This first part of the piece has also been structured according to the continuous rotation of shots picturing the inside Trotsky's room and shots of Frank Jackson outdoors, while the statesman's voice remains firmly anchored to the sound stage. The alternation in this visual sequence provide the basis on which Macchi defined the three sync points.

Macchi inserted two interventions that break the homogeneous sound surface of the opening, also in response to another visual event. In fact, the first intervention of the woodwinds occurs in bar 8. It is then repeated at bar 11, with the addition of the second vocal intervention, which is entrusted this time to a polarised form of execution dividing the song between the low and middle registers, before proceeding to the enunciation of four different consonants as in Document 21. These are two central interventions at the core of the sequence, because they serve to draw attention to the murder weapon as Delon comes across it almost unexpectedly in a market. The music paradoxically guides both our gaze and that of the actor towards this very important object, that we also recall from the shot of the mural at the beginning of the sequence.

By design, the centrality of this synchronisation effect is also evidenced – in pencil and blue ballpoint pen – by other textual layers in the score set in at least two different moments, during the phase of recording and synchronisation with the images. Following the last bar on the first page, Macchi added a series of additional notes in pen, mostly related to timing indications. In bar 8, he moved up the reference indicating the duration of the next bar, probably due to the page turn; and then, starting from the second page, he rewrote the time points in a larger format. The numbers remain the same as those that he already marked in pencil, which means that these are not chronometric variations, but rather visual aids to help with the concerted effort required to facilitate the coordination of the sound dimension with the visual one. In fact, in addition to the numbers showing the timing, there are also some horizontal pen strokes marking salient details before structural sync points. For example, these visual aids are present in bars 9 and 10, in a moment of musical expectancy, before the intervention of the sopranos and wind instruments coinciding, with Delon taking hold of the pick in the film. They appear again in bar 15 during a moment of sound stasis before the entrance of the cellos, which paves the way for the next frame change (b. 19) depicting the "flash" of Delon and Schneider in front of the fireplace.

Macchi continued to revise the timing on the third page of the fair copy, writing in ballpoint pen up to 1', 42". Marking the place where an editing cut takes us from Trotsky's room to that of the assassin, this point was already circled in pencil in the first draft, and now it has also been written in pen. The final intervention of the flute is linked to this new frame, which is synchronised with the end of the zoom that focusses on Delon's profile seen through a mirror (1', 55"). From the position of the two notes of the flute, written initially in pencil and then crossed out, we can infer that this musical gesture was meant to lead to the next shot, of Trotsky's empty room, that concludes the sequence. Described in Macchi's notes as Delon's own mental projection, a final pedal on the C sharp up to 2', 22" was planned for the entire duration of this last shot. However, a different solution was chosen during recording; that is, to eliminate all sound from the statesman's empty room, thereby reducing the overall duration of the M. 8/1 piece as it was initially planned. The last two indications have been duly cancelled out with a blue ballpoint pen, and the new total time of 2', 03" has been written in pencil. As we said before, after Macchi completed the fair copy, he made two more interventions, in ballpoint pen and then in pencil. The order of these adjustments can be easily deduced from the timing indications (1', 30") in bar 23, written first in pen and then circled in pencil.

After making some overall changes, Macchi returned to the draft to fine-tune some details apparently did not work so well in performance. This explains the long pencil stroke at bar 10, which underlines the entrance of the cellos (in order to remind Macchi the conductor), immediately followed by the sopranos and winds. Agogic indications «accelera [accelerate]» (bb. 20-21), in preparation for the new entrance of the sopranos at bar 23, have also been added during this second phase of "performative" revision. This time they sing a low G on the vowels "u" and "o" (always according to the Italian alphabet) – followed immediately by wind instruments at bar 25. As on the previous page, the two pencil strokes aid in managing the audiovisual balance of the sequence and facilitate synchronisation during recording. The scene of the window being closed assumes a strong expressive value similar to the one on the previous page when Delon takes hold of the murder weapon. At the end of the film, this is the very window where we see a petrified Delon who has just killed Trotsky with the pickaxe. Again in pencil, Macchi used an arrow to emphasise the anticipation of the flute at the end of the piece.

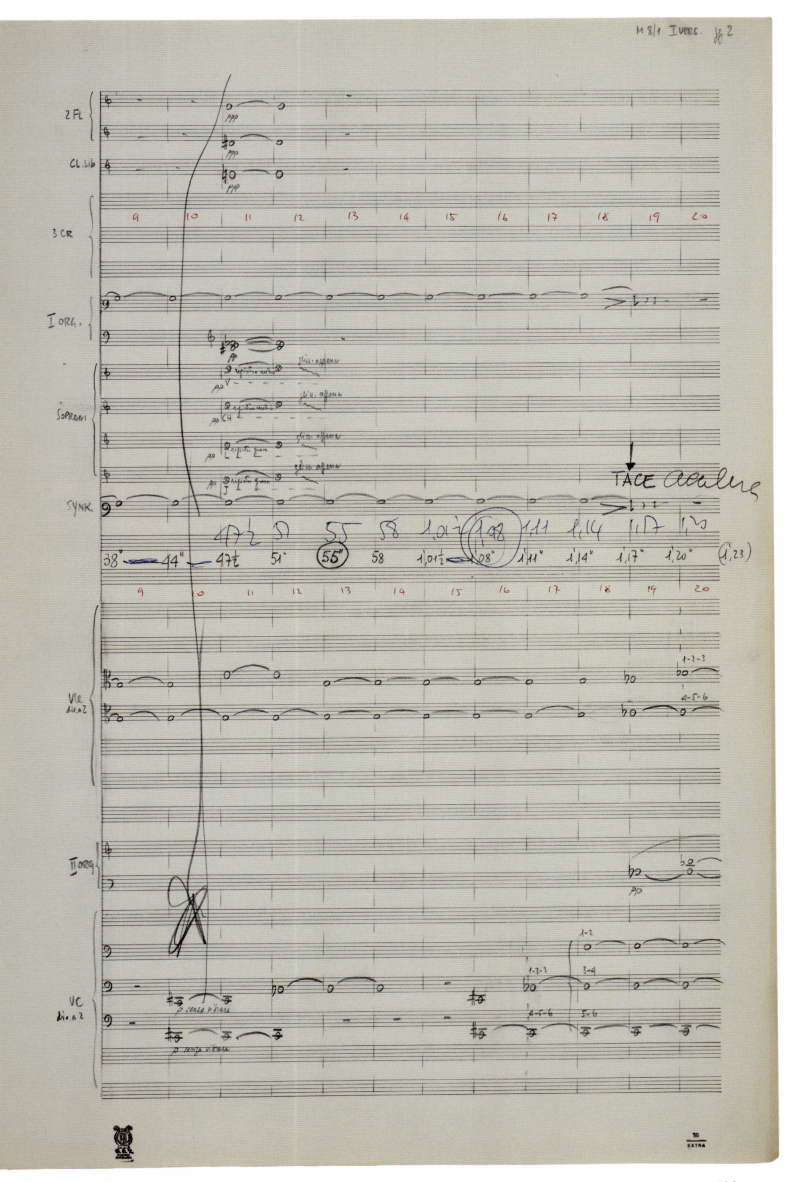

Document 23, Br («2»)

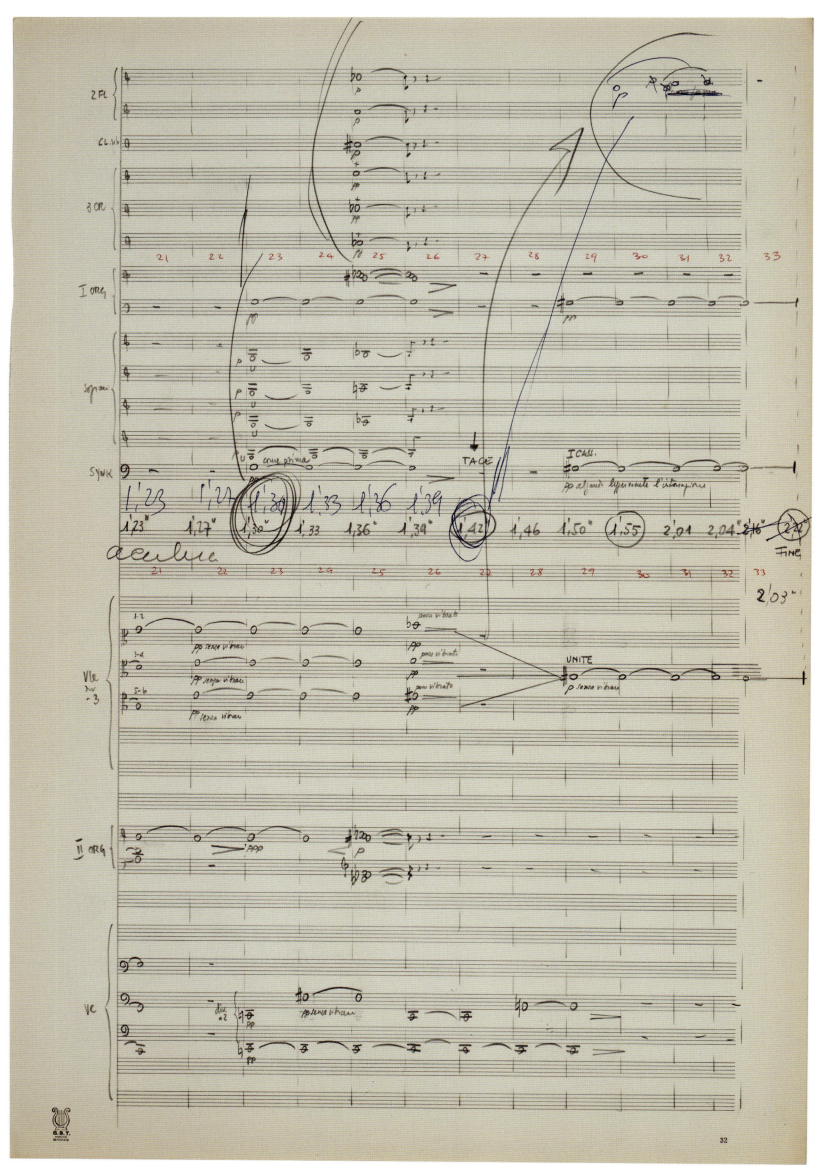

Document 24: M. 8/1 II versione, draft
EMC, 2 ff. (blank Bv). Pencil on staff paper, ca. 220 x 319 mm

The flyleaf of the second version of M. 8/1 immediately provides us with two pieces of information. Firstly, the indication «non fatto [not done]» tells us straightaway that this version of the sequence does not appear in the film. The second and more interesting piece of information has to do with the role that the sequence plays within the film. The annotation «grande sequenza [grand sequence]» confirms the importance of this piece in the film's framework and in the director's imagination. Compared to the previous draft, the document in which Macchi began to plan the second version of M. 8/1 is much neater and spread over two pages. On the first page the music is distributed over three systems: the first system consists of five staves, while the others have only two; the other page instead has two four-part systems. Macchi most likely began this draft after he had finished drafting the first version, giving him the opportunity to think about the instruments he required and the eventual timbric solutions at his disposal by way of this group of instruments, seemingly identical in both versions. As in the first version, prior to the changes made during in-studio editing (which, as we have seen, led to the shortening of the piece), the duration is set at 2', 22". If we compare the timing of the two versions, we can see that, generally speaking, the chronometric articulation of the entire sequence is more or less the same, with three distinct sync points that are also found in the first version (1', 27", 1', 30", and 1', 42"), especially at the end of the piece.

The fact that the second version puts the previous compositional experience to good use can easily be seen in the way Macchi treated the voices. In the prior draft their presence is rather ambiguous, while their impact within the piece in the second version is now crystal clear. In this case, Macchi gave a precise definition of the timbral effect he desired from the voices, to be obtained through the «mano ribattuta sulla bocca [hand tapping on the mouth]», while each of the eight singers sings a letter – the five Italian vowels and the consonants "j" and "l" – in a sequence of pitches spanning an octave. On the contrary, the note written next to the voices on the second and third staves is not so easy to decipher. It seems to better define a number of performative elements: the dynamics in *pianissimo*; a possible rhythmic expression of the repeating hand gestures; and ultimately, the indication «zona acuta [high zone]» which seems to specify the intonation of the vocal register, along with notes indicated on the staff. Compared to the first version, in which each intervention included a change of emission, it is now clear from the draft that the idea was to define a stable structure that could then to be recalled in other parts of the piece, through the simple indication «soprani come inizio [sopranos like the beginning]». It is interesting to note that although the interventions of the soprano are described in detail, at this stage in planning they do not seem to be tied to precise sync points. The recall of these voices has been placed within a wider interval of a few seconds: between the time points 38" and 44" in the second system of the first page; whereas, in the first system on the second page, they were initially noted generically between 1', 36" and 1', 42", and then specifically at 39". However, the appearance of the sopranos between 50" and 56" is quite different, having been built on the same letters, but only around the note of E. As was partly the case in the first version, here, in all three cases there is a clear intention to link the voices to the winds, who perform the same hexatonic collection in all three occurrences. However, while the sopranos and the voices enunciate a series of events marked by a localised chord impression, there are other elements that suggest an expansion of the sound in the horizontal sense. Macchi certainly envisaged this dimension through the indication «eco [echo]», written on several occasions on the draft, in association with single notes or bichords played by the cellos. Thus, the draft provided him the ideal moment not only to plan the primary parameters for the composition of a piece, but also to imagine the sound using so-called secondary parameters.

141

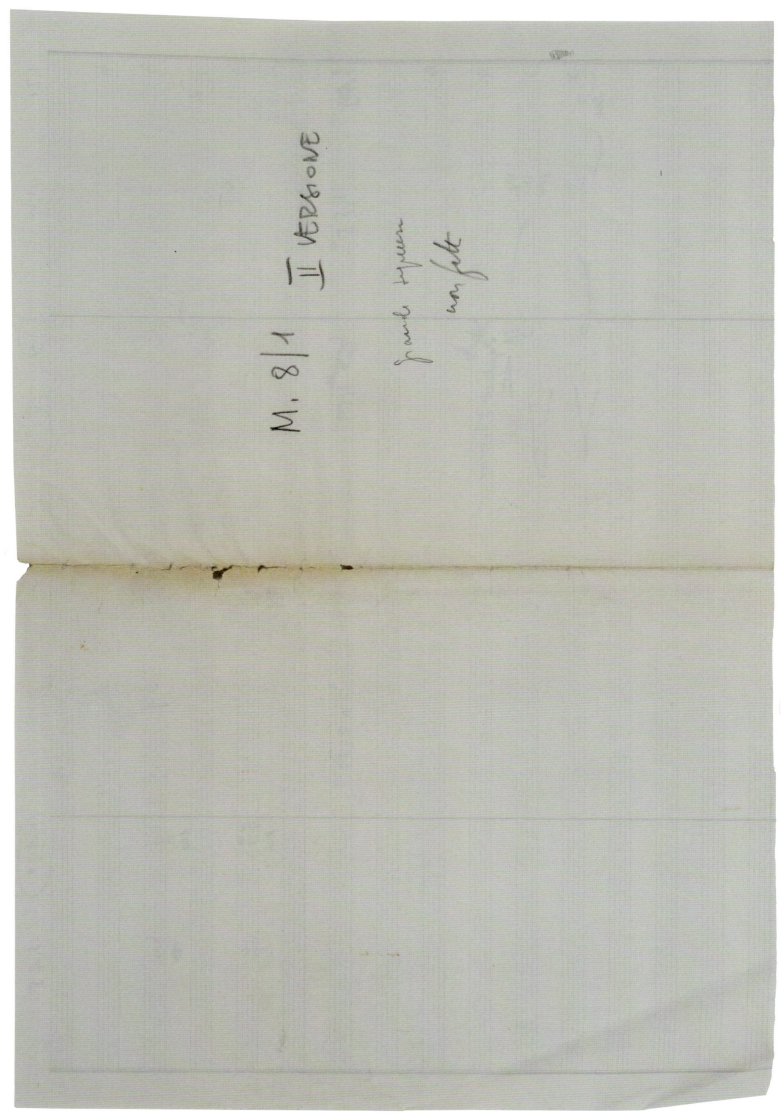

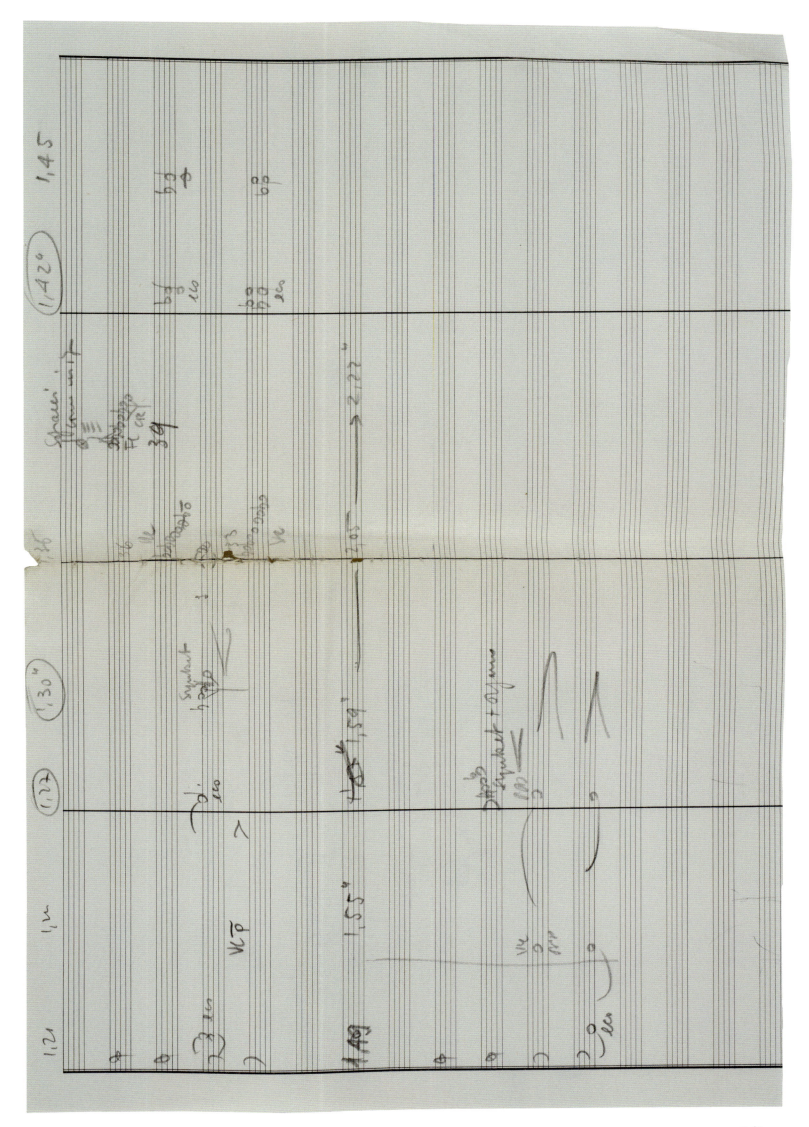

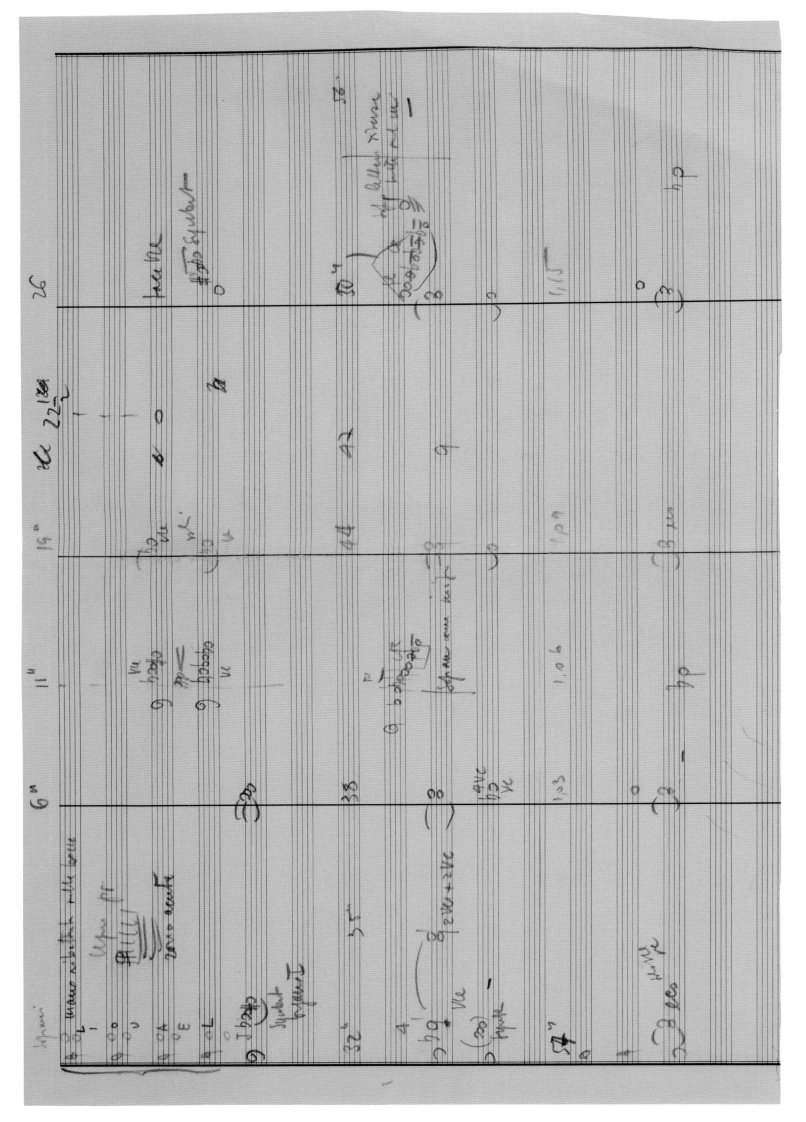

Document 25: M. 8/1 II versione, fair copy
EMC, 4 ff. (all versos blank). Pencil and red ballpoint pen on staff paper, 470 x 325 mm

Upon comparison with the fair copy of the first version, we can conclude that the second version of M. 8/1 was most likely never tested in sync with the images in the recording studio. This is less due to the fact that the duration of the piece remains fixed at 2', 22" – Macchi and Losey had planned to give sound to the entire sequence – but mainly because this version lacks any additional markings that testify to Macchi's standard process of "rewriting" the music within an audiovisual context during the recording phase. The fair copy, therefore, only bears traces of the passage from draft to score. As previously noted, this implies the definition of all the functional details in order to organise the sound in the most accurate manner possible, especially with regards to the dynamic indications. In fact, the second version, more so than the first, explores a dynamic sound range that never extends beyond *piano* and tries to soften the points of attack and the diminuendo as much as possible, with to verbal indications such as «eco [echo]» and «sparire [disappear]» which give the performers an idea of the effect to be obtained when playing.

As noted in our comparison of the two versions of M. 3/3 (Documents 17-19), when Macchi worked on a new version, not only did he try to adopt different compositional strategies in a strictly musical sense, he also defined different relationships between the various expressive elements of the film. From this point of view, the beginning of the film is a good example of this creative approach, because it shows how it can be possible to arrive at completely different audiovisual interpretations, while maintaining the same sync points (here too Macchi circled the time points set at 6" and at 19"). As we have already gathered from the draft, the three initial shots of the mural are characterised by the vocal interventions of the sopranos, who quickly tap their mouth with their hands. In the transition to the fair copy, Macchi clearly indicated the pitch to be sung by each of the voices, covering the diatonic collection within an F3-F4 octave. However, more importantly, he added a new sound layer to the first bar. In fact, by «legno battuto velocissimo [wood very fast beaten]» playing the whole hexatonic collection both the violas and cellos contribute to defining the timbral effect, initially imagined only for voice. Hence, contrary to what happened in the first version, there are six introductory seconds based on a sound layer that lacks directionality, but exhibits a jagged sound surface. The chordal harmonisation of the Synket and the organ on three notes a semitone apart also contributes to defining this sound layer. They play a fundamental role as the only transitional elements at the very beginning of the sequence, which starts with Trotsky's speech in voiceover, while Delon's character walks down the street. And his use of Synket pedal shows Macchi's clever application of this alternative version to also test a different way of managing the balance between music, image and voice. In the first version, the G pedal was the sound consistently associated with the statesman's speech, whether in the in- or over- position. Though, having described his acting style as charged with tension, in the second version Macchi used the Synket-organ pedal to mark Delon's presence. In correspondence with bars 4-5, the segment during which Burton's voice is deacusmatised, the Synket and the organ disappear, only to reappear again at 26" with the frame change to Delon.

As the sequence progresses, we can then observe several different strategies that Macchi used to manage the salient sync points. For example, the moment in which Delon is about to pick up the murder weapon (32"-38") is indeed marked by a different figuration of the sound layer – the descending fourths of organ II – but there is a complete lack of deviation from the timbric point of view, an effect that was created in the previous version by the entry of the flutes. On the contrary, in this version, the entire segment that leads to Delon picking up the axe is far more dramatic. In the first version he only emphasised the gesture, while in the second version of M. 8/1, Macchi dramatised the whole segment from when the actor begins to closely observe a pair of skis on a stall (41") right up to the culminantion of the pickaxe (50"). The beginning and end of this audiovisual segment are marked by two interventions by the sopranos, no longer accompanied by the strings – as in the first bar – but by the winds. Although no sound recording of this piece exists, we can see that in terms of timbre, the first intervention, which mixes the effect of the repeated mouth-tapping vocals with the blend of woods and brasses, is more incisive in terms of fulfillment mechanisms than the second, more conventional version. In fact, for the last strong synchronised effect at bar 29, Macchi returned to annotating the first intervention to record the action of Trotsky shutting the window.

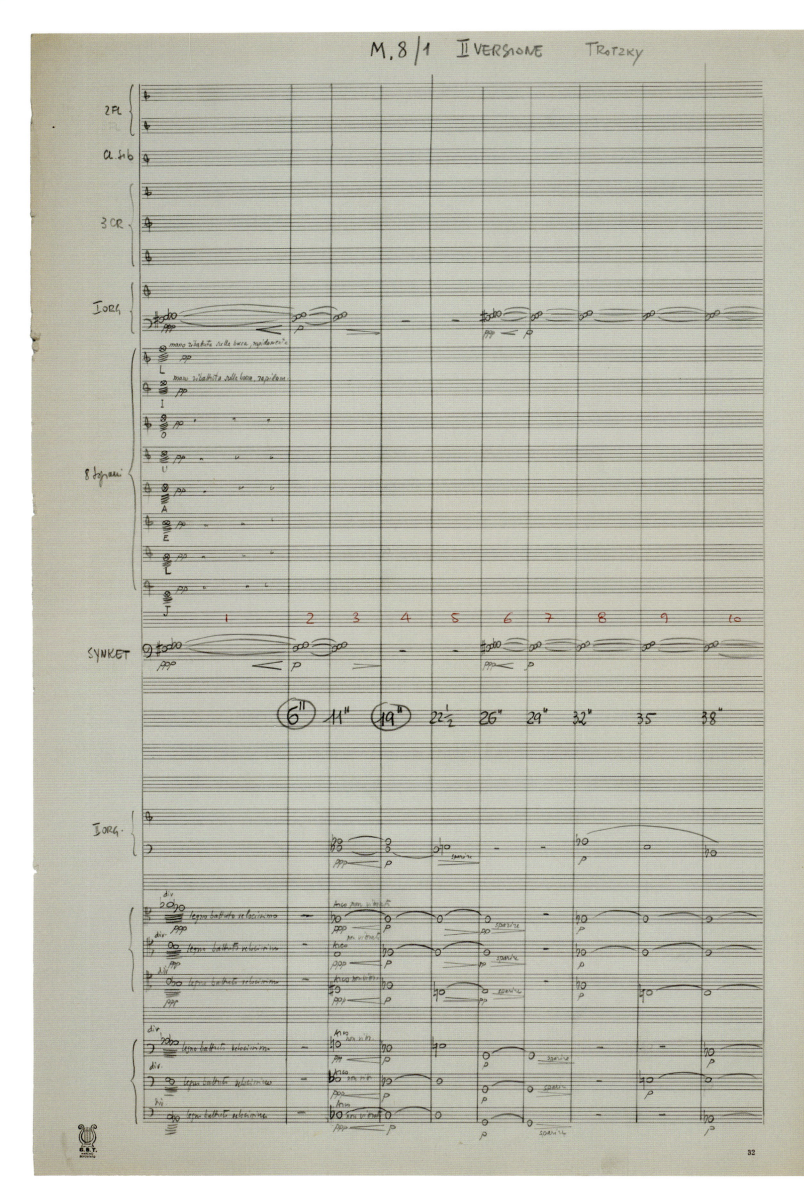

Document 25, Br («2»)

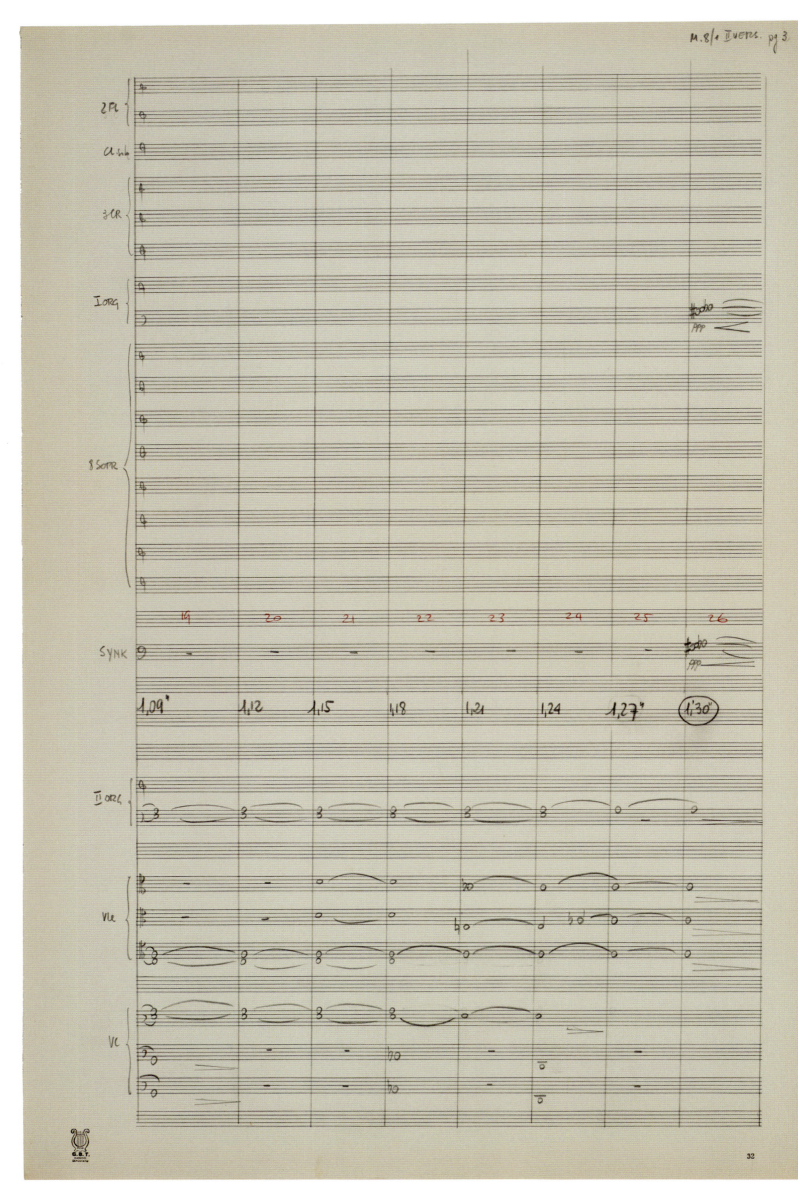

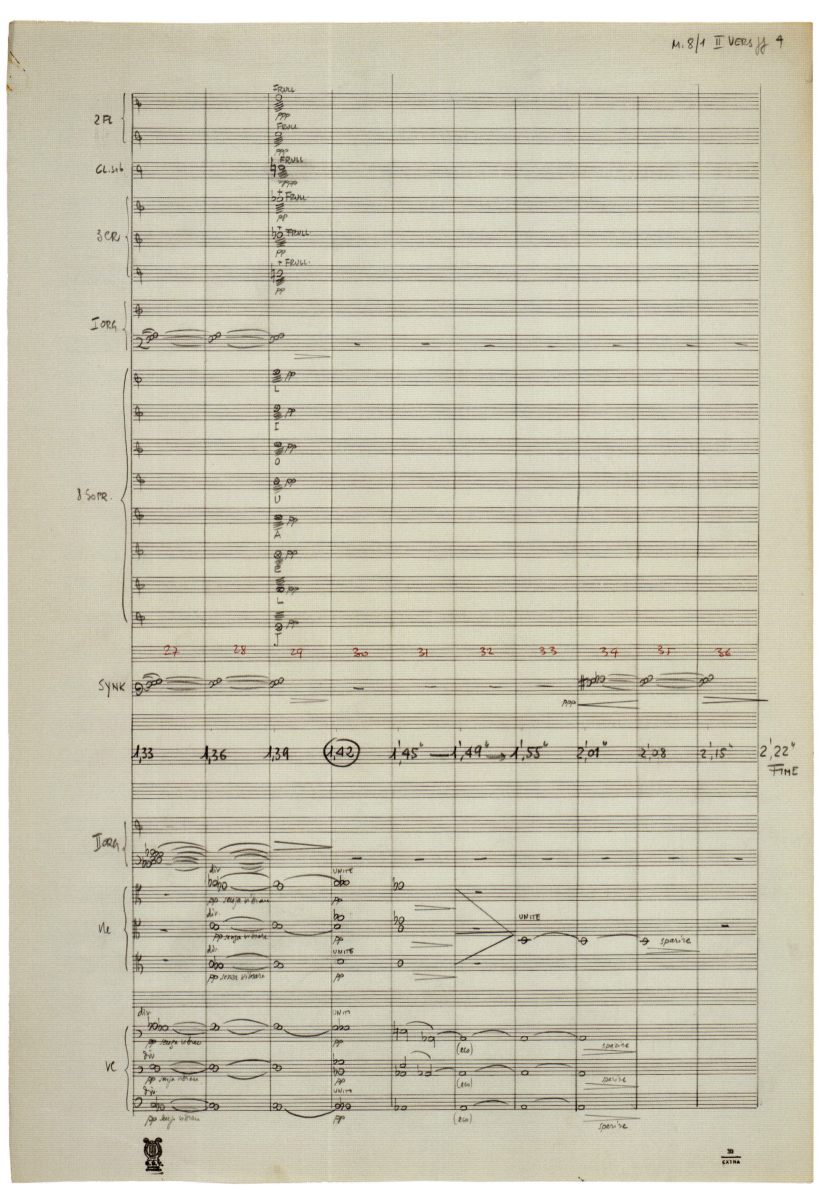

BIBLIOGRAPHY

Primary sources
Egisto Macchi Collection, Giorgio Cini Foundation, Venice.
Joseph Losey Collection, British Film Institute, London.

Interviews and published documents
Felice Chilanti, *Trotzky vivo: l'assassinio di un intellettuale contemporaneo*, Bologna: Cappelli, 1972.
Marco Cosci, *«Acts of wisdom and trust»: Sheets, Tapes and Machines in Egisto Macchi's Film Music Composition*, «Musica/Tecnologia», VIII-IX, 2014-2015, pp. 135-155: 152-155.
Alain Delon, *Témoignage sur Losey*, «Positif», 583, September 2009, pp. 56-58.
Joseph Losey, *L'œil du Maître*, Textes réunis et présentés par Michel Ciment, Paris-Arles: Institut Lumière/Actes Sud, 1994.
Egisto Macchi, *Appunti per [una] conferenza*, in Daniela Tortora, *Nuova Consonanza 1989-1994*, Lucca: Lim, 1994, pp. 159-162.
Emanuela Martini, Giorgio Rinaldi, Paolo Vecchi (eds), *Incontro con Joseph Losey: «Tutti politici i miei film»*, «Cineforum», 193, April 1980, pp. 176-179.
Gene D. Phillips, *Rencontre avec Joseph Losey*, «Séquences», 72, April 1973, pp. 18-21.
Tony Rayns, *Losey & Trotsky*, «Take One», III/8, March 1973, pp. 13-15.
Sebastian Schadhauser, *Conversazione con Joseph Losey*, «Filmcritica», 222, February 1972, pp. 66-69.
Giuseppe Sibilla, «Lo dico che anche la rabbia è un dovere», «Radiocorriere TV», 41, November 1976, pp. 22-24.
Il cinema come si fa. La musica, 8 November, 1993, Rai Tre.
Avanguardie 60, Per es. Nuova Consonanza (Episode n. 3), 17 September 1969, Rai Uno.

Secondary literature
Theodor W. Adorno, Hanns Eisler, *Composing for the Films*, New York-London: Continuum, 2005.
Theodor W. Adorno, Hanns Eisler, *Komposition für den Film*, Frankfurt am Main: Suhrkamp, 2006.
Maria Francesca Agresta, *Il suono dell'interiorità. Daniele Paris per il cinema di Liliana Cavani, Luigi Di Gianni, Lorenza Mazzetti*, Lucca: Lim, 2010.
Marco Alunno, *Compositori d'area colta nel cinema del secondo Novecento*, in Roberto Giuliani (ed.), *La musica nel cinema e nella televisione*, Milan: Guerini Studio, 2011, pp. 51-63.
Adriano Aprà, *Itinerario personale nel documentario italiano*, in Lino Miccichè (ed.), *Studi su dodici sguardi d'autore in cortometraggio*, Turin: Associazione Philip Morris Progetto Cinema-Lindau, 1995, pp. 281-295.
Arved Ashby, *Modernism Goes to the Movies*, in Id. (ed.) *The Pleasure of Modernist Music: Listening, Meaning, Intention, Ideology*, Rochester: Rochester University Press, 2004, pp. 345-386.
Jacques Aumont, *Moderne: comment le cinéma est devenu le plus singulier des arts*, Paris: Cahiers du cinéma, 2007.
Sergio Bassetti, *Alla voce jungla*, «Segnocinema», IX/49, May-June, 1991, pp. 49-53.
André Bazin, *What is Cinema?*, vol. 1, Berkeley-Los Angeles: University of California Press, 2005.
Marco Bertozzi, *Storia del documentario italiano. Immagini e culture dell'altro cinema*, Venice: Marsilio, 2008.
Sally Bick, *Unsettled Scores: Politics, Hollywood, and the Film Music of Aaron Copland and Hanns Eisler*, Urbana: University of Illinois Press, 2019.
Claudio Bisoni, *Gli anni affollati. La cultura cinematografica italiana (1970-79)*, Rome: Carocci, 2009.
Nicola Bondanese, *Musica e generi documentaristici in Italia tra gli anni Cinquanta e Settanta*, in Roberto Giuliani (ed.), *La musica nel cinema e nella televisione*, Milan: Guerini Studio, 2011, pp. 177-217.
Gianmario Borio, *Riflessioni sul rapporto tra struttura e significato nei testi audiovisivi*, «Philomusica on-line», VI/3, 2007.
Gianmario Borio, *Sound as Process: Scelsi and the Composers of Nuova Consonanza*, in Franco Sciannameo (ed.), *Music As Dream: Essays on Giacinto Scelsi*, Lanham: Scarecrow Press, 2013, pp. 41-52.
Gianmario Borio, Giordano Ferrari, Daniela Tortora (eds), *Teatro di avanguardia e composizione sperimentale per la scena in Italia: 1950-1975*, Venice: Fondazione Giorgio Cini, 2017, pp. 235-257.
Roberto Calabretto, *Lo schermo sonoro. La musica per film*, Venice: Marsilio, 2010.
Roberto Calabretto, *Luigi Nono e il cinema. «Un'arte di lotta e fedele alla verità»*, Lucca: Lim, 2017.
Roberto Calabretto, Giovanni De Mezzo, *Il paesaggio sonoro nel cinema sardo. Banditi a Orgosolo di Vittorio De Seta e Padre padrone dei fratelli Taviani*, «L'avventura. International Journal of Italian Film and Media Landscapes», 4/1, 2018, pp. 19-40.

Bibliography

Roberto Calabretto, Marco Cosci, Elena Mosconi (eds), *All'ascolto del cinema italiano: musiche, voci, rumori*, «Quaderni del CSCI», 15, 2019.

David Caute, *Joseph Losey: A Revenge of Life*, London: Faber and Faber, 1996.

Alessandro Cecchi, *Creative Titles. Audiovisual Experimentation and Self-Reflexivity in Italian Industrial Films of the Economic Miracle and After*, «Music, Sound, and the Moving Image», VIII/2, 2014, pp. 179-194.

Alessandro Cecchi, *Tecniche di sincronizzazione nella musica per film di Angelo Francesco Lavagnino: una prospettiva musicologica*, «Musica/Tecnologia», 8-9, 2014-2015, pp. 57-93.

Alessandro Cecchi, Maurizio Corbella (eds), *Film Music Histories and Ethnographies: New Perspectives on Italian Cinema of the Long 1960s*, «Journal of Film Music», VIII/1-2, 2015 [2019].

Michel Chion, *Audio-vision. Sound on Screen*, New York: Columbia University Press, 1994.

Michel Chion, *La musique au cinéma*, Paris: Fayard, 1995.

Marcia Citron, *Opera on Screen*, New Haven: Yale University Press, 2000.

Nicholas Cook, *Between Process and Product: Music and/as Perfomance*, «Music Theory Online», VII/2, 2001.

Nicholas Cook, *Beyond the Score. Music as Performance*, Oxford – New York: Oxford University Press, 2013.

Maurizio Corbella, *«Filmcritica»: 1960-1970. Bilancio di un decennio d'interesse per il suono cinematografico*, unpublished work.

Maurizio Corbella, *Paolo Ketoff e le radici cinematografiche della musica elettronica romana*, «Acoustical Art and Artifacts: Technology, Aesthetics, Communication (AAA TAC)», 6, 2009, pp. 65-75.

Maurizio Corbella, *Gino Marinuzzi Jr: Electronics and Early Multimedia Mentality in Italy*, «Musica/Tecnologia», 8-9, 2014-2015, pp. 95-133.

Marco Cosci, *La voce del padrone e i suoni del popolo. Identità musicali e processi d'ibridazione tra universi etnici, colti e popular in* Padre Padrone, «Cinema e Storia», III/1, 2014, pp. 55-68.

Marco Cosci, *Verdi secondo Macchi: smontare il melodramma, ricostruire l'Italia*, «L'Avventura. International Journal of Italian Film and Media Landscapes», I/1, 2015, pp. 41-54.

Marco Cosci, *Listening to Another Italy: Egisto Macchi's New Music for Italian Documentaries of the 1960s*, «Journal of Film Music», VIII/1-2, 2015 [2019], pp. 109-125.

Marco Cosci, *La scena media(tizza)ta: teatro, cinema e televisione in* A(lter)A(ction), in Gianmario Borio, Giordano Ferrari, Daniela Tortora (eds), *Teatro di avanguardia e composizione sperimentale per la scena in Italia: 1950-1975*, Venice: Fondazione Giorgio Cini, 2017, pp. 235-257.

Marco Cosci, *Vancini, Macchi and the Voices for the (Hi)story of Bronte*, «Archival Notes», 2017, pp. 65-81.

Marco Cosci, *Un mondo di suoni. Il documentario italiano 1931-1965*, in Roberto Calabretto, Marco Cosci, Elena Mosconi (eds), *All'ascolto del cinema italiano: musiche, voci, rumori*, «Quaderni del CSCI», 15, 2019, pp. 75-81.

Annette Davison, *Hollywood Theory, Non-Hollywood Practice*, Aldershot: Ashgate, 2004.

Luciano De Giusti (ed.), *Joseph Losey. Senza re, senza patria*, Milan: Il castoro, 2010.

Giovanni De Mezzo, *Teoria e prassi negli scritti cinematografici di Vittorio Gelmetti*, «Musica e Storia», XVII/3, 2009, pp. 637-677.

Giorgio De Vincenti, *Il concetto di modernità nel cinema*, Parma: Pratiche Editrice, 2000.

Domenico Ferraro (ed.), *Tra magia e realtà: il meridione nell'opera cinematografica di Luigi Di Gianni*, Rome: Squilibri, 2001.

Colin Gardner, *Joseph Losey*, Manchester: Manchester University Press, 2004.

Colin Gardner, *La storia senza pietà:* Mr. Klein *e i cristalli del tempo*, in Luciano De Giusti (ed.), *Joseph Losey. Senza re, senza patria*, Milan: Il castoro, 2010, pp.160-178.

Roberto Gervasio, Roman Vlad, *La musica nel documentario*, in Enzo Masetti (ed.), *La musica nel film*, Rome: Bianco e Nero Editore, 1950, pp. 69-77.

Mark Graham, *Padre Padrone and the Dialectics of Sound*, «Film Criticism», 1, 1981, pp. 21-30.

Mirko Grasso (ed.), *Scoprire l'Italia: inchieste e documentari degli anni Cinquanta*, Calimera (LE): Kurumuny, 2007.

Daniel Goldmark, Lawrence Kramer, Richard Leppert (eds), *Beyond the Soundtrack. Representing Music in Cinema*, Berkley-Los Angeles: University of California Press, 2007.

William Kinderman, Joseph E. Jones (eds), *Genetic Criticism and the Creative Process. Essays Music, Literature and Theater*, Rochester: University of Rochester Press, 2009.

James Leahy, *L'arte di Joseph Losey: un viaggio personale*, in Luciano De Giusti (ed.), *Joseph Losey. Senza re, senza patria*, Milan: Il castoro, 2010, pp. 74-92.

Luca Lombardi, *Conversazioni con Petrassi*, Milan: Suvini Zerboni, 1980.

Patricia Losey, *Mes années avec Joseph Losey*, Paris: Éditions L'Âge d'Homme, 2015.

Gino Marinuzzi Jr, *Aspetti della musica per film*, in Enzo Masetti (ed.), *La musica nel film*, Rome: Bianco e Nero Editore, 1950, pp. 35-39.

Emanuela Martini (ed.), *Joseph Losey*, Milan: Il castoro, 2013.

Alessandro Mastropietro, *A Survey of New Music Theatre in Rome, 1961-1973: 'Anni favolosi'?*, in Robert Adlington (ed.), *New Music Theatre in Europe: Transformations between 1955-1975*, New York: Routledge, 2019, pp. 177-202.

Olivia Mattis, *Varèse's Multimedia Conception of "Déserts"*, «The Musical Quarterly», LXXVI/4, 1992, pp. 557-582.

Marshall Mcluhan, *Understanding Media: The Extensions of Man*, Cambridge: MIT Press, 1964.

Ilario Meandri, *Internatinal Recording (1959-1969). Indagine sulle memorie orali*, Turin: Kaplan, 2013.

Sergio Miceli, *Musica per film: storia, estetica, analisi, tipologie*, Lucca-Milan: Lim-Ricordi, 2009.

Sergio Miceli, *Musica e cinema nella cultura del Novecento*, Rome: Bulzoni, 2010.

Ennio Morricone, Sergio Miceli, *Composing for the Cinema: The Theory and Praxis of Music in Film*, Lanham: Scarecrow Press, 2013.

Mario Nascimbene, *Malgrè moi, musicista*, Spinea: Edizioni del Leone, 1992.

Roberto Nepoti, *L'età d'oro del documentario*, in Sandro Bernardi (ed.), *Storia del cinema italiano: 1954-1959*, Venice: Marsilio, 2004, pp. 185-194.

David Neumeyer (ed.), *The Oxford Handbook of Film Music Studies*, Oxford-New York: Oxford University Press, 2014.

Bill Nichols, *Representing Reality: Issues and Concepts in Documentary*, Bloomington: Indiana University Press, 1991.

Bill Nichols, *Introduction to Documentary*, Bloomington: Indiana University Press, 2010.

James Palmer, Michael Riley, *The Films of Joseph Losey*, Cambridge: Cambridge University Press, 1993.

Ivelise Perniola, *Vittorio De Seta tra antropologia visiva e poesia*, in Sandro Bernardi (ed.), *Storia del cinema italiano: 1954-1959*, Venice: Marsilio, 2004, pp. 275-281.

Goffredo Petrassi, *Autoritratto. Intervista elaborata da Carlo Vasio*, Rome-Bari: Laterza, 1991.

Luigi Pizzaleo, *Il liutaio elettronico. Paolo Ketoff e l'invenzione del Synket*, Rome: Aracne, 2014.

Armando Plebe, *La musica per film e l'avanguardia musicale*, «Filmcritica», XIV/135-136, July-August 1963, pp. 447-451.

Maurizio Porro, *Joseph Losey*, Milan: Contemporanea cinema, 1978.

Michael Renov, *Towards a Poetics of Documentary*, in Id. (ed.), *Theorizing Documentary*, New York-London: Routledge, 1993, pp. 12-36.

Francesco Maria Ricci, *La musica di Roman Vlad per il cinema, la televisione e il teatro*, «Nuova Rivista Musicale Italiana», IV, 2008, pp. 499-522.

Holly Rogers (ed.), *Music and Sound in Documentary Film*, New York-London: Routledge, 2015.

Friedemann Sallis, *Music Sketches*, Cambridge: Cambridge University Press, 2015.

Elena Salza, *Egisto Macchi and Antonin Artaud: from* A(lter)A(ction) *to* München-Requiem *and Beyond*, «Archival Notes», 3, 2018, pp. 97-118.

Gianluca Sciannameo, *Nelle Indie di quaggiù: Ernesto De Martino e il cinema etnografico*, Bari: Palomar, 2006.

Daniela Tortora, *Nuova Consonanza. Trent'anni di musica contemporanea in Italia*, Lucca: Lim, 1990.

Daniela Tortora (ed.), *Egisto Macchi*, «Archivio Musiche del XX secolo», Palermo: CIMS-Centro di iniziative musicali in Sicilia, 1996.

Leon Trotsky, *History of the Russion Revolution*, trans. by Max Eastman, Chicago: Haymarket Books, 2008.

Robert Van der Lek, *Concert Music as Reused Film Music: E. W. Korngold's Self-arrangements*, «Acta Musicologica», LXVI/2, 1994, pp. 78-112.

Breixo Viejo, *Música moderna, para un nuevo cine. Eisler, Adorno y el Film Music Project*, Madrid: Akal, 2008.

Giada Viviani, *Nino Rota: La dolce vita. Sources of the Creative Process*, Turnhout: Brepols, 2018.

James Wierzbicki (ed.), *Double Lives: Film Composer in the Concert Hall*, New York: Routledge, 2020.

Ben Winters, *Catching Dreams: Editing Film Scores for Publication*, «Journal of the Royal Musical Association», CXXXII/1, 2007, pp. 115-140.

Reviews of *The Assassination of Trotsky*

Rodolphe Bacquet, *L'impossible miroir: étude comparée de trois portraits de figures politiques modernes*, «CinémActìon», 139, June 2011, pp. 137-142.

Luigi Bini, *L'assassinio di Trotsky*, «Letture», XXVII, 6-7, June-July 1972, pp. 532-534.

Michelangelo Buffa, *L'assassinio di Trotski* [sic], «Filmcritica», 223, March 1972, pp. 150-151.

M. Ca., *L'assassinio di Trotsky*, «Avanti!», 26 April 1972.

Ugo Casiraghi, *L'assassinio di Trotsky*, «L'Unità», 25 April 1972.
Jacques Chevallier, *L'assassinat de Trotsky*, «Image et Son», 261, May 1972, pp. 90-91.
Richard Combs, *Human Ceremony*, «Listener», CXII/2873, 30 August 1984, p. 33.
Derek Elley, *The Assassination of Trotsky*, «Focus on Film», 11, Fall 1972, p. 10.
Jean-René Ethier, *The Assassination of Trotsky*, «Séquences», 72, April 1973, pp. 41-42.
Ugo Finetti, *L'assassinio di Trotzkij* [sic], «Cinema Nuovo», 217, May-June 1972, pp. 218-220.
Guy Hennebelle, *L'assassinat de Trotsky*, «Écran», 8, September-October 1972, p. 61.
José Carlos Huayhuaca, *El asesinato de Trotsky*, «Hablemos de Cine», X/66, 1974, pp. 40-41.
Gérard Legrand, *La mort en ce jardin. Sur The Assassination of Trotsky*, «Positif», 139, June 1972, pp. 19-22.
Claudio Lucato, *L'assassinio di Trotzky*, «Cineforum», 113, April 1972, pp. 63-74.
Nicholas Mosley, *Paradoxes of Peace, or the Presence of Infinity*, «Vertigo», IV/3, Summer 2009, pp. 50-51.
Gene D. Phillips, *Recontre avec Joseph Losey*, «Séquences», 72, April 1973, pp. 18-21.
Pietro Pintus, *L'assassinio di Trotsky*, «Sipario», 313, June 1972, p. 51.
Tony Rayns, *Losey & Trotsky*, «Take One», III/8, March 1973, pp. 13-15.
P. Séry, *L'assassinat de Trotsky. Dialectique de la fatalité*, «Cinéma 72», 166, May 1972, pp. 122-126.
Brad Stevens, *The infiltrator*, «Sight & Sound», XIX/6, June 2009, p. 37.
Philip Strick, *The Assassination of Trotsky*, «Sight & Sound», XLI/4, Fall 1972, pp. 230-231.
Margaret Tarratt, *The Assassination of Trotsky*, «Films and Filming», XIX/2, November 1972, p. 44.
Ugo Ulive, *El asesinato de Trotsky*, «Cine al Dia», 16, April 1973, pp. 33-34.
Carlo Felice Venegoni, *Fedele alla cronaca ma generico. L'assassinio di Trotsky di Joseph Losey*, «Cinemasessanta», XII/90, July-August 1972, pp. 61-62.
Charles Vildrac, *The Assassination of Trotsky*, «Monogram», 6, October 1975, pp. 20-22.

Video and audio recordings
Joseph Losey, *El Asesinato de Trotsky*, Barcelona: Solomon Pictures, 2010.
Joseph Losey, *L'assassinat de Trotsky*, Paris: StudioCanal, 2010.
Joseph Losey, *L'assassinio di Trotsky*, Milano: Ricordi Video, 1988.
Joseph Losey, *The Assassination of Trotsky*, London: London Films, 2000.
Egisto Macchi, *L'assassinio di Trotsky - Il delitto Matteotti*, Beat Records – CDCR 15, 1990.